Praise for *Anatomy of a Business Plan*

"A tremendously useful tool…easy to follow, concise, and produces results."

—Anthony Robbins, Author of *Awaken the Giant Within* and *Unlimited Power*

"Recently, I had the opportunity to review two loan applications that included business plans. The most noteworthy item in both of these applications was the business plan. After reading each one, my confidence in the applicant was greatly boosted. Each applicant stated that your software and book were easy to use. By the way, both loans were approved."

—Nancy Russell, First Union Small Business Capital (formerly The Money Store)

"Simply put, *Anatomy of a Business Plan* is the best step-by-step guide to starting, building, and raising capital for your business. We have raised over $20 million for our clients by using this guide, and we have an additional $15 million pending. Use it; it works!"

—Thomas Jay Wacker, Board Member, Centaur Holdings Corporation

"This book helps the entrepreneur write a credible, comprehensive business plan and helps to understand why each element is essential to business success."

—Jan Norman, Author of *What No One Ever Tells You About Starting Your Own Business*
(Preview it at www.smallbusinessresources.com.)

"*Anatomy of a Business Plan* is the best source for my community college students to produce a successful business plan in both oral and written form. The authors have created a source for those interested in 'growing a business' that is very thorough, yet nonthreatening in its approach to the reader. This book serves as the cornerstone of my Introduction to Entrepreneurship class, in which my students have produced hundreds of viable business plans, many of which have been successfully implemented. Hats off to Pinson and Jinnett for making this latest version even better!"

—Michael L. Bejtlich, Associate Professor, Cape Cod Community College

"*Anatomy of a Business Plan* is a great business planning resource. Get the basics, go to the sources, find the materials, and put it all together. This is a wonderful guide to learn how to write a business plan."

—Patricia Heartsfield, Self-Employment Training Coordinator, Illinois Central College

"A definitive and critical tool for any business plan writer! This concise step-by-step guide demystifies the torture of developing and writing a business plan. The sample plans and worksheet templates simplify the process and provide excellent comparisons. This is the most comprehensive and realistic business plan resource available. No business owner should be without this book!"

—Mark S. Deion, President, Deion Associates & Strategies, Inc.

"I am convinced that *Anatomy of a Business Plan* is the best book on the market for business plan development. It is an excellent resource for the full gamut of entrepreneurs, from start-up to experienced business owners who are seeking investors or a loan. The latest version adds up-to-the-minute Internet resources that will open a new array of research tools to help create innovative marketing plans. It also serves as an outstanding textbook for any small business curriculum that addresses strategies for developing a business plan. Sample worksheets and preplanning exercises provide the ideal structure to guide students through the analysis of their business goals and the direction of their research efforts. The book is comprehensive and easy to follow, with examples that enlighten individuals in the full range of product and service ventures."

—Bernadette Tiernan, President, Tiernan Associates/Author of *E-tailing*

Praise for *Anatomy of a Business Plan, 4th Edition*

"Abundant in explanation and example, consistent in direction, clear in guidance for sound decision making, *Anatomy of a Business Plan* is a worldly and practical guide for success in business. Students like the results they achieve by following the steps in this book."

—Tony Ortega, Director, Business Development Academy,
California State Polytechnic University, Pomona

"Whether in manufacturing or service, this new edition of *Anatomy of a Business Plan* gives business professionals the necessary tools to write an intelligent and complete business plan in order to lead a business into the 21st century. It's a reference guide to buy and keep."

—Dorothy L. Dreher, President, Organizational Concepts, Inc.

• •

Other books and software by the same authors:

Automate Your Business Plan (see page ix)

Keeping the Books

Target Marketing

Steps to Small Business Start-Up

Anatomy of a Business Plan

FOURTH EDITION

A Step-by-Step Guide to
Starting Smart, Building the Business,
and Securing Your Company's Future

Linda Pinson
and
Jerry Jinnett

DEARBORN™
A **Kaplan Professional** Company

Acquisitions Editor: Jean Iverson
Managing Editor: Jack Kiburz
Cover Design: Scott Rattray, Rattray Design
Interior Design: Eliot House Productions

Published by Dearborn, a Kaplan Professional Company

99 00 01 10 9 8 7 6 5 4 3 2 1

Library of Congress Cataloging-in-Publication Data
Pinson, Linda.
    Anatomy of a business plan: a step-by-step guide to starting smart, building the business, and securing your company's future/Linda Pinson and Jerry Jinnett.—4th ed.
       p.   cm.
    Includes index.
    ISBN 1-57410-127-7 (paper)
    1. Business planning. 2. New business enterprises—Planning. I. Jinnett, Jerry.
II. Title.
HD30.28.P5 1999
658.4'012—dc20
                                           99-26126
                                          CIP

Dedication

· ·

It is with a great deal of pleasure that we dedicate this book to Tom Drewes, the former President of Quality Books, Inc., our mentor and friend. His kindness and encouragement were our inspiration in 1986. Because of his belief in us, our books are now being used in libraries across the nation. Thank you, Tom, for your many years of tireless dedication to independent publishers and for your willingness to share yourself with so many and ask for nothing in return.

Table of Contents

AUTOMATE YOUR BUSINESS PLAN

1999 9.0 FOR WINDOWS

The SBA's chosen format for your winning business plan

WRITE YOUR BUSINESS PLAN WITH AN EXPERT AT YOUR SIDE

AUTOMATE YOUR BUSINESS PLAN   Master Plan
File Options Main Menu Research Help

Cover Sheet
Table of Contents
Statement of Purpose
Part I - Organizational Plan
Part II - Marketing Plan
Part III - Financial Documents
Financial Statement Analysis
Supporting Documents

Select the part of the plan you wish to work on

"**Automate Your Business Plan**, has an integrated word processor and spreadsheets that could pass for popular programs like Microsoft Word and Excel. The owners of Lookers, Inc. recently used AYBP to raise $200,00 to open a second restaurant and say the program's financial sections are particularly powerful." *Inc. Magazine*

"Automate Your Business Plan" assumes you know nothing about writing a business plan. We walk you through the process and make your job easier.

☐ *Our step-by-step planning process will enable you to organize your industry expertise into a working business plan that will attract capital and ensure success.*

■ Easy instructions guide you through each part of your plan.

Bonus *Special Web page "hot links"* you to marketing & financial research sites

■ Two complete real-life business plans serve as examples to help you overcome writer's block.

■ **Automate Your Business Plan** is a stand-alone software program -- not a set of templates depending on someone else's software for compatibility and support. If you have questions, call us.

ATTRACT LENDERS & INVESTORS WITH A CUSTOMIZED BUSINESS PLAN

AUTOMATE YOUR BUSINESS PLAN   Master Plan
File Options Main Menu Research Help

Part II: Marketing Plan

Marketing Plan
Target Market Worksheet
Competition Evaluation

Instructions
Example
Build/Edit

See an example of a complete marketing plan

Investors are turned off by canned plans that look and sound like everyone else's. A customized working business plan is a plan to succeed.

☐ *Your plan will be tailored to your specific industry and situation.*

■ We help you research and write a winning marketing plan.

■ We help you develop a valid set of financial projections.

☐ *These are some of the great features you will like about our software:*

■ Instructions, examples, and pre-formatted files for all parts of your plan

■ All files pre-set with headers, fonts, margins, and print commands

■ Master Plan & multiple plan capabilities; import/export to or from Word® & Excel.®

SAVE 100+ HOURS WITH FORMATTED & FORMULATED FINANCIAL STATEMENTS

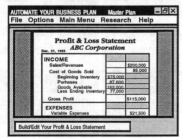

AUTOMATE YOUR BUSINESS PLAN   Master Plan
File Options Main Menu Research Help

Profit & Loss Statement
ABC Corporation
Dec. 31, 1995

INCOME		
Sales/Revenues		$200,000
Cost of Goods Sold		85,000
Beginning Inventory	$75,000	
Purhases	87,000	
Goods Available	162,000	
Less Ending Inventory	77,000	
Gross Profit		$115,000
EXPENSES		
Variable Expenses		$21,500

Build/Edit Your Profit & Loss Statement

"**Automate Your Business Plan** and *Anatomy of a Business Plan* are thorough, practical, and easy-to-understand." *Sandy Sutton, District Director*
Santa Ana District Office, U.S. Small Business Administration

We help you develop realistic financial projections so you can make the right decisions for a successful and profitable business future.

☐ *You will move with ease through your entire financial plan.*

■ We set up and formulate all of your financial spreadsheets.

■ We show you how to customize them and input your numbers.

■ We automatically do all of your calculations for you.

Bonus *Amortizing Software* calculates loan principal & interest payments.

☐ *Your lender/investor will be happy to see the following financial information:*

■ Sources & Uses of Funds
■ Pro-Forma Cash Flow Statement
■ Three-Year Income Projection
■ Break-Even Analysis

■ Quarterly Budget Analysis
■ Profit & Loss Statement
■ Balance Sheet
■ Ratio Analysis

© 1996, 1997, 1998 & 1999

**OUT OF YOUR MIND...
AND INTO THE MARKETPLACE™**

FOR INFORMATION ON BUSINESS BOOKS & SOFTWARE:

Write To: 13381 White Sand Drive, Tustin, CA 92780
Telephone: (714) 544-0248   Fax: (714) 730-1414

Home Page - http://www.business-plan.com

Acknowledgments

··

Dearborn would like to acknowledge the works of Small Business Development Centers (SBDCs) around the country for their untiring support of start-ups and small business owners. Most notably, the Illinois SBDC Network has entered into a partnership with Dearborn to provide high quality materials such as *Anatomy of a Business Plan* and other titles, to enhance the training and counseling of entrepreneurs in their state. It is the type of public/private partnership that will make today's small businesses prosper.

It is always good to utilize the talents of experts who specialize in areas that are beyond your specific expertise. John P. Neal helped develop the material on exit strategies in Chapter 1. John is the founder of RCG Management in San Diego, a pioneer in providing management services to growing companies. He is CEO of ACE Group, Inc., one of Southern California's largest resellers of accounting, manufacturing, human resource, and sales management systems. He serves on several for profit and not-for-profit boards and is chairman of the Small Business Committee of the California Chamber of Commerce.

"Product-Market Analysis" on pages 40–44 was written and contributed by Donald R. McCrea, who is the Director of Executive Education at the University of California, Irvine. This is a very valuable tool for focusing on your target market. We would like to thank Mr. McCrea for allowing us to utilize his material in *Anatomy of a Business Plan*.

Preface

. . . .

One of the principal reasons for business failure is the lack of an adequate plan. When we consider the concept of business planning, three critical facts always seem to surface:

1. **All businesses need a business plan.** You can fly by the seat of your pants, but you will probably get torn pants. Successful business owners are usually those who have taken the time to evaluate all the aspects of their businesses and to map their plans for the future.

2. **All lending institutions require a business plan.** Lenders and investors are sharing the risk in your business. They want to know that you are going to be successful. Your business plan is the only way they have to evaluate whether or not they should take that risk.

3. **Few business owners know how to write a business plan!** Everyone hears the terms "cash flow," "marketing plan," "fixed assets," "break-even analysis," etc. Even if a business owner understands some of these terms, it is not often that he or she has the concept of how to put them together into a workable plan. The thought of having to research and combine all of this information into a working business plan can be a heavy burden.

It is the goal of this book to take away the mystery in the business planning process. We want to give you a clear, concise, and easy-to-understand format to help you prepare a plan that will aid you either as a new business owner planning for start-up or as a currently operating business owner who needs a vehicle for implementing changes throughout the life of your business.

Anatomy of a Business Plan was designed with the simplification of your task as its primary purpose. The first thing you should do is read the book to give you a general overview of the format and content. After reading, begin with the Organizational Plan section and complete each part before proceeding to the next topic. If any forms are needed for your work, you will find them following the text relating to that item. If you follow this step-by-step method, you will soon have a completed business plan.

Two full-length business plans are also included in this book to help you see the results that were obtained by business owners who followed our format. You will find them in the back of the book under Appendix I: Marine Arts of California Business Plan and Appendix II: Dayne Landscaping Business Plan. We thank Bob Garcia of "Marine Art of California" for his generosity in sharing his business plan with us and with you. A special note of thanks also goes to Robin Dayne, marketing specialist and owner of rtd Marketing International, Inc., who researched and wrote the Dayne Landscaping, Inc. business plan for us.

Thank you for choosing our book to help you accomplish your goal. We wish you success in writing your business plan!

—**Linda Pinson and Jerry Jinnett**

Business Plan Considerations

. . . .

A well-written business plan will provide a pathway to profit for any new or existing business. Your business plan will also provide the documentation that a lender or investor requires if you find it necessary to seek outside funding sources for your business.

This chapter is designed to give you some background information and guidelines to consider prior to writing your business plan.

Why do you need a business plan? If you need access to additional capital, what does the lender or investor need to know? What are the key words that make your plan more effective? These questions will be addressed in the following pages.

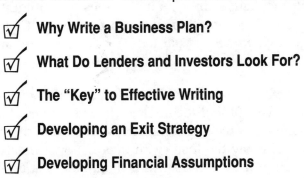

☑ **Why Write a Business Plan?**

☑ **What Do Lenders and Investors Look For?**

☑ **The "Key" to Effective Writing**

☑ **Developing an Exit Strategy**

☑ **Developing Financial Assumptions**

Why Write a Business Plan?

Every business can benefit from the preparation of a carefully written plan. There are three main purposes for writing that plan. There is an additional benefit if you do business internationally.

Financial statements: documents that show your financial situation.

1. Your business plan will serve as your guide during the lifetime of your business. It is a blueprint of your business and will provide you with the tools to analyze your business and implement changes. To be of value, your business plan must be kept up-to-date. While plans presented to lenders must be bound, you may choose to keep your working copy of the plan in a loose-leaf binder. Then you may add current financial statements, updated rate sheets, recent marketing information, and other data as they become available.

2. A business plan is a requirement if you are planning to seek financing. It will provide potential lenders or investors with detailed information on all aspects of your company's past and current operations and provide future projections. Obviously, if you are a new business, you will not have a history. The business plan for a new company seeking funding will have to rely on the credit records and financial statements of the individuals involved in the business. These will give the lender or investor insight into the ways in which personal business is conducted. The manner in which company business is conducted often reflects one's personal management style.

3. If you do business internationally, a business plan provides a standard means of evaluating your business potential in a foreign marketplace. More than ever before, world trade is essential to the health of the American economy and to the growth of most U.S. companies. No business today can afford to overlook the potential of international commerce brought about by changes in communications, technology, and transportation. The development of a business plan will demonstrate ways in which your business can compete in this global economy.

Capital: money available to invest or the total of accumulated assets available for production.

If you are seeking capital, the business plan details how the desired investment or loan will further the company's goals. Every banker or investor wants to know how the loan will improve the worth of your company and enable you to repay the loan (with interest) on a timely basis. You will have to detail how the money will be used and back up your figures with solid information such as estimates, industry norms, rate sheets, etc. Bankers have access to statistics that are considered normal for various industries, so be sure that your projections are reasonable.

One of the principal reasons for business failure is lack of planning. Remember:

> *"The business that fails to plan, plans to fail."*

Take the time to write a clear, concise, and winning business plan. The success of your business depends on it!

What Do Lenders and Investors Look For?

If you are looking for lenders or investors, it is to your advantage to understand the elements that they would most want to see in a well-written business plan. Investors (or venture capitalists) will become equity partners in your company. They will need to justify to themselves that the money they are investing in your company will essentially result in the desired return on their investments. Remember that bankers are people, too. Just as you will have to present your business plan to them, they will have to present your plan to their bank's loan committee. We all fear rejection. You are afraid of having your loan denied. The loan officer is fearful of presenting your plan to the committee and having it rejected. You can increase your chances of success with lenders and investors by considering the following items. Keep them in mind as you write your plan and review them when your plan has been completed.

Loan: money lent at interest.

1. *What is your credit history?*

   Provide a personal credit report that demonstrates you are a good risk. If you are an existing business, provide information about your payment history. A past bankruptcy or a history of late payments can serve as a "red flag" and send out a warning signal that you may be a bad risk. You will have to prove through a well-prepared Financial Section that you understand all of the costs involved in your business and that you have a complete understanding of cash flow. If you are a new business, your personal financial history will be examined. You may be required to submit a personal balance sheet and income tax returns for the previous three years. The banker determines your character based on your financial history.

Cash flow: the actual movement of cash into and out of a business.

2. *What collateral do you have?*

   What assets do you have and what are you willing to risk for the success of your business? You may be asked to use your home as collateral. You may have money in CD's or other investments that will qualify. The collateral you provide shows your commitment to your company and removes risk on the part of the investor (your new equity partner) or the lender (the bank that is granting you loan request). You will generally be

Collateral: something of value given or held as a pledge that a debt or obligation will be fulfilled.

required to provide collateral in an amount equal to one third of the loan value.

3. ***What is your repayment plan?***

Lenders and investors want to know that you appreciate their needs and that you have given consideration to your company's ability to fulfill their goals.

a. *If you are seeking a lender:*

Your lender (banker) wants to know that your company can repay the loan plus interest and, for the period of the loan, maintain a positive cash flow that will allow you to continue to operate your business.

If the loan is to increase assets, any asset that you want to finance must last at least as long as the loan period. For example, you cannot get a five-year, $25,000 loan on a piece of electronic equipment that is expected to become obsolete within two years of the date of purchase.

The asset should generate the repayment of funds. Show in your Financial Section (specifically in your Cash Flow Projections and in your Three-Year Projected Income Statement) that the object of the loan will increase sales, increase efficiency, or cut costs and will, in turn, generate added revenue for repayment of the loan plus interest.

If the loan is for working capital, you will need to show how the loan plus interest can be repaid through cash (liquidity) during the next year's full operating cycle, generally one year.

b. *If you are seeking an investor:*

Venture capitalists and other equity investors will frequently require that you provide them with an exit strategy. They are most concerned with the profit potential of your company and will ultimately want to know where the business is heading. The investor will want to see a financial plan that shows how the company will move toward its goals and produce the desired profit to be distributed to them under a predetermined agreement. As an equity partner, the investor has a say in how the company is operated and will be the hardest to satisfy because he is putting his own money at risk.

4. ***Is there a demand for your product or service?***

Be prepared to show evidence that your product or service is in demand by your target market (your customers). You can demonstrate demand through a favorable sales history, accounts receivable information, or purchase orders. If you are a new service company or a business with a new product, show

Interest: the cost of borrowing money.

Asset: anything of worth that is owned. Accounts receivable are an asset.

Account receivable: a record of what is owed to you.

customer acceptance through questionnaire and survey data and testimonials. To be valid, the responses must come from your target market and not from friends and family. Test market your product and get some evaluations. Ask for testimonial letters.

You must clearly define your target market and your pricing strategy, and compute your potential revenue. These are educated "guesstimates" based on careful and thorough research. Your trade and professional associations can provide statistics regarding average sales, consumer demand, new trends, and competition. Use these statistics to validate your conclusions.

5. *Have you established a proprietary position?*
   This means that you have secured your position in the market in some manner. There is something unique about your business, and you have protected this uniqueness in some way. This may be through copyright, trademark, or patent. Include a copy of the document verifying such protection. If you are located in a mall or shopping center, you may be able to work with management to limit competition in some manner. For example, location of competition may be written into the terms of the lease. You may be able to ensure that you will be the only donut shop in a small shopping center or have it specified in the terms of your lease agreement that you will have no direct competition within a given radius of your store. Include a copy of your lease in the Supporting Documents section of your plan and stress any proprietary rights when you write about your location.

6. *Are your projections realistic?*
   In business planning, we make assumptions. Assumptions are based on statistics and industry information. For example, if we state that we are going to capture an additional 15 percent of the market, we must be prepared to prove that 15 percent of the market is currently not being served or that the total market is going to grow by that amount. Demographic studies from the local Chamber of Commerce or the Economic Development Corporation may project a 20 percent increase in population through the year 2005. If this added population base fits your customer profile, you can indicate in your business plan this population increase will lead to an increase in your customer base and in your revenues. Remember that lenders and investors judge your plan and goals in terms of your industry's practices and trends.

7. *Do you have a strong marketing plan?*
   When a lender or an investor is reviewing your business plan, one of the primary areas of focus will be your marketing

plan. As you write your marketing plan, you will learn that much of the emphasis is placed on the development of a highly targeted market that can be effectively served by your business—customers who need what you have to offer and who will choose you and pay you to solve their problems and fill their needs.

The lender will make an assessment regarding the logic of your marketing plan and will decide whether or not it is probable that, during the term of your loan, you will be able to sell to those customers in a volume that is sufficient to repay your loan plus interest.

An investor (or venture capitalist) will not only be looking at your marketing plan in terms of your current plans. As a potential equity partner, he or she will also focus on your long-term marketing goals, making a determination as to whether or not it is likely that the company can continue to increase its market share accordingly and generate the desired return on investment.

The "Key" to Effective Writing

The text of the business plan must be concise and yet must contain as much information as possible. This sounds like a contradiction, but you can solve this dilemma by using the key word approach. Write the following key words on a card and keep them in front of you while you are writing:

Who	**When**	**Unique**
What	**Why**	**Benefit to the Customer**
Where	**How**	**How Much**

Answer all of the questions asked by the key words in one paragraph at the beginning of each section of your business plan. Then expand on that thesis statement by telling more about each item in the text that follows. Stress any uniqueness and benefit to the customer that may pertain to the section in which you are writing. Examples will be given in the following chapters to give you guidance. Keep in mind, if you are seeking financing, that the lender's or investor's time is limited and that your plan is not the only one being reviewed. Often the first paragraph following a heading will be the only area read; therefore, it is very important to include as much pertinent and concise information as possible in that first paragraph.

Effective Use of Your Time

There is no set length to a business plan. The average length seems to be 30 to 40 pages, including the Supporting Documents section. Break the plan down into sections. Set up blocks of time for work with target dates for completion. You may find it effective to spend two evenings per week at the library. You will not be interrupted by the telephone or tempted by the refrigerator or television set. An added bonus is that the reference material you need will be close at hand. It takes discipline, time, and privacy to write an effective business plan.

Supporting Documents

You will find it time-saving to compile your list of Supporting Documents while writing the text. For example, while writing about the legal structure of your business, you will realize the need to include a copy of your partnership agreement. Write "partnership agreement" on your list of Supporting Documents. When it comes time to compile that section of your plan, you will already have a listing of necessary documents. As you go along, request any information you do not have, such as credit reports. If you take care of gathering the necessary documents in this manner, the materials you need to complete the Supporting Documents Section will be available when you are ready to assemble it.

Business Plan Outline

With the previous considerations in mind, you are ready to begin formulating your plan. The pieces of a business plan in this book are as follows:

- ◈ **Cover Sheet**
- ◈ **Executive Summary (or Statement of Purpose)**
- ◈ **The Organizational Plan**
- ◈ **The Marketing Plan**
- ◈ **Financial Documents**
- ◈ **Supporting Documents**

Each of the areas of the business planning process is covered in a separate chapter of the book. *Anatomy of a Business Plan* is designed to help you write a complete, concise, and well-organized plan that will guide you and your company toward a profitable future.

Before you go any further, the following are two subjects that will help you to focus on your goals and write your business plan more effectively.

Developing an Exit Strategy:
Start the Race with the Finish Line in Sight[*]

Before you begin the business planning process, you need to think about the concept of planning your exit strategy. An exit strategy is not a plan for failure. It is a plan for success. Developing an exit strategy before you write your business plan will enable you to make the best decisions for your business. As you read the following pages, you will understand what an exit strategy is and how you can apply it to the business planning process.

Where Is the Finish Line?

Have you ever seen runners line up for a race not knowing where the finish line is? This would never happen, right? Whether you are starting a new business or expanding a current business, the implication is the same. *Before you begin the race, you need to know where you expect to finish.*

Businesses are started for many reasons. Some of the more common reasons include:

- ❖ To build a business for yourself instead of for someone else
- ❖ To pursue a passion (e.g., "I've always wanted to own a restaurant.")
- ❖ To be your own boss and the master of your own time
- ❖ To earn money doing what you really like to do (woodworking, quilting, photography, writing, etc.)
- ❖ To capitalize on an invention
- ❖ To replace income from the loss of a job
- ❖ To create net worth (long-term capital appreciation)

It is also inherent in the makeup of entrepreneurs to think early on about future expansion of their enterprises. What new products or services can be added? Can new markets be reached? Can the business use more employees? Can it open more offices?

The list of reasons for start-up and expansion could go on and on. What's really important, though, is to understand that, in all cases, it is critical to develop an *exit (liquidity) strategy*.

---

[*] Reprinted with permission of John P. Neal, CEO, ACE Group, Inc. See Acknowledgments.

Developing an Exit Strategy Is the Secret

It is a given that professional investors (i.e., venture capitalists) will require a well thought-out exit strategy as part of the business plan for any venture in which they plan to invest. However, most entrepreneurs, intent on creating an immediate source of income or just caught up in the excitement of launching or expanding their businesses, have a habit of overlooking the "finish line." Consequently, they are unprepared for this "certain-as-taxes" event.

So, what should your strategy be? Before we go any further, you need to understand that there are no right or wrong strategies, only different ones. *Your* strategy should fit *your* goals. The logical place to start is with your long-term goals. The most obvious and often cited goal is retirement. Some entrepreneurs like to develop one business and then leave it to start another venture. You may have other reasons that you foresee will eventually cause you to exit your own business. Whatever your goals may be, there are three questions you need to answer before you begin to build a better business plan:

1. Where are you headed?
2. When do you want to get there?
3. What will your business look like when you arrive?

What Are Some of the Forms of Exit?

Some of the potential forms of exit include:

◈ *Selling all or a portion of the business*: It may be possible to sell the business outright to an independent buyer. If this is the case, you will want to maximize the net income of the business and avoid having assets tied up in the business that you would intend to later keep in your personal possession.

◈ *Passing the business to a family member*: This can be a good way to transfer value to your heirs in a way that minimizes estate taxes. Proper structuring is important; as well as determining who will run the business.

◈ *Selling to an Employee Stock Ownership Plan (ESOP)*: This can be a valuable vehicle when the new owner group is comprised of key employees in the business. There are certain tax advantages to ESOPs. Existence of the ESOP can also add to the value of the enterprise by giving employees a sense of ownership in the business.

◆ ***Taking the company public***: For those interested in gaining liquidity quickly while having the option to share in future stock appreciation, this might be a good option. The complexities of this form of exit are substantial, as is the demand on management's time leading up to and continuing on after the "event." This option is not for the faint of heart!

◆ ***Liquidation***: In some cases, the best option to gain liquidity may be to simply discontinue conducting business, sell off the business assets, pay off creditors, and keep the proceeds (after taxes, of course). While this is, in some respects, the simplest option, it often yields the least return to the owners because there is little or no value given for the "going concern" or goodwill of the business. This is often the method used when the business value is closely tied to real estate or other productive assets. It is also common for sole proprietor service businesses where income production is dependent solely on the owner practicing his or her skills.

Each of the above involves a variety of considerations. For instance, if you plan to sell the business, what kind of market can you expect for your type of business? How big might it need to be to achieve optimal value? If you plan to pass it on to a family member, who will that be? How will you train them to run the business? Will whomever you have in mind to succeed you be interested in taking over when you are ready to get out? When will you need to begin the transition? Many of these questions are difficult to answer, but ultimately your successful exit will depend on it.

Making Decisions Based on Your Exit Strategy

If you will take the time to think about and answer some of these questions, a clear picture of your business will begin to take form. Three of the major decisions you will be better prepared to make will be those of (1) selecting the source, type, and amount of capital you will need for your business, (2) deciding on the current form of organization, or legal structure, (sole proprietorship, partnership, or corporation) that will best serve your needs, and (3) considering tax issues that will impact your business.

Financing Your Business

Your choice of financing (source of capital) is important and will directly influence your choice of exit. Keep in mind, when considering financing options, not only the ease with which you can raise the funds you require to reach your goals, but the costs of each type of financing in terms of both money and relationships. In the simplest sense, capital is available from four sources: (1) yourself, (2) friends and family, (3) financial institutions, and (4) the public at large. The monetary cost of each of these options is generally inversely proportional to its personal or "relationship" cost.

◆ *Yourself (owner financing)*: The first question you should ask yourself is, "Do I really need additional financing to meet my goals, or do I just need to manage my cash flow effectively?"

◆ *Friends and family*: Friends and family can be the easiest, quickest, and least expensive form of financing. However, the emotional or relationship cost can be very high. What if your business fails and you are unable to repay your friends and family? Receiving funds from a traditional lender or a venture capital firm will take far longer, but failure to repay them isn't likely to affect your family gatherings.

◆ *Financial institutions (debt capital)*: In the middle is the traditional bank or finance company. Like the venture capitalist (below), they want to see a completed business plan before loaning any money to you. However, they don't tend to focus on *your* exit. Instead they focus on *their* exit, which is repayment of the loan when it is due along with interest and other applicable fees. These lenders want to see that management will be able to generate sufficient income and manage cash flow in such a way as to ensure timely repayment. They typically require personal guarantees of the owners and often will require additional collateral, such as a lien on your house or other property, to further ensure repayment.

◆ *Venture capitalists (equity capital)*: Venture capitalists typically invest in opportunities in which they expect to earn a high compound rate of return and that will provide an exit (return of their capital along with a return, or profit, on that capital) within five to seven years. They require a complete business plan with a strong exit strategy. Exit in this case, is usually via an Initial Public Offering (IPO) or acquisition by a larger, often public, company. In either case, such an exit typically results in a change of management and loss of control of the entity by the founders. While the venture capital option can be attractive, obviously it is not appropriate under many circumstances.

Dealing with Legal and Tax Issues

It is always a good idea to seek the advice of an experienced corporate attorney and a business accounting professional. Since laws vary from state to state, it is best to choose advisers familiar with the state in which the business will operate.

The determination of financing needs has a direct bearing on the form of legal structure you will need for your business. Thinking about your exit strategy will provide the basis for determining the form or organization that will best serve your needs as you pursue your goals. If you are a new business and the choice is not clear-cut, your attorney and tax adviser can help you make the best decision. Alternately, if you are a current business that is planning to expand through the use of debt or equity capital, you may be advised that you need to change to a legal structure that will enable you to protect your personal assets and to ensure your ability to deal with your lender or investor.

1. *A few of the legal issues that you and your advisers need to consider:*
   - *Liability of owners, directors, and officers*: Owners, directors, and officers may become liable for the actions and debts of the company in certain events. Reasonable protection from such liability can be achieved by a combination of effective use of elections and structuring alternatives and supplemented with Directors and Officers (D&O) insurance.
   - *Applicability of state and federal securities laws*: Rules regarding solicitation of investors are complex and require close compliance to avoid civil and criminal penalties.
   - *Rights of minority owners*: Access to books and records and minimum disclosure requirements create obligations requiring strict compliance.
   - *Ease and cost of transfer of ownership*: Depending on your time frame for exit, some legal structures are easier to deal with than others are.
   - *Buy-sell agreements among partners or shareholders*: Terms and conditions for buying out a partner/shareholder or their heirs should be spelled out clearly up front to avoid later disputes.

2. *Some of the tax issues to be considered:*
   - *Treatment of capital gains upon the sale/transfer of the business*: Tax events need to be planned far in advance. This includes available tax elections to minimize taxes incurred when all or a portion of your interest in a business is sold.

- *Corporate and personal taxes*: Proper structuring can strike an optimal balance between corporate and personal taxes and avoids double taxation.

- *Title to any real property owned*: Certain property may be best owned by partners/shareholders individually and leased to the business in order to achieve the lowest overall tax bill.

- *Reasonable compensation limits*: The IRS and state taxing authorities can set limits on the level of salaries to owner employees. Payments in excess of these limits become dividends that are taxable to the owner and not allowed to be deducted by the corporation.

- *Retirement plans*: A strong retirement plan can be a key tool for attracting high quality employees as well as providing for the owners' retirement. A wide variety of plans exist ranging from simple IRAs to complicated 401(K) plans. Each has advantages and limitations.

- *Unrelated business income*: If you are planning to start a "not-for-profit" corporation, which is not subject to normal income taxes, you will need to follow specific guidelines restricting the types of revenue you can generate. Sales of products unrelated to your not-for-profit business purpose may subject the organization to taxation.

Exit Planning Just Makes Good Sense!

By now you can see that thinking in terms of your future exit strategy will help you with your financing decisions and your legal and tax considerations as you write your business plan. Obviously, the less complex your business is, the fewer decisions you will have to make.

It does not matter whether you are writing a business plan for a new business or for an existing business that is moving in a new direction. Business planning is an ongoing process. As you continue to operate, your goals may change radically. The current and future goals and their impact on your exit strategy need to be continually reflected in your business plan.

With your vision established and sound financial, legal, and tax strategies decided upon, you can confidently build your business plan and ...

start the race with the finish line in sight!

Developing Financial Assumptions

What Are Financial Assumptions?

Financial assumptions are the rationale upon which you base the numbers you enter in your financial statements. A simplified example would be explaining that a marketing expense projection of $28,000 is based on sending out four mailings during the year (January, April, August, and October) at a cost of $10,000 for the initial mailing and $6,000 for each subsequent mailing.

Adding Financial Assumption Explanations to Your Business Plan

When you are writing the text portion of your business plan, each part of the plan should be developed not only as a conceptual idea, but in terms of how it will generate revenues and/or incur expenses. When you decide which legal structure suits your purpose, go one step further and find out what costs you will incur during the process. When you make decisions on who your management will be and what their jobs will entail, plan also what their compensation and your costs will be in terms of salary, taxes, and benefits. When you are considering a marketing campaign, determine its costs, probable response, and projected revenues.

In essence, every financial statement could have a sheet appended to it that explains how you arrived at your numbers. However, there are several scenarios you can choose to follow.

1. On all financial statements, you can add explanations at the bottom to clarify any items that would be confusing to the reader. In this instance, you would make no reference at the bottom to numbers that you feel need no clarification.

2. You can include a page of labeled "Financial Assumptions" either before or after your financial documents (or at some other location that is documented in your table of contents). On this page(s), you can list your financial assumptions. It is best in this instance to divide them into categories: revenues, inventory expenses, fixed and variable expenses, loans received, loan repayments, fixed asset purchases, etc. Also have a start-up cost category if you are a new business.

3. You can develop a full sheet of assumptions for your pro forma cash flow statement and append it to the back of the cash flow statement. On the other statements you can clarify only items that need explanation. This method puts the clarification in close proximity to the number it describes.

Having the pro forma cash flow statement fully explained has an additional advantage if you are approaching a lender or investor. The pro forma cash flow statement is of the highest priority in determining the validity of your request for funding. If you take the time to develop a full assumptions sheet for your cash flow statement, it saves the lender or investor valuable time in trying to determine the premises upon which your numbers are based.

What Is the Process for Developing Your Assumptions?

There is a logical process for creating financial assumptions. The steps are as follows:

1. As you develop each piece of your business plan, remember to develop it in terms of revenues you expect to generate and expenses you expect to incur (as in the examples above).

2. Keep a piece of paper at your side. As you determine the revenue and expense dollars related to the task you are working on, jot down the assumptions that you have developed. Be sure to include explanations of when revenues will be realized and when expenses will be incurred.

3. When you are ready to develop your financial plan, gather your assumptions together in one place and use them as the basis for the dollar amounts you input. Finally, append your assumptions to your financial statements, where they are needed, for clarification.

Oh, No! Another Job to Do!

Every time this book comes up for revision there is always something more to add to the business planning process. The reader may cringe because there is one more job to do. Going through the Financial Assumption Process will prove to be extremely valuable to you.

One of the most frequent errors made by people writing a business plan is that what they say in the text portion of the plan does not correlate with the numbers that they use in their financial documents. In fact, some people try to develop their financial plans first and then develop their organizational and marketing plans. **This is a fatal error.** You must develop the qualitative information and then quantify it in your financial plan. If the numbers do not work out, then you go back to the drawing board and make new decisions that will give you better financial results.

By utilizing the financial assumption process, you will be developing your plan the right way—write the text, thinking in terms of revenues and expenses; list the assumptions on a sheet of paper; transfer the numbers into your financial documents; append any assumptions that are needed for clarification of numbers to your financial documents.

The financial assumption process will do two things for you. It will save you time, because you will have all of your numbers at your fingertips when you are ready to develop your financial plan. The most important benefit, however, will be that your business plan will have absolute continuity between what you say in words in the text portion of your plan and what you say in numbers in the financial plan. In other words, *the qualitative part of your plan will say the same thing as the quantitative part of your plan and the plan will be both credible and defensible.*

Qualitative = Quantitative = Credibility + Defensibility

Note: On page 45 of the Dayne Landscaping, Inc. sample business plan (Appendix II), you will find an example of one way of documenting a list of financial assumptions. The writer in this example chose to include it as one of the Supporting Documents. You can also see an example of a clarification of a single line item in the pro forma cash flow statement at the bottom of page 30 of the same plan.

CHAPTER 2

The Cover Sheet

The cover sheet of your business plan is like the cover of a book. It needs to be attractive and should contain some important information.

The next two pages cover the following:

 What to Include

 Sample Cover Sheet

What to Include

The first page of your business plan will be the cover sheet. It serves as the title page and should contain the following information:

- ◆ **Company name**
- ◆ **Company address**
- ◆ **Company phone number (including area code)**
- ◆ **Logo, if you have one**
- ◆ **Names, titles, addresses, and phone numbers of the owners or corporate officers**
- ◆ **Month and year in which plan is issued**
- ◆ **Number of the copy**
- ◆ **Name of the preparer**

The company name, address, and phone number should appear in the top one-third of the page. If you have a logo, it may appear in the upper left-hand corner of the page or wherever you choose.

Information regarding the owners or corporate officers of the business will appear in the center of the page.

The bottom third of the page will contain the remaining information. The month and year in which the plan was written lets the lender or investor know if it is up-to-date. For instance, your plan is five months old, the lender or investor may request an update on certain financial information. Many lenders and investors prefer that one or more of the business owners or officers write the plan. This signifies a hands-on approach to the running of the company. Numbering your copies helps you keep track of them.

Keep a log with the following information: number of copy, name of person reviewing the copy, reviewer's phone number, and date submitted. This way you can keep up with the reviewing process and can make follow-up calls to the lender if necessary.

A sample cover sheet follows for your use. As you can see, this one-page contains a lot of information. It provides the name, location, and phone number of your business. By listing the sole proprietor, partners, or corporate officers, a lender or investor will know the legal structure of the business and how to contact key people directly for additional information. Keep in mind that lenders and investors must review many business plans in a limited amount of time. It is to your advantage to help them by making your plan thorough and concise.

Sample Cover Sheet

AEROTECH, INC.

372 East Main Street
Burke, NY 10071
(555) 555-4319

*AERO*TECH, INC.

John Smith, President
742 South Street
Jamestown, NY 10081
(555) 555-0221

Mary Blake, Vice-President
86 West Avenue
Burke, NY 10071
(555) 555-1213

Edwardo Rodriguez, Secretary
423 Potrero Avenue
Jessup, NY 10602
(555) 555-1648

Steve Wang, Treasurer
321 Nason Street
Adams, NY 10604
(555) 555-0201

Plan prepared January, 2000
by the Corporate Officers

Copy 2 of 6

Executive Summary

•••

The executive summary is the thesis statement of your business plan. It summarizes who you are, what your company does, where your company is going, why it is going where it is going, and how it will get there. If you are seeking funding, it specifies the purpose of the funding you seek and justifies the financial feasibility of your plan for the lender or investor.

Although the executive summary appears near the front of the plan, it is most effectively written after the rest of your business plan is complete. At that time, your concepts will be well developed and all the information and financial data needed will be available.

Use the **Key Word** approach mentioned earlier in the book. In a concise, one-page statement you will sum up the essence of your business plan by including answers to the following questions:

- ☑ **What?**
- ☑ **Where?**
- ☑ **Why?**
- ☑ **How?**
- ☑ **When?**

Executive Summary

The executive summary is the thesis statement of your business plan. It summarizes the content and purpose of your finished business plan, specifying who you are, where you are going, and how you plan to get there. If a lender or investor were to read only the executive summary, he would know the name and nature of your business, its legal structure, the amount and purpose of your loan request, and a repayment statement. If your business plan is for internal use only and you are not seeking funds, this statement would be a summary of your business and its goals for the future.

Use the **key word** approach mentioned earlier in this book. Be concise and clear. The executive summary is generally contained on one page. As you write your business plan and refine your ideas, you will probably discover new ideas and information that you will want to incorporate into your business plan to make your business more effective and profitable. For this reason, the executive summary is most effectively written after your plan has been completed. At that time, all the information and financial data will be available and you can draw it from the written text and financial spreadsheets.

The following is an example of how the key words may be used to help you form your executive summary as seen on page 26:

What?

What is the business name?
(Aerotech, Inc.)

What is its legal structure?
(S Corporation)

What product or service is involved?
(Manufacturer of specialized parts for the aerospace industry)

What will the loan do for the company?
(Modernize equipment, which will result in a 35 percent increase in production and decrease the unit cost by 25 percent)

What will be used for collateral?
(Property at 372 E. Main Street, Burke, NY, with an assessed valuation of $800,000 in 1998)

Where?

Where is the business located?
(372 E. Main Street, Burke, NY 10071)

Why?

Why is the loan needed?
(To increase growth capital)

How?

How much money is needed?
($250,000)

How will the loan be used?
(For the purchase of new and more modern equipment and
to train personnel in the use of the new equipment)

How will the loan be repaid?
(The end result will be a net profit increase sufficient to
repay the loan and interest within three years)

When?

When was the business established?
(1990)

When is the loan needed?
(Funding is needed so equipment can be delivered and in
place by May 23, 2000. There is a two-month period
between order placement and delivery date.)

When can repayment begin?
(Within 30 days of receipt of funds)

If you are writing your plan to serve as a guide for your business, and not
planning to seek a lender or investor, writing an executive summary will
help you to formulate a good summary picture of where you are planning
to go in your business.

If you are planning to approach a lender, address the question of loan
repayment and be specific about the use of funds. You want to show the
lender your company's ability to meet interest expense as well as principal repayments. Some lenders like to see "two ways out" (two different
sources of repayment). Support the amount requested with information
such as purchase orders, estimates from suppliers, rate sheets, and marketing results. Include this information in the Supporting Documents
section. For example, if you are purchasing a piece of equipment in
order to increase production or expand services, you must not only show
figures on its cost, but must also demonstrate a ready market for the
additional products or services. The rest of the plan must back up your
summary statement.

If you are hoping to attract an investor (venture capitalist), you will need to address how you will meet his or her goals for growth and profitability. Remember that an investor will be an equity partner in your company.

When you have answered the key word questions, you are ready to present that information in a few concise paragraphs.

Executive Summaries

If you are not planning to seek a lender or investor. The Best-CARE Company executive summary is for a company whose goal does not involve seeking financing from a lender or investor. It is different from the second example in that it does not involve justification of financing or a schedule for receipt of funds, repayment of a loan, or plans for return on investment to a venture capitalist (equity partner).

If you are planning to seek a lender or investor. The executive summary for Aerotech, Inc. is for a company whose goal is to seek financing from a lender or investor. Unlike the BestCare example, this executive summary will have to address the financing needs of the company in terms of how much money is needed, when it is needed, how the company plans to use the funds, how the use of those funds will achieve a desired outcome, and how and when repayment will take place to the lender. In the case of venture capital, you will address the investor's profit potential (return on investment).

BestCARE Company Executive Summary

BestCARE Company is a partnership established in 1995, whose purpose is to provide quality full-time care to the elderly through licensed residential board and care homes.

The company is administratively located at 1234 Hillside Drive in the city of Laguna Hills, California, the home of Jennifer Lopez, R.N., one of the two partners. In addition to attending to the administration and accounting duties, Ms. Lopez also oversees medical services for the elderly residents. Her partner, Henry Johnson, oversees maintenance of the homes and does all of the shopping for food, furniture, patient supplies, etc.

BestCARE Company owns and operates three five-bedroom homes within Orange County, California. Each home provides 24-hour per day, full-care services for up to six residents. Two fully-trained caregivers have been hired for each home and live on the premises. Contract-service caregivers work on the live-ins' days off.

The three current homes have now been running profitably for the last three years. Current research shows that there are twice as many families seeking board and care homes as the preferred lifestyle for their elderly parents than was the case in 1995. This has created a high demand where the supply is short.

BestCARE Company is now planning to expand by purchasing two more homes over the next five years. The two new homes will be mortgage free. They will be purchased with cash from previous profits from the company that have been retained and invested by the partners.

This business plan will serve as a five-year plan that will guide the company through the administrative, marketing, and financial issues that are inherent in reaching a growth goal that will double the size of the company.

Executive Summary for Aerotech, Inc.

Formed in 1990, Aerotech, Inc. is an S Corporation operating from a 25,000-square-foot manufacturing and warehousing space in Aerospace Tech Park, a light-industrial park, located at 372 E. Main Street, Burke, New York. In the past two years, the Economic Development Corporation (EDD) of Burke has been successful in encouraging large aerospace and technology corporations to relocate to the Tech Park. Aerotech, Inc. has developed excellent working relationships with the relocated companies. The company currently serves 20% of the total market with gross revenue of $650,000.

Aerotech, Inc. custom designs and manufactures specialized parts for the aerospace industry. The company is seeking growth capital in the amount of $250,000 for the purpose of purchasing automated equipment and for training existing personnel in the use of that equipment. Modernization of equipment will result in a 35% increase in production and will decrease the unit costs by 25%.

Burke EDD projections through the year 2005 indicate a 30% increase in tenancy in the Tech Park by aerospace companies. Federal Government statistics project a 25% increase in the United States in aerospace development through the year 2020. Information from engineering and aerospace trade associations indicate that automation is needed to allow the company to remain competitive. By building on past working relationships with current companies and by actively marketing to new residents of the Tech Park, Aerotech, Inc. will be able to capture an additional 15% of the market; the Corporation's share will be 35% of the total market.

Funding is needed in time for the equipment to be delivered and in place by May 23, 2000. There is a two-month period between order placement and delivery date. Training of employees on the new equipment is projected to cover a two-week period following equipment placement.

The company is expected to break-even 24 months after completion of the employee training period. Repayment of the loan and interest can begin promptly within 30 days of receipt of funds. The loan can be secured by company-owned real estate that has a 1999 assessed valuation of $800,000.

Part I
The Organizational Plan

The first major section of your business plan covers the organizational details of your business. Include information about your industry in general and your business in particular.

Again using the key words, address all of the following elements. There is no set format for their arrangement. You may cover each item in an order that seems logical to you.

- ☑ **Description of the Business**
- ☑ **Products or Services**
- ☑ **Management and Personnel**
- ☑ **Legal Structure**
- ☑ **Location**
- ☑ **Accounting and Recordkeeping**
- ☑ **Insurance**
- ☑ **Security**

Begin this section with a one-page summary addressing the key elements of your business. If you are seeking funding, the lender or investor should have a clear picture of the origins and objectives of your company. Indicate where the company is going and how it is going to get there. The text following your business summary will expand on each area presented. Be prepared to back up statements and justify projections with data in the Supporting Documents section.

You may formulate the organizational plan by again using the key word system. Answer the questions as they relate to each of the areas to be addressed in this section. There is no set format for their arrangement. Cover each topic in an order that seems logical to you. Remember, you are writing a summary. Be concise.

Description of the Business

This is the section of the plan in which you present a brief summary of the organization of your business, its business history, its present status, and your future projections for research and development. Stress the uniqueness of your product or service and state how you can benefit the customer. Project a sense of what you expect to accomplish three to five years into the future.

Answer such questions as when and why this company was formed, the nature of the services or products provided, how the company developed, and what is being projected for the future.

Example: The following is a sample Description of Business statement for Aerotech, Inc.:

> Aerotech, Inc. was established in 1990 to meet the demand for specialized parts for the aerospace industry. This industry experienced moderate growth with an increase in contracts beginning in 1998. Industry projections indicate a growing demand for the type of products the company manufactures. Aerotech, Inc. maintains a competitive edge with prompt order fulfillment, excellent customer relations, and custom design capabilities. The company is adequately housed in a 25,000-square-foot facility and desires to meet the growing demand for its products through the purchase of new and more modern equipment, which will provide the opportunity for broader scope bidding, increased custom design capabilities, lower per unit costs, and faster turnaround time.

After completing the Description of Business statement, expand on each of the following topics in an order that seems logical to you.

Products or Services

If you are the manufacturer and/or wholesale distributor of a product. Give a detailed description of the development of that product from raw materials to finished item. The development of a flowchart will help you identify the various stages of production and will serve as a visual representation of product development for a lender or investor.

Wholesale: selling for resale.

The flowchart will help you develop a time line to demonstrate when raw materials must be ordered, how much time is needed in the production process, and how much time is involved in inventory storage and in shipping and handling. What raw materials are used, and how much do they cost? Who are your suppliers, where are they located, and why did you choose them? Include cost breakdowns and rate sheets in the Supporting Documents section to back up your statements. Although you may order from one main supplier, include information on alternate suppliers. Address how you could handle a sudden increase in orders or a loss of a major supplier. How will the work get done, by whom, and at what cost? Project peak production times and determine when money will be needed for key purchases. You will use labor cost projections again when you develop a Cash Flow Statement in your Financial Documents section.

Describe your equipment and facilities. Information on vehicles, equipment, and buildings owned by your company will appear as Balance Sheet items in the Financial Documents section of your plan. When preparing your Balance Sheet, you will refer to this section for information on current values.

If you are developing a product for export or are anticipating importing raw materials or finished products for sale in this country, expand your business plan to include global information. The development of a flowchart will help you identify the steps involved in bringing goods into this country or in shipping them overseas along with the time and costs involved. You may be working with foreign manufacturers and agents. You will deal with freight forwarders and custom brokers. The cost of their services and the time and method of payment will transfer to the Cash Flow Statement in the Financial Documents section of your plan.

If you are a retailer. Describe the products you sell and provide information about your primary and secondary sources of supply. Describe your product selection process and explain why specific suppliers or vendors were chosen. Include product descriptions and rate sheets in the Supporting Documents section.

Retail: selling directly to the consumer.

You may want to develop a flowchart to demonstrate the distribution process. How do the products you sell in your shop get from the manu-

Inventory: a list of assets being held for sale.

Service business: a retail business that deals in activities for the benefit of others.

Management: the art of conducting and supervising a business.

facturer through your industry's normal distribution channels, into your store, onto your shelves, and into your customers' hands?

Do you have a system for managing and tracking inventory? What volume of goods do you stock in inventory, how do you determine the value of your inventory, who will be responsible for checking the inventory? Refer back to this section for information on inventory when completing the Business Financial Statement or Loan Application form from the lender.

If you provide a service. Tell what your service is, why you are able to provide it, how it is provided, who will be doing the work, and where the service will be performed. Tell why your business is unique and what you have that is special to offer to your customers. If you have both a product and a service that work together to benefit your customer (such as warranty service for the products you sell), be sure to mention this in your plan. State where you will be getting your supplies and why those suppliers were chosen. Project the costs of overhead and vehicle expense. Will you be providing service in the customer's home or will you work from an office or shop? How much time is involved in the service you will be doing, and how many of those hours are billable to the client?

In all cases. List future products or services that you plan to provide as you grow your business. Try to anticipate potential problem areas and work out a plan of action. You should state any proprietary rights, such as copyright, patent, or trademark in this section. You will need to back up your statements by including copies of photos, diagrams, and certificates in the Supporting Documents section.

Management and Personnel

Potential lenders or investors in a new business will ask, "Why should your management team be entrusted with our money?" As a business owner, some of the questions you will ask are, "What are the key areas of management in my business"; "How will the organization be structured?"; "Who will manage the business?"; "What outside help may be required?"; "How many employees will be needed and when should they be hired?" These questions can be answered with the development of a realistic organizational plan.

Your management and personnel needs will be determined by the capabilities of the business owners, by the amount of time they will be able to commit to the business, and by the demands of the marketplace. Small businesses usually start up with the owners doing most of the work. As the business grows and sales increase, staff is added. Project how your company will grow and when additional employees will be added. Hiring policies, job descriptions, and employee contracts are all part of an organizational plan. Tell how employees will be compensated: salaries, benefits, bonuses, vacation time, stock purchase plans.

An organizational chart can visually show areas of responsibility and the personnel in charge of each section along with the number of employees they will manage. For example, you may need key people in charge of marketing, administration, finance, and operations. Each of these individuals may have employees that they will supervise. The lender will be able to identify the key people in your business, and you will have a graphic representation of your management and personnel.

Stock: an ownership share in a corporation; another name for a share; accumulated merchandise.

Companies involved in international trade will require additional team members. Knowing the language of the country you work with is important in building strong business ties. You may need the services of a translator. Imported products need permits and documentation. Customs brokers and freight forwarders take care of documentation and ensure that the shipment will arrive on time, intact, and at the agreed-upon price. They will handle freight costs, port charges, consular fees, and insurance costs.

Customs broker: a licensed individual who, for a fee, handles the necessary papers and steps in obtaining clearance of goods through the customs.

You may consider using an export management company or contracting for foreign representation. The International Trade Administration (ITA) will prepare custom evaluations, called World Traders Data Reports, on your potential trading partners. Its overseas commercial staff checks the firm's standing in the local business community, credit-worthiness, and overall reliability and suitability as a trade contact. The ITA is administered through the U.S. Department of Commerce.

Becoming a successful importer or exporter depends on the determination and commitment of your entire company. Your management team and work force should understand the procedures involved in international commerce. Your local Trade Administration office, the Department of Commerce, and the U.S. Customs Service can provide information on specific trade laws that will affect your business.

Legal Structure

Next, provide a description of the legal structure of your business. If you are a sole proprietor, tell about your abilities and include your resume. Be honest about areas in which you will need help and state how you will get that help. Will you hire an office manager, work with an accountant, or seek the advice of someone in marketing?

If you have formed a partnership, explain why the partners were chosen, what they bring to the company, and how their abilities complement each other. Show their experience and qualifications by including copies of

Partnership: a legal business relationship of two or more people who share responsibilities, resources, profits, and liabilities.

Corporation: a voluntary organization of persons, either actual individuals or legal entities, legally bound together to form a business enterprise.

Articles of Incorporation: a legal document filed with the state that sets forth the purposes and regulations of a corporation.

their resumes. Include a copy of your partnership agreement in the Supporting Documents section. Your agreement should include provisions for partners to exit and for the dissolution of the company. It must spell out the distribution of the profits and the financial responsibility for any losses. Explain the reasoning behind the terms of your agreement.

If you have incorporated, outline the corporate structure and give detailed information on the corporate officers. Who are they, what are their skills, why were they chosen, and what will they bring to the organization? Include a copy of the charter and articles in the Supporting Documents section.

If you anticipate changing your legal structure in the future, make projections regarding why you would change, when the change would take place, who would be involved, and how the change would benefit the company. Refer back to this section for information on legal structure when completing the Business Financial Statement or Loan Application form from a lender.

Best- and Worst-Case Scenarios

You may hear a lender refer to the worst-case scenario. This means that the lender wants you to be able to identify potential problems and to work out solutions before these difficulties occur. It is also to your advantage to prepare for the unexpected so that your business can continue to run smoothly. If sales projections are not achieved, are there other ways in which you can generate revenue? Will you be required to reduce staff or will they be able to fill other positions? For example, if sales drop off at your sporting goods store, could personnel increase revenue by teaching in-store classes or by holding sports clinics.

Some businesses fail because they become too successful too soon. Therefore, it is also good to plan for the best-case scenario. If you are inundated with orders, your business plan should contain the information needed to locate and hire added employees and contact additional suppliers. For example, if you project a volume of business that would warrant hiring additional staff in six months, project the additional salaries and transfer those amounts to the Cash Flow Statement. Your business plan is your key to responding promptly to the unexpected in order to keep your business progressing smoothly.

Location

If location is a marketing consideration, it will not be included in this section. For example, if you are opening a retail shop and need to be directly accessible to your customers, your choice of location will be determined by your target market and would therefore need to be addressed in your Marketing Plan (see Chapter 5). If you are a manufacturer, however, and ship by common carrier, such as United Parcel Service, your location may not be directly tied to your target market. In that case, you would discuss location here in your Organizational Plan. You may begin with a sentence such as:

> Aerotech, Inc. is housed in 25,000 square feet of warehouse space located at 372 E. Main Street, Burke, New York. This space was chosen because of accessibility to shipping facilities, good security provisions, low square-footage costs, and proximity to sources of supply and to the target market.

Now expand on each reason and back up your statements with a physical description of the site and a copy of the lease agreement. Your lease or rental agreement will contain the financial information needed for monthly cost projections for the Cash Flow statement. The value of property owned will be transferred to a Balance Sheet in the Financial Documents section.

Give background information on your site choice. List other possible locations and tell why you chose your location. You may want to include copies of pictures, layouts, or drawings of the location in the Supporting Documents section.

A **Location Analysis Worksheet** is included at the end of this section. You may duplicate it for your own use in gathering data needed to make a decision regarding the location of your business. This worksheet is intended as a guideline for writing a location (site) analysis. Cover only those topics that are relevant to your business.

Marketing: all the activities involved in the buying and selling of a product or service.

Target market: the specific individuals, distinguished by socio-economic, demographic, and interest characteristics, who are the most likely potential customers for the goods and services of a business.

Lease: a long-term rental agreement.

Accounting and Recordkeeping

Tell what accounting system will be used and why the system was chosen. What portion of your accounting will be done internally? Who will be responsible for keeping your records? Will you be using an outside accountant to maximize your profits? If so, who within your company will be skilled at reading and analyzing the financial statements provided by the accountant?

It is important to show not only that your accounting will be taken care of, but that you will have some means of using your financial statements to implement changes to make your company more profitable. After reading this section, the lender or investor should have confidence in your company's ability to keep and interpret a complete set of financial records. Information regarding accounting and auditing of your books is

Accountant: a highly trained professional who is skilled at keeping business records.

often requested on the Business Financial Statement from the lender or investor.

If you are involved with international trade, keep up with changes in currency by reading the foreign exchange reports regularly. A knowledge of currency exchange rates and awareness of devaluation and escalation of the dollar can mean the difference between a profit and loss for your company. Understand the methods of payment for the countries with which you are dealing. Do they require foreign bank checks, will they accept credit cards, will you need a letter of credit from your bank, how will they be invoicing? You may need in-country agents to process monetary transactions.

Insurance

Insurance is an important consideration for every business. Product liability is a major consideration, especially in certain industries. Service businesses are concerned with personal liability, insuring customers' goods while on the premises or during the transporting of those goods. If a vehicle is used for business purposes, your insurance must reflect that use. If you own your business location, you will need property insurance. Some types of businesses require bonding. Partners may want life insurance naming each other as the beneficiary.

Exporters may reduce risks by purchasing export credit insurance from the Export-Import Bank of the U.S. agent, the Foreign Credit Insurance Association. Policies available include insurance for financing or operating leases, medium term insurance, the new-to-export policy insurance for the service industry, and the umbrella policy.

Consider the types of coverage appropriate to your business. Tell what coverage you have, why you chose it, what time period it covers, and who the carrier is.

Keep your insurance information current. An **Insurance Update Form** has been included at the end of this section. Use it to maintain information on alternate insurance companies. If your premiums are suddenly raised or your coverage is canceled, you will be able to refer to your worksheet in order to find another insurance carrier. The Business Financial Statement from the lender asks for information that can be taken from this section.

Letter of credit: instrument issued by a bank by which the bank substitutes its own credit for that of an individual or business.

Liability insurance: risk protection for actions for which a business is liable.

Security

According to the U.S. Chamber of Commerce, more than 30 percent of business failures result from employee dishonesty. This includes not only theft of merchandise, but also theft of information.

Address the issue of security as it relates to your business. For example, if you are disposing of computer printout data, a small paper shredder may be cost-effective. We have all seen the sensing devices used in clothing stores. Anticipate problem areas in your business, identify security measures you will put into practice and tell why you chose them, and what you project they will accomplish. Discuss this area with your insurance agent. You may be able to lower certain insurance costs while protecting your business.

Summary

You have now covered all the areas that should be addressed in the Organizational Plan. Use the key words, be thorough, anticipate any problem areas, and be prepared with solutions. Analyze industry trends and be ready to project your business into the future. Chapter 11, "Information Resources," contains listings of resource materials available to you. Most are available at your public or college library. Use them to gather the information needed to write a comprehensive business plan. When the Organizational Plan section has been completed, you are ready to go to the next chapter and begin formulating the Marketing Plan.

Location Analysis Worksheet

1. Address: _____

_____

2. Name, address, phone number of realtor/contact person: _____

_____

3. Square footage/cost: _____

_____

4. History of location: _____

_____

5. Location in relation to your target market: _____

_____

6. Traffic patterns for customers: _____

_____

7. Traffic patterns for suppliers: _____

_____

8. Availability of parking (include diagram): _____

_____

_____

9. Crime rate for the area: _____

_____

10. Quality of public services (e.g., police, fire protection): _____

_____

Location Analysis Worksheet
continued

11. Notes on walking tour of the area: _____

_____

_____

12. Neighboring shops and local business climate: _____

_____

_____

13. Zoning regulations: _____

_____

14. Adequacy of utilities (information from utility company representatives): _____

_____

15. Availability of raw materials/supplies: _____

_____

16. Availability of labor force: _____

_____

17. Labor rate of pay for the area: _____

_____

18. Housing availability for employees:_____

_____

19. Tax rates (state, county, income, payroll, special assessments): _____

_____

20. Evaluation of site in relation to competition: _____

_____

_____

Insurance Update Form

Company Name: Aerotech, Inc.   **Updated as of January, 1999**

Company	Contact Person	Coverage	Cost Per Year
Best Insurance Company 123 E. Blank Street Anytown, USA 12345	Sam Smith 555-123-4567	General Business Policy (see attached)	$ 750
Ace Insurance Agency 345 W. 11th Avenue Everytown, USA 23456	Lydia Likable 555-456-7890	Worker's Compensation	$ 617
AAA Life Insurance Co. Route 7, Box 2222 Ruraltown, USA 77777	Pete Farmer 555-987-6543	$200,000 Universal Life Policy Beneficiary: John K.	$ 1,642
BBB Life Insurance Co. 4444 Any Street Best Town, USA 22222	Susan Swift 555-876-5432	$200,000 Universal Life Policy Beneficiary: Joe	$ 1,576
Best Insurance Company (address: see above)	Sam Smith 555-123-4567	Auto Vehicle 1 (see current policy)	$ 634
Best Insurance Company (address: see above)	Sam Smith 555-123-4567	Auto Vehicle 2 (see current policy)	$ 583
Industry Insurance Specialists 465 Insurance Blvd., Suite A Sue Town, USA 66666	Roy Ripoff 555-666-6666	Product Liability	$ 1,270
1. TOTAL ANNUAL INSURANCE COST			**$ 7,072**
2. AVERAGE MONTHLY INSURANCE COST			**$ 589**

Notes:

1. *Make sure to take out $1,000,000 Umbrella Policy when John retires from the company.*
2. *Check into Employee Benefits; Association is planning to offer new coverage June, 1999.*

CHAPTER 5

Part II
The Marketing Plan

• •

The second major section of your business plan covers the details of your marketing plan. In this section you will include information about the total market with an emphasis on your own target market.

Again using the key words, address all of the following elements. There is no set format for their arrangement. Cover each item in an order that seems logical to you.

- ☑ **The Product-Market Analysis**
- ☑ **Target Market**
- ☑ **Competition**
- ☑ **Methods of Distribution**
- ☑ **Promotion**
- ☑ **Pricing**
- ☑ **Product Design**
- ☑ **Timing of Market Entry**
- ☑ **Location**
- ☑ **Industry Trends**

The Product-Market Analysis*

Before you write your Marketing Plan, the most important thing you need to do is to analyze your market and make a product-market decision. There are two parts to this decision:

1. **The choice of which customer needs you will satisfy**—as reflected in the specific product or service you will sell to your customers.
2. **The choice of the specific customers to whom you wish to sell your product or service** (your target market segment).

Once you have made these decisions, you will be ready to write your marketing plan, as described in the next part of this chapter. If you take the time to do this analysis and carefully choose which customers you will market your product or service to, you will find that almost every prospect you talk to will have a need for what you're selling.

Choosing a group of customers to sell to—i.e., selecting a target market segment—means selecting potential customers according to some criteria you have determined are related to the likelihood these customers will want to buy your product or service. These criteria might include demographic factors such as age, income, or where they live; or lifestyle factors such as interest in sports, antique collecting, reading mystery novels, or seeing foreign movies. Your job as a businessperson is to determine what factors relate to your customers' likelihood of buying your product or service.

Follow the Four Rules for Marketing and Sales Success

The following four rules for marketing and sales success are designed to help you analyze your market and choose the customers who are more likely to want to buy your product or service. Focusing your marketing and selling efforts on these customers will make finding and keeping new customers easier for you than if you are targeting less selectively.

 Note: These rules apply whether you are selling to consumers or to other businesses. They also apply to you whether you are a start-up or an existing business.

Rule #1: Find Potential Customers Who Want Your Product or Service

If your potential customers are consumers, will they recognize that they have a need or want? If your customers are businesses, will they

---

* Reprinted with permission of Donald R. McCrea, Director of Executive Education, University of California, Irvine.

recognize that they have a business problem to solve or an opportunity to exploit?

If the group of customers you have chosen to sell to clearly recognizes their need, want, problem, or opportunity, then they are more likely to want to buy your product or service. Note, though, that it's not enough that *you* recognize that your prospects have a need or problem: you will have to determine if they will recognize this, as well.

If your prospects do not recognize their need or problem, then the first action plan of your marketing and selling activities will be to create or heighten your prospects' awareness of their need or problem. This will require specific effort on your part, and is typically done through an integrated marketing communications program.

It's far simpler and less costly, however, if (during your analysis) you can identify that there is a selected group of potential customers who *already* recognize their need or problem. This group then validates your plan by becoming your *target market segment*, and your marketing and selling tasks become easier with this group.

The question you must answer is: What are the characteristics of your potential customers that are related to their need or desire for your product or service? The **Target Market Worksheet** at the end of this chapter will help you answer this question. For example, if you are selling an electric toothbrush, people who visit a dentist regularly are more likely to be interested in your toothbrush than those who don't visit the dentist very often. Customer characteristics that relate to likelihood of visiting a dentist might include income and education. You might therefore choose to sell your electric toothbrush only to individuals making more than $50,000 a year and with at least a four-year college degree.

Rule #2: Identify Customers Who Are Ready to Buy

Will the want/need/problem/opportunity cause your prospects enough pain or the prospect of enough pleasure that they will be willing to take action?

If your prospects are ready to act to fill their need or solve their business problem, then they will be more likely to buy your product or service. On the other hand, if your potential customers' need or problem is not strong enough to motivate them to take action, then you will be required to expend more sales and marketing efforts to convince them that they will benefit from filling the need or solving the problem. Keep in mind that your prospects probably have several needs or problems, so you must show them that the one you can fill or solve is of high enough priority that they should fill it before the others. This again will require specific effort your part, and will become another requirement for your integrated marketing communications program. You will be able to save yourself much of this effort, however, if you plan to refine your target market segment to include only those prospects who already recognize their need or problem *and* who are willing to act on that need or problem.

To continue your analysis, then, the next question you must ask yourself is: Are there additional customer characteristics that will tell me that these customers will be ready to buy? To expand on the example above—of those who visit the dentist regularly—those with a higher likelihood of gum disease may be more ready to buy your electric toothbrush than those with healthy teeth and gums. One customer characteristic that is related to a higher incidence of gum disease is age. You might therefore choose to sell your electric toothbrush to those individuals who are over 45 years of age.

When you combine this characteristic with the income and education characteristics we selected previously, your analysis has determined that your target market segment would now become those individuals earning $50,000 or more per year, with four or more years of college education, and who are over 45 years of age.

To complete your analysis, there are two more rules to apply once you have identified your target market segment. Both rules will help your business achieve success.

Rule #3: Let the Customers Know that You Can Fill Their Need

Will your prospects recognize that you can fulfill their need or want, or solve their business problem? If you are an existing business, do your prospects already recognize your ability to fill their need or want, or solve their business problem?

If you are an existing business, and they do, then your marketing communications program has already done its job, or you have already built good relations with these prospects. You can move on to Rule #4.

If your prospects do not yet recognize your ability to meet their need or solve their problem, then you must figure out how to demonstrate to them your ability to do so. This activity will become a part of your marketing communications program, and will form the core of your initial selling activities. Your prospects must recognize that you have a solution to their need or problem before they will commit to spending time or resources with you.

If you have chosen a target market segment satisfying Rules #1 and #2, then the bulk of your marketing and sales activities and expenditures will be dedicated to satisfying Rule #3 and Rule #4. Rule #3 will be satisfied by your advertising and promotional activities.

Once you have figured out how to educate your prospects on your ability to satisfy their need or solve their problem, you can move on to Rule #4.

Rule #4: Find Customers Who Will Pay

Will your prospects pay you *to meet their need or solve their business problem?*

There are two parts to this Rule: (1) Will your prospect *pay*? And (2) Will your prospect *pay you*? Even though your prospects recognize their need or problem, are motivated to take action, and recognize that you have a solution, they may not be ready or able to pay, or to pay you.

You must ensure your prospect will have funds budgeted or available to fill this need or solve this problem. You also must ensure you are dealing with the decision-makers. In the case of a family, the husband and wife may make joint decisions, especially on large purchases. In the case of a business, several individuals may comprise the "buying center," including a purchasing agent, an executive, a financial officer, and possibly others.

Once you have determined your prospect's ability and willingness to pay, you must ensure they will willing to pay you—i.e., they recognize you can fill their need or solve their problem in a way that no other competitor or substitute product can. They must clearly see greater value in what you have to offer them and trust you to stand behind your product or service's ability to meet their need or solve their problem. If your prospects can't distinguish you from your competitors, don't trust you, or can't distinguish your product or service from other products or services offered to them, then a portion of your marketing and sales activities will have to be spent on educating them about your uniqueness and trustworthiness. Of course, uniqueness and trustworthiness must have value to your prospects before they will be willing to pay for them. Utilize the **Competition Analysis Worksheets** at the end of this chapter.

Conclusion

If you are a new business analyzing your market, remember that every firm must satisfy these four rules for marketing and sales success. If you have an existing business and you are having difficulty finding customers to purchase your product or service—or—you are spending a lot of time "convincing" your prospects to buy, consider targeting your market segment to satisfy Rules #1 and #2. Then, you'll find that almost every prospect you talk to will have a need for what you're selling. You'll then be able to concentrate your marketing and sales efforts on satisfying

Rules #3 and #4, to ensure that they easily see how you can fulfill their needs better than any of your competitors.

If the results of your product-market analysis show that there are valid customers for your product or service, you are now ready to write your marketing plan. The benefit to you of following the four rules will be shorter sales cycles, a higher percentage of prospects converted to customers, and more productive use of your marketing and sales dollars

◆ ◆ ◆ ◆ ◆

What Is a Marketing Plan?

Now that you have made a product-market decision, you are ready to write the actual Marketing Plan. Your Marketing Plan is the section of your business plan that is devoted to getting your product or service to your customer or "target market." You might like to think of marketing as **the Three Rs Process**. You will need to **(1) research**, **(2) reach**, and **(3) retain** your target market. The elements included in this chapter should help you to organize needed information into a workable plan that will do just that.

A good marketing plan is essential to your business development and success. It will be necessary for you to include information about the total market with emphasis on your target market. You must take the time to identify your customers and find the means to make your product or service attractive and available to them. The key here is time. It takes time to research and develop a good marketing plan, but it is time well spent.

Most of the information you need will be found in the public library and in the publications of the U.S. Department of Commerce, the U.S. Small Business Administration (SBA), and the U.S. Census Bureau (see Chapter 11, "Information Resources," for specific resources). Remember, you need a clear understanding of who will purchase your product, who will make use of your service, why they will choose your company, and how they will find out about it.

Begin this section with a one-page summary covering the key elements of your marketing plan. The text following will expand on each area presented in the summary. Back up statements and justify projections with data in the Supporting Documents section. Again, the key word approach will help you to thoroughly cover each area. The topics may be covered in any order that seems logical to you.

Target Market

The target market has been defined as "that group of customers with a set of common characteristics that distinguishes them from other customers."

You want to identify that "set of common characteristics" that will make those customers yours.

Tell how you did your market research. What were your resources and what were your results? What are the demographics of your target market? Where do your customers live, work, and shop? Do they shop where they live or where they work? What is their psychological make-up? Are they impulse purchasers? If you are in the business of VCR repair, how many VCRs are owned within a specific radius of your shop? Would in-home service be cost-effective and a benefit to your customers? What are their demographics in terms of age, sex, and income? What do they do in their leisure time? Back up your findings with census reports, questionnaires, test marketing results. State how you feel you can serve this market in terms of your resources, strengths, and weaknesses. Focus on reasonable, believable, and obtainable projections regarding the size of your potential market.

Companies involved in international trade will identify products or services suitable for import or export. What are their selling features? What needs do they satisfy? Profile the country or countries in which you plan to do business and outline your strategy for reaching those markets. Just as markets are different, so are the needs of your potential customers. Variations in climate, physical environment, personal income, spending habits, religious beliefs, and national traditions will influence the types of goods and services foreign customers need and find acceptable.

Note: A **Target Market Worksheet** has been included at the end of this chapter for your use in identifying your customers. Complete the questions asked on the worksheet in outline format. Then formulate the information gathered into text. After reading this section, the lender or investor must know that you have identified your customers, and that you have data to support your findings.

Competition

Direct competition is a business offering the same product or service to the same market. **Indirect competition** is a company with the same product or service, but with a different target market. For example, a gift shop is in direct competition with another gift shop and in indirect competition with a catalog company that offers the same products. If you are a CPA who goes to the client, your indirect competition will be CPAs working in an office. The difference between direct and indirect competition is most often determined by the method of delivering your product or service.

Evaluate both types of competitors. You want to determine the competitors' images. To what part of the market are they trying to appeal? Can you appeal to the same market in a better way? Or can you find an untapped market?

Use the **Competition Evaluation Worksheet** at the end of this section to compile, organize, and evaluate information about your competition. Your analysis of this information will help you plan your market entry. What is the competition's current market share (what percent of the total customer base is theirs)? Can you tap into this share or will you need to carve out your own market niche (your wedge of the pie)? Make a comparison of your competitor's pricing structure and product or service quality.

To help you with your research, we have also provided a **Competition Reference List for Locating Information on Companies**.

After completing a competition analysis, you and your lender will know who your competitors are, where they are located, what products or services they offer, how you plan to compete, how your customers can access your business, and why you can provide a unique and beneficial service or product.

Methods of Distribution

Distribution is the manner in which products are physically transported to the consumer and the way services are made available to the customer. Distribution is closely related to your target market.

Establish the purchasing patterns of your customers. If you are selling a product, do your customers purchase by direct mail, buy through catalogs, or make in-store purchases? Will you sell directly through a manufacturer's representative? If you are shipping the product, who will absorb the shipping costs and what carrier will be used?

Contract: an agreement regarding mutual responsibilities between two or more parties.

Use the **key words** to answer questions regarding your distribution plan. Back up decisions with statistical reports, rate sheets for shippers, contracts with manufacturer's reps, or any other supporting documents.

If you are involved in a service business, will you provide in-shop service? Will you make house calls, and if so, how will mileage costs be handled? What is your planned response time to fill your customers' needs?

Tariff: duties imposed on exports and imports.

If you plan to import or export merchandise, you need to be aware of distribution practices, import regulations, and licensing requirements for countries with which you are doing business. Check on tariffs, quotas, and other government-imposed trade restrictions. You should also be familiar with a country's legal system and regulatory framework including contract law, taxation, currency restrictions, and restrictions on foreign investment and operations. This information is available from the U.S. Department of Commerce International Trade Administration.

List the pros and cons of the various methods of distribution and give the reasons for your choices. Keep in mind the **worst-case scenarios** mentioned in the Organizational Section. Present alternatives. For example, if your mobile service van breaks down, do you have a vehicle that could be used as a back-up? If you are the only service provider, how will you keep your customer happy if you are ill or away from your business for a period of time? Provide for a smooth business flow. Projects costs for one year and break them down into monthly expenditures. These amounts will be transferred to a Cash Flow Statement.

If you plan to import or export merchandise, you need to be aware of the distribution practices and trade regulations for countries with which you are doing business. Fulfillment will involve a combination of sea, air, and land container service, and you will need the advice of an experienced freight forwarder.

Freight forwarder: company responsible for handling transport of imported and exported goods; deal with documentation, permits, and transport.

Promotion

Promotion of your business involves using all means available to get the message to your customers that your product or service is good and desirable.

You will have identified what is **unique** about your business and how that uniqueness will **benefit the customer**. The uniqueness and benefits of your products or services will carry through all of your promotion and will develop your image. The following paragraphs discuss some types of promotion to be considered while you are writing your plan:

Note: Be sure to develop your promotion plan in terms of projected costs and expected response (i.e. return on investment). A promotion plan is only effective if it generates revenues to justify the expense.

A. **Paid advertising** is one means of promotion and is available through radio, television, newspapers, and magazines. To be effective, your promotion must be tailored for your target market. What magazines and newspapers do they read? Analyze your competitors' advertising in these publications. Your marketing research will have spelled out which television programs, radio stations, and publications are of interest to your target market. In the example of Aerotech, Inc., trade publications and the business section of your key newspapers would be appropriate. Be ready to back up your decisions. Tell the lender or investor where you will put your advertising dollars, why you chose those methods, how your message will reach your customers, when your advertising campaign will begin, how much your plan will cost, and what format your advertising will take. Include copies of your advertisements and rate sheets in the Supporting Documents section.

B. **Directory listings** such as the telephone Yellow Pages or trade and professional directories are another means of promoting your business. Be aware that directories are published at various times of the year. What is their publication schedule, what costs will be incurred for the listing, what are the circulation figures, what segment of your target market has access to these directories, and how will this be cost-effective? Costs and expected reveunues will be transferred to your Cash Flow Statement.

C. **Publicity** is "free" media coverage you have received or plan to seek. Include samples of press releases you will send and a plan for contacting key media people. You will find listings of media in the reference section of your library. Include copies of media coverage you have received in the Supporting Documents section. Explain who you plan to contact, when you plan to contact them, what promotional angle you will present, and how you plan to capitalize on that publicity. Publicity can be very valuable to your business and can greatly enhance your credibility. When you pay for an advertisement, you are telling the customer that your product or service is good. When a member of the media or someone else outside of your organization gives your product or service a boost, it is perceived as impartial judgment and may be worth several paid advertisements.

D. **Direct mail** can be an effective way to deliver specific information to large numbers of people. Direct mail can take the form of inexpensive fact sheets, letters, promotional gimmicks, contests, discount coupons, and brochures. Tell how you will choose your mailing list, what will be sent, and what response you expect. If you have already used direct mail, detail the results. How large was the mailing? How many responses were received? Was it cost-effective? Would you use direct mail in the future? Include samples of all promotional pieces in the Supporting Documents section.

E. **Business and community involvement** through participation in trade shows and community events and membership in civic and business organizations is another means of promotion. Membership dues, subscriptions to trade publications, and fees for conference attendance and participation are all costs that should be projected and included on the Cash Flow Statement.

F. **Web page and Internet marketing** can be an effective channel for selling and marketing your goods. Consumers can be attracted to your site by linking your Web page to other sites providing information on your industry. Currently, businesses providing software, computer hardware, publications, entertainment, travel, and online information seem to be creating a demand for their products and services. Be sure to look at stats on Internet usage and sales by category to project potential revenue from this marketing strategy. Look carefully at the cost of Web page development, linkage, and management. The potential revenue must justify the expense.

International companies will have to determine which media will effectively promote their products or services throughout the foreign market. Local assistance can be critical to the success of your advertising and publicity plan. Individuals familiar with the local culture should aid in the design of your promotional materials. For example, sales and warranty messages must be translated into locally understood languages. Make sure that your company name and the names of your products and services do not lead to translating problems. In some countries, television and radio do not carry advertising.

In summary. If you are seeking financing, tell the lender or investor where you plan to put your promotional dollars, why you have chosen those avenues, how your message will reach your target market, when your promotional campaign will begin, how much your plan will cost, and what format your advertising will take. Your timing of market entry or when you will actually start your business or introduce a new product or service may be tied to your promotional schedule. For example, if you plan to start your business during the holiday season and the new phone directories are published in November, you may be required to place your ad in July for inclusion. Since Aerotech, Inc. plans to increase production by 35 percent beginning in May of 2000, the company will have to commit to certain advertising and promotion in the preceding months in order to be timely and effective in creating additional buyers. Contact your promotional resources to determine their publication schedules.

Pricing

Your pricing structure is critical to the success of your business and is determined through market research and analysis of financial considerations. Basic marketing strategy is to price within the range between the price ceiling and the price floor. The market determines the price ceiling.

Profit: financial gain; returns over expenditures.

Bad debt: money owed to you that you cannot collect.

Customs duty: tax levied on goods imported into the U.S.; may also refer to tax on goods exported.

It is the highest cost a consumer will pay for a product or service and is based on perceived value. What is the competition charging? What is the quality of the product or service you are offering? What is the nature of the demand, and what is the image you are projecting? The price floor is the lowest amount at which you can offer a product or service, meet all of your costs, and still make your desired profit. Consider all costs: manufacturing costs, variable expenses, office overhead, interest expenses, and tax expense. The price floor will also have to take into account your desired annual profit. In addition to paying your costs, the revenues of the business must generate a profit. The viable business operates between the price ceiling and price floor. The difference allows for discounts, bad debt, and returns. Justify your pricing schedule based on the above considerations. Be specific as to how you arrived at your pricing structure and leave room for some flexibility.

In addition to normal pricing considerations, businesses involved in foreign trade must factor in added costs specifically related to foreign sales. These include higher promotional and product delivery costs, duties, customs broker fees, and appropriate local value added taxes. How much of these costs can be built into the price and how much will be billed separately?

Positioning or predetermining the perceived value in the eyes of the consumer can be accomplished through promotional activities. To be successful, you must decide what your product or service offers that your competitor's does not and promote it as the unique benefit. Very few items on the market have universal appeal—your product or service cannot be all things to all people. However, if you focus and position your product or service properly, prospective purchasers or users will immediately recognize its benefits to them. A "market mix" involving complementary products or total package services can benefit the customer and may enable you to charge an acceptably higher price.

Product Design

Packaging and product design can play a major role in the success of your business. It's what first catches the customer's eye. Consider the tastes of your target market in the ultimate design of your product and your package. Decide what will be most appealing in terms of size, shape, color, material, and wording. Packaging attracts a great deal of public attention. Be advised of the Fair Packaging and Labeling Act, which established mandatory labeling requirements. The Food and Drug Administration has strict procedures for labeling of items falling within its jurisdiction. The packaging guidelines can be obtained by contacting the agency or referring to a copy of the regulations in the library.

Exporters must be concerned with the quality, safety, and technical standards that may be unique to the country with which they will be dealing. Appropriate packaging must be considered for protection against breakage and spoilage in transport. Voltage differences and metric conversion must be regarded. Do your product's technical specifications and codes ensure compatibility with locally manufactured products?

Follow the same format of using key words to answer questions regarding your product design and packaging. Include sketches or photos. Also include information on any proprietary rights such as copyright, trademark, or patent. Be sure to interpret your plans in terms of financial requirements and use that information to help you determine projections on cost of goods to be sold.

Timing of Market Entry

The timing of your entry into the marketplace is critical and takes careful planning and research. Having your products and services available at the right time and the right place is more a matter of understanding "consumer readiness" than your organizational schedule. The manner in which the consumer receives a new product can be affected by the seasons, the weather, and the holidays.

Early January and September are the best times to mail fliers and catalogs as consumers seem to be more receptive to mail order purchasing in those months. The major gift shows are held in the summer months (June, July, and August) and again in January and February. Most wholesale buying takes place at these shows. November and December are not good months for introducing most new service businesses unless they relate in some way to the holiday season. Spring is a better time to introduce a service. There may also be other considerations that come into play. For example, if your main avenue of advertising is the Yellow Pages and it comes out in November, you will need to plan your market entry accordingly.

Information from your trade journals and trade associations will help you determine the timing patterns for your industry. Tell when you plan to enter the market and how you arrived at your decision.

Location

If your choice of location is related to your target market, you will cover it in this section. For example, the location of a retail store is a marketing decision. It must be located near its target market or customers, provide adequate parking, and satisfy zoning regulations.

List the reasons for your choice of location. What is the character of the neighborhood? Does the site project your business image? Where is the competition in the area? What is the traffic pattern? What are the terms of the lease? What services, if any, does the landlord provide? What is the occupancy history of your location? Did any companies in the area go out of business within the past few months? If so, try to find out if it was related to location. Does a strong economic base support the area in which you plan to locate? What alternate sites were considered? The chambers of commerce, police departments, and city planning commissions may be able to supply you with information that will help you to determine the best location.

When you are planning the location of your business, look at all of the financial implications of your choice in order to have the information for your projections. If you will be leasing space, get a copy of the proposed lease agreement. You can also get estimates on other expenses related to your location (i.e., utilities, insurance, maintenance, etc.) and include them in projected expenses

 Note: Use the **Location Analysis Worksheet** provided at the end of the Organizational Plan section. You may also refer to "Location" in Chapter 4 for additional information.

Industry Trends

Be alert to changes in your industry. The wise business owner follows industry trends, analyzes the economy, projects "best and worst case scenarios," and looks for ways to keep the business healthy.

Trade and professional associations and their journals and industry reports for your field will help you to write about this area. New technology may bring new products into the marketplace, which will generate new service businesses. Project how your market may change and what you plan to do to keep up. For example, the rapid technological advances in the computer industry paired with worldwide web connectivity have caused significant changes in the photographic industry. Every major camera manufacturer is now fighting to keep ahead of their competitors in the design of digital cameras—cameras that will not only take pictures, but will enable the user to load the images into their computer, print them out, and send them, at the click of a mouse, via e-mail attachments to their friends, family, and business associates in various parts of the globe.

Analyze the economy and be aware of financial and political forecasts. For example, Aerotech, Inc. manufactures specialized parts for the aerospace industry. Will there be a continued demand for such parts? If there are cutbacks in the federal budget, could Aerotech retool and go after commercial contracts? Read government reports and business magazines and newspapers.

Project some best- and worst-case scenarios for the future. Do some analysis regarding how much time and money would be spent in changing the focus of your business in order to remain competitive. These considerations can be translated into financial projections in order to determine if the business can remain viable.

Answer questions such as: How can the business remain competitive? What is the best-case scenario for the business? What are some of the worst-case scenarios? What costs will be incurred in order to keep growing my business? Include copies of industry reports in the Supporting Documents section as back-up for your decisions.

Potential Revenue

Potential revenue refers to the gross income that you project your company will earn. For example, you have a pest control business that is owner-operated, you can provide pest control service to five homes per day, and you work five days per week. The average income per job is $75. The potential revenue from your business is $1,875 per week. Computing five homes per day for each of the five days per week that you are open for business may be unrealistic. You must consider your administrative duties: recordkeeping, ordering supplies, and marketing. Review an average week, account for time spent on running your business, consider seasonal problems such as winter rains that cause downtime, and realistically project your potential revenue.

By computing the size of your target market and the average sale per customer, you can project the revenue potential for your company. Your local Chamber of Commerce, Small Business Development Center, Economic Development Department, and trade and professional associations can provide the statistical information and assistance you need to make this determination.

Worksheets and References

The following pages contain the worksheets mentioned in this chapter. Use the "Reference Section" of this book to identify sources that will help you gather information for answering your key word questions. When you have covered all of the areas addressed in the Marketing Plan, you will be ready to begin work on the Financial Documents section.

The income and expense numbers generated through market research and the development of Part I/The Organizational Plan and Part II/The Marketing Plan will now be transferred onto spreadsheets in Part III/Financial Documents. Analysis of these spreadsheets will determine the viability of your business.

Target Market Worksheet

1. WHO ARE MY CUSTOMERS? _____

    a. Economic level (Income range): _____

    b. Sex: _____

    c. Age range: _____

    d. Psychological makeup (Lifestyle): _____

    e. Buying habits: _____

2. LOCATION: _____

    a. Where do my customers live? _____

    b. Where do they work? _____

    c. Where do they shop? _____

3. PROJECTED SIZE OF MARKET: _____

4. WHAT ARE THE CUSTOMERS' NEEDS? _____

    a. _____

    b. _____

    c. _____

    d. _____

    e. _____

5. HOW CAN I MEET THOSE NEEDS? _____

    a. _____

    b. _____

    c. _____

    d. _____

    e. _____

6. WHAT IS UNIQUE ABOUT MY BUSINESS? _____

_____

Note: Complete the questions asked on the worksheet in outline format. Then formulate the information gathered into text.

Competition Reference List
(For locating information on companies)

Is the company publicly owned or privately owned/closely held?
1. *Directory of Companies Required to File Annual Reports with the SEC.*

Does the company have a parent company or subsidiaries?
1. *Directory of Corporate Affiliations.*
2. *International Directory of Corporate Affiliations.*
3. *America's Corporate Families.*

Do you need to know the company's type of business, executive officers, number of employees, annual sales?
1. *Standard & Poor's Register of Corporations.*
2. *Dun and Bradstreet's Million Dollar Directory.*
3. *Ward's Business Directory of Largest U.S. Companies.*
4. *Career Guide: Dun's Employment Opportunities Directory.*
5. *Standard Directory of Advertisers.*

Do you need the company's corporate background and financial data?
1. *Standard & Poor's Corporate Records.*
2. *Moody's Manuals.*
3. *Walker's Manual of Western Corporations.*

Is the company newsworthy?
1. *Predicasts F & S Index.*
2. *Business Periodicals Index.*

Is the company listed in a specialized directory?
1. *Thomas Register of American Manufacturers.*
2. *Best's Insurance Reports.*
3. *Standard Directory of Advertising Agencies.*
4. *U.S.A. Oil Industry Directory.*
5. *Who's Who in Electronics.*
6. *World Aviation Directory.*
7. *Medical and Healthcare Marketplace Guide.*

How does the company rank in the industry?
1. Annual issues of *Fortune, Forbes, Inc.,* and *Business Week.*
2. *Dun's Business Rankings.*

Note: Contact the reference librarian in the business section of your community or college library for availability and use of these references. Many libraries have computer services and databases available.

Competition Evaluation Worksheet

1. COMPETITOR: _____
   _____

2. LOCATION: _____
   _____

3. PRODUCTS OR SERVICES OFFERED: _____
   _____

4. METHODS OF DISTRIBUTION: _____
   _____

5. IMAGE: _____
   a. Packaging: _____
   b. Promotional materials: _____
   c. Methods of advertising: _____
   d. Quality of product or service: _____

6. PRICING STRUCTURE: _____
   _____

7. BUSINESS HISTORY & CURRENT PERFORMANCE: _____
   _____

8. MARKET SHARE (number, types, and location of customers): _____
   _____

9. STRENGTHS (the strengths of the competition can become your strengths): _____
   _____

10. WEAKNESSES (looking at the weaknesses of the competition can help you find ways of being unique and of benefiting the customer):
    _____
    _____

Note: A Competition Evaluation Worksheet should be made for each competitor. Keep these records and update them. It pays to continue to rate your competition throughout the lifetime of your business.

CHAPTER 6

Part III
Financial Documents

· ·

You learned earlier that the body of a business plan is divided into three main sections. Having completed the Organizational and Marketing Plans, you are now ready to develop the third area of your plan.

Financial Documents are those records used to show past, current, and projected finances. In this section, we will cover the major documents you will want to consider and include in your business plan. They will consist of both pro forma (projected) and actual financial statements. Your work will be easier if these are done in the order presented.

- ☑ **Summary of Financial Needs**
- ☑ **Dispersal of Loan Funds Statement**
- ☑ **Cash Flow Statement (Budget)**
- ☑ **Three-Year Income Projection**
- ☑ **Break-Even Analysis**
- ☑ **Balance Sheet**
- ☑ **Profit & Loss Statement**
- ☑ **Loan Application/Financial History**
- ☑ **Financial Statement Analysis**

· · · · · ·

Take a Look Back

Before you begin work on your financial statements go back to Chapter 1 and reread the section on "Developing Financial Assumptions." Remember that the numbers in your financial plan are derived through the development of organizational and marketing concepts in terms of revenues that will be generated and expenses that will be incurred.

Warning on the Order of Preparation

You are now beginning the Financial Document section of your business plan. We would strongly suggest that you prepare these documents in the order that we have presented them because it will simplify the process. In the same way that a house builder must lay the foundation, build the walls, and finally put on the roof, you will find that your financial statements will build on each other. Each one will use information from the ones previously done. If you try to jump ahead, you will make your task more difficult.

Purpose of Financial Documents

In the first two sections, you have written about the physical setup of your operation and your plans for finding and reaching your customers. The Financial Documents section is the quantitative interpretation of everything you have stated in the text portion of your plan. Well-executed financial statements will provide you with the means to look realistically at your business in terms of profitability. Financial Documents is often the first section examined by a potential lender or investor.

The financial documents included in your plan are not just for the purpose of satisfying a potential lender or investor. The primary reason for writing a business plan is so that it will serve as a guide during the lifetime of your business. It is extremely important that you keep it updated it frequently. This means examining your financial statements on a periodic basis, measuring your actual performance against your projections, and revising your new projections accordingly.

Types of Financial Documents

There are three types of financial documents covered in this section. Before you begin your work, it is best to understand what they are and the purpose of each type.

Statements of your needs and uses of funds from a lender or investor. The first two documents covered are the "Summary of Financial Needs" and the "Loan Fund Dispersal Statement." These two documents are the only ones that are written in paragraph form rather than as spreadsheets in rows and columns. They are included only if your business is seeking funds from a lender or investor (or other source).

Pro forma statements. The word "pro forma" in accounting means "projected." These are the statements that are used for you to predict the future profitability of your business. You are not magic and will not be able to be 100 percent right. However, your projections should be based on realistic research and reasonable assumptions. The most frequent error made during the business planning process is the overstating of revenues and the understanding of expenses.

Actual performance statements. These are the historical financial statements reflecting the past performance of your business. If you are planning a new business, you have no history. Therefore, you will not have these statements to include. However, once you have been in business for even one accounting period, you will have a Profit & Loss Statement and a Balance Sheet for those periods.

Financial statement analysis. Once you have completed the financial documents described above, it is also important to use them as tools to look at your business and enable you to make future decisions that will make your business more profitable. Financial Statement Analysis utilizes the income statement and the balance sheet and is the study of relationships and comparisons of single components in single or comparative financial statements. In the last section of this chapter, you will learn how to use your income statement and balance sheet to prepare a financial statement analysis of your business.

Profit & loss statement: a list of the total amount of sales (revenues) and total costs (expenses). The difference between them is your profit or loss.

How to Proceed

The financial documents will be presented in the order discussed in the paragraphs above. It will be necessary for you to determine your individual situation and decide which documents to include. Below are five descriptions. Decide which one fits your business and proceed accordingly:

1. *If yours is a new business and you are going to seek a lender or investor:*
   Include the "Application of Loan Funds" and the "Loan Fund Dispersal Statement." You will also include all of the pro forma statements. You have no financial history and cannot include actual performance statements. Financial statement analysis will be based on projections only and will utilize your three-year profit & loss (income) projection and projected balance sheet.

2. *If yours is a new business and you are not going to seek a lender or investor:*
   You will not include the "Application of Loan Funds" and the "Loan Fund Dispersal Statement." You will include all pro forma statements. Again, financial statement analysis will be based on projections and will utilize the three-year profit & loss (income) projection and projected balance sheet.

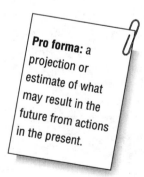

Pro forma: a projection or estimate of what may result in the future from actions in the present.

3. *If yours is an existing business and you are going to seek a lender or investor:*
   You will need to include all financial documents discussed in this chapter.

4. *If yours is an existing business and you are not seeking a lender or investor:*
   You will include all financial documents discussed in this chapter with the exception of the "Application of Loan Funds" and the "Loan Fund Dispersal Statement."

5. *If this business plan is being written for a division within a larger business:*
   Consider your division as being a business within a business and include as indicated in 1–4.

◆ ◆ ◆ ◆

Now You Are Ready to Prepare Your Financial Documents

The three types of financial documents will be presented in the following order:

- ◆ **Statements of financial needs and uses of funds from a lender or investor**
- ◆ **Pro forma statements**
- ◆ **Actual financial statements**

The examples on the following 30 pages are not related to each other.

Each of the worksheets and financial statements on the following pages serve as examples and relate only to the text material describing that particular document. They have no correlation with each other. For example, the numbers on the pro forma cash flow statement on page 77 do not match the numbers on the quarterly budget analysis on page 79.

Please do not try to follow numbers from one spreadsheet to the next.

In Appendices I and II, we have provided you with two complete business plans. By examining the financial documents in those plans, you can readily see how the numbers build on each other throughout the entire financial plan. These plans have 100 percent correlation between all the spreadsheets.

Statements of Financial Needs
and
Uses of Funds from a Lender or Investor

The two financial text documents covered on the following pages describe your needs for capital to be infused into your company through borrowed or invested funds. They also outline your intended use of those funds.

Include these two statements only if you are seeking funds from a lender or investor.

The two documents are:

☑ **Summary of Financial Needs**

☑ **Loan Fund Dispersal Statement**

Summary of Financial Needs

If you are applying for a loan, your lenders and investors will analyze the requirements of your business. They will distinguish among the three types of capital as follows:

Working capital. fluctuating needs to be repaid through cash (liquidity) during the business's next full operating cycle, generally one year.

Growth capital. needs to be repaid with profits over a period of a few years. If you seek growth capital, you will be expected to show how the capital will be used to increase your business profits enough to be able to repay the loan (+ interest) within several years (usually not more than seven).

Equity capital. permanent needs. If you seek equity capital, it must be raised from investors who will take the risk for dividend returns or capital gains, or a specific share of the business.

Keeping the above in mind, you must now prepare a Summary of Financial Needs. This document is an outline giving the following information:

1. **Why** you are applying for a loan.

2. **How much** you need.

 Note: A sample Summary of Financial Needs follows on the facing page.

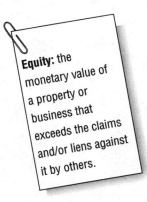

Equity: the monetary value of a property or business that exceeds the claims and/or liens against it by others.

Sample Summary of Financial Needs

Summary of Financial Needs

I. Genesis Multimedia[*] is seeking a loan to increase growth capital in the following areas of production:

    A. Equipment (new and more modern)

    B. Training of personnel in operation of above

II. Funds needed to accomplish above goal will be $100,000.

    A. See "Loan Fund Dispersal Statement" for distribution of funds and back-up statement.

---

[*] Company name is fictitious.

Loan Fund Dispersal Statement

Uses of financing. The potential lender or investor will require a statement of how the money you intend to borrow will be used. It will be necessary for you to:

1. Tell how you intend to utilize the loan or investment funds.

2. Back up your statement with supporting data.

> **Note:** Number 2 will show the lender that you have done your homework properly.

The following are two examples that will help to clarify your understanding of the above.

Example 1

How money will be used. Funds for advertising.

Back-up statement. Refer to the advertising section of your plan. That section must contain a breakdown of how you intend to do your advertising and a projection of the response you expect to get as a result. Rate sheets should be included in the Supporting Documents.

Example 2

How money will be used. Funds for expansion. (Include a concise statement explaining how you intend to expand.)

Back-up statement. Include the following information:

a. Projected costs of carrying out plans.

b. Projections as to how that expansion will ultimately result in increased profits for your business and thereby enable you to repay your loan. If you are seeking venture capital, remember that the venture capitalist will be looking for an exit strategy that will provide a return of capital plus a profit within five to seven years.

c. References to other sections of your business plan that relate to projected expansion.

> **Note:** A sample Loan Fund Dispersal Statement has been included on the facing page.

You must be sure that your supporting data can be easily found by the loan officer who is examining your application. If your information is not well-organized and easily retrievable, you will risk having your loan turned down simply because information cannot be located. The necessity of having a well-written Table of Contents will be discussed in Chapter 10, "Putting Your Plan Together."

Sample Loan Fund Dispersal Statement

Loan Fund Dispersal Statement

1. **Dispersal of Loan Funds**

   Genesis Multimedia will utilize anticipated loan funds in the amount of $100,000 to modernize its production equipment. This will necessitate the purchase of two new pieces of equipment and the training of present personnel in the operation of that equipment.

2. **Back-Up Statement**

   a. The equipment needed is as follows:

      (1) High-speed F-34 Atlas Press (purchase price: $123,000)

      (2) S71 Jaworski Ebber (purchase price: $110,000)

   b. The training is available from the manufacturer as a three-week intensive program (cost: 10 employees @ $1,200 = $12,000).

   c. The remaining $5,000 of loan funds will be used to make the first monthly installment on loan repayment (a period of low production due to employee training off the premises).

   d. The equipment will result in a 35% increase in production and will decrease unit cost by 25%. The end result will be a net profit increase sufficient to repay the loan and interest within three years with a profit margin of 15%.*

*Note: Refer to page 17 for production plan of Genesis Multimedia. See pages 27 and 28 of the marketing section for market research and projected trends in the industry. (See footnote at bottom of page.)

Note: Page numbers in the example above are hypothetical and do not refer to page numbers in *Anatomy of a Business Plan*.

In the example above, the business plan writer's production plan would include a description of the equipment, how the work will be done, by whom, and at what cost.

Market research would show projected demand for the product, and thus would show how increased production will result in increased sales and ultimately in the company's capability to repay the loan in a timely fashion.

Pro Forma Statements

◈ ◈ ◈ ◈

The financial statements that follow are pro forma statements. They show your projections for the future profitability of your business.

All business plans must contain the following pro forma statements:

- ☑ **Cash Flow Statement**
- ☑ **Three-Year Income Projection**
- ☑ **Break-Even Analysis**

We have included blank forms of all three pro forma statements in Appendix III. They are ready for you to customize and input your numbers.

> **Balance sheet:** an itemized statement that lists the total assets and the total liabilities of a given business to portray its net worth at a given moment in time.

A **Projected Balance Sheet may also be required.** A potential lender or investor may require that you include a Pro Forma (or Projected) Balance Sheet for specific target dates in the life of your business (e.g.: "day-1," "end of year 1," etc.). You will find instructions for the development of a balance sheet under "Actual Financial Statements" in the next part of this chapter. There are also examples in our sample business plans in Appendices I and II.

Also included in this section are:

> **Analysis:** breaking an idea or problem down into its parts; a thorough examination of the parts of anything.

- ◈ **Cash to Be Paid Out and Sources of Cash worksheets.** These worksheets will help you to develop your cash flow statement and may be included in your business plan.

- ◈ **A Quarterly Budget Analysis spreadsheet.** This is your tool for comparing your company's projections with its actual performance. Your cash flow statement will be effective only if it is revised quarterly, reflecting the results of a budget analysis.

If you are a new business, you have no actual performance to measure against projections. Therefore, you will not have a quarterly budget analysis until you have been in business for three months.

If you have been in business for one or more quarters: do a quarterly budget analysis, revise your cash flow statement accordingly, and insert the revised cash flow statement in your business plan.

Pro Forma Cash Flow Statement (Budget)

It is a fact that a third or more of today's businesses fail due to inadequate cash flow. The cash flow statement is usually the first thing a lender or investor examines in your business plan. What is cash flow?

What Is a Cash Flow Statement?

The Pro Forma Cash Flow Statement is the financial document that **projects** what your business plan means in terms of dollars. A cash flow statement is the same as a budget. It is a pro forma (or projected) statement used for internal planning and estimates how much money will flow into and out of a business during a designated period of time, usually the coming tax year. Your profit at the end of the year will depend on the proper balance between cash inflow and outflow.

The **Cash Flow Statement** identifies when cash is expected to be received and when it must be spent to pay bills and debts. It also allows the manager to identify where the necessary cash will come from.

This statement deals only with **actual cash transactions** and not with depreciation and amortization of goodwill or other noncash expense items. Expenses are paid from cash on hand, sale of assets, revenues from sales and services, interest earned on investments, money borrowed from a lender, and influx of capital in exchange for equity in the company. If your business will require $100,000 to pay its expenses and $50,000 to support the owners, you will need at least an equal amount of money flowing into the business just to maintain the status quo. Anything less will eventually lead to an inability to pay your creditors or yourself.

The availability or nonavailability of cash **when** it is needed for expenditures gets to the very heart of the matter. By careful planning, you must try to project not only **how much** cash will have to flow into and out of your business, but also **when** it will need to flow in and out. A business may be able to plan for gross receipts that will cover its needs. However, if those sales do not take place in time to pay the expenses, your venture will soon be history unless you plan ahead for other sources of cash to tide the business over until the revenues are realized.

Time period. The Cash Flow Statement should be prepared on a monthly basis for the next tax year (or more) of your business. To be effective, it must be analyzed and revised quarterly to reflect actual performance in the preceding three months of operations.

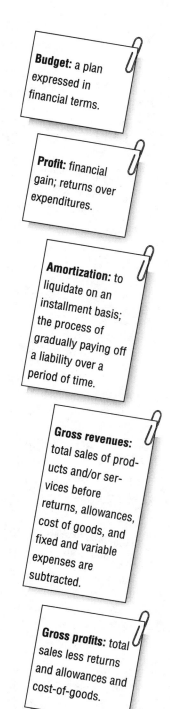

Budget: a plan expressed in financial terms.

Profit: financial gain; returns over expenditures.

Amortization: to liquidate on an installment basis; the process of gradually paying off a liability over a period of time.

Gross revenues: total sales of products and/or services before returns, allowances, cost of goods, and fixed and variable expenses are subtracted.

Gross profits: total sales less returns and allowances and cost-of-goods.

Planning Worksheets

To Help You Prepare Your Pro Forma Cash Flow Statement

Before preparing your budget, it might be useful to compile individual projections and budgets. They might be as follows:

- ◆ **Revenue Projections (product and service)**
- ◆ **Inventory Purchases**
- ◆ **Variable (Selling) Expense Budget (w/Marketing Budget)**
- ◆ **Fixed (Administrative) Expense Budget**

Pre-Planning Worksheets

Because the cash flow statement deals with cash inflow and cash outflow, the first step in planning can be best accomplished by preparing two worksheets.

Cash: money that is readily available: cash in bank or petty cash.

1. *Cash to Be Paid Out*

   This worksheet documents the cash flowing out of your business. It identifies categories of expenses and obligations and the projected amount of cash needed in each category. Use the information from your individual budgets (inventory purchases, direct expenses, administrative expenses, owner draws, etc.).

   These expenditures are not always easy to estimate. If yours is a new business, it will be necessary for you to do market research. If you are an existing business, you will combine information from past financial statements with trends in your particular industry.

2. *Sources of Cash*

   Use this worksheet to document the cash flowing into your business. It will help you to estimate how much cash will be available from what sources. To complete this worksheet, you will have to look at cash on hand, projected revenues, assets that can be liquidated, possible lenders or investors, and owner equity to be contributed. This worksheet will force you to take a look at any existing possibilities for increasing available cash.

Liquidate: to settle a debt or to convert to cash.

Sample Worksheets

On the next four pages, you will see examples of the two worksheets along with accompanying information explaining each of the categories used. The worksheets are filled in for a fictitious company, Genesis Multimedia, to help you understand the process.

Please note that the Cash to Be Paid Out Worksheet shows a need for $131,000. It was necessary in projecting Sources of Cash to account for $131,000 without the projected sales because payment is not expected to be received until November and December (too late for the cash needs of January through October). Next year, those revenues will be reflected in cash on hand or other salable assets.

When you do your own worksheets:

◈ Try to be as realistic as possible. Do not overstate revenues and/or understate expenses, a deadly error frequently made during the planning process.

◈ Be sure to figure all of your estimates on both worksheets for the same time period (i.e. annually, quarterly, monthly).

Note: Blank forms of the two worksheets are provided in Appendix III.

Explanation of Categories
Cash to Be Paid Out Worksheet

> **Variable and Fixed Expense Categories Must Be Determined by You**
>
> Every business has expenses that are specific to its industry. You will have to customize your variable and fixed expense categories to match your business. We have suggested some in our examples to get you started. You will type in your own headings in the working spreadsheets. As you begin to operate your business, you will be better able to determine what your true expenditures are. However, for your business plan, you will need to set your expense headings beginning with this worksheet and use the same ones throughout your spreadsheets. You can change later if you find that your current categories do not meet your needs.

1. *Start-Up Costs*
   These are the costs incurred by you to get your business underway. They are generally one-time expenses and are capitalized for tax purposes.

2. *Inventory Purchases*
   Cash to be spent during the period on items intended for resale. If you purchase manufactured products, this includes the cash outlay for those purchases. If you are the manufacturer, include labor and materials on units to be produced.

3. *Variable Expenses (Selling or Direct Expenses)*
   These are the costs of all expenses that will relate directly to your product or service (other than manufacturing costs or purchase price of inventory).

4. *Fixed Expenses (Administrative or Indirect Expenses)*
   Include all expected costs of office overhead. If certain bills must be paid ahead, include total cash outlay even if covered period extends into the next year.

5. *Assets (Long-Term Purchases)*
   These are the capital assets that will be depreciated over a period of years (land, buildings, vehicles, equipment). Determine how you intend to pay for them and include all cash to be paid out in the current period. **Note**: Land is the only asset that does not normally depreciate and will be listed at cost.

6. *Liabilities*
   What are the payments you expect to have to make to retire any debts or loans? Do you have any accounts payable as you begin the new year? You will need to determine the amount of cash outlay that needs to be paid in the current year. If you have a car loan for $20,000 and you pay $500 per month for 12 months, you will have a cash outlay of $6,000 for the coming year.

7. *Owner Equity*
   This item is frequently overlooked in planning cash flow. If you, as the business owner, will need a draw of $2,000 per month to live on, you must plan for $24,000 cash flowing out of your business. Failure to plan for it will result in a cash flow shortage and may cause your business to fail.

 Note: Be sure to use the same time period throughout your worksheet.

Cash to Be Paid Out Worksheet

Business Name: Genesis Multimedia   Time Period Covered: Jan 1–Dec 31, 2000

1. START-UP COSTS		1,450
Business license	30	
Accounting fees	500	
Legal fees	920	
Other start-up costs:		
a.		
b.		
c.		
d.		
2. INVENTORY PURCHASES		
Cash out for goods intended for resale		32,000
3. VARIABLE EXPENSES (SELLING)		
Advertising/marketing	8,000	
Freight	2,500	
Fulfillment of orders	800	
Packaging costs	0	
Sales salaries/commissions	14,000	
Travel	1,550	
Miscellaneous	300	
TOTAL SELLING EXPENSES		27,150
4. FIXED EXPENSES (ADMINISTRATION)		
Financial administration	1,800	
Insurance	900	
Licenses and permits	100	
Office salaries	16,300	
Rent expense	8,600	
Utilities	2,400	
Miscellaneous	400	
TOTAL ADMINISTRATIVE EXPENSE		30,500
5. ASSETS (LONG-TERM PURCHASES)		6,000
Cash to be paid out in current period		
6. LIABILITIES		
Cash outlay for retiring debts, loans, and/or accounts payable		9,900
7. OWNER EQUITY		
Cash to be withdrawn by owner		24,000
TOTAL CASH TO BE PAID OUT		**$131,000**

Explanation of Categories
Sources of Cash Worksheet

1. ***Cash on Hand***
   Money that you have on hand. Be sure to include petty cash and moneys not yet deposited.

2. ***Sales (Revenues)***
   This includes projected revenues from the sale of your product and/or service. If payment is not expected during the time period covered by this worksheet, do not include that portion of your sales. Think about the projected timing of sales. If receipts will be delayed beyond the time when a large amount of cash is needed, make a notation to that effect and take it into consideration when determining the need for temporary financing. Include deposits you require on expected sales or services. To figure collections on Accounts Receivable, you will have to project the percentage of invoices that will be lost to bad debt and subtract it from your Accounts Receivable total.

Accounts receivable: a record of what is owed to you; all of the credit accounts taken together.

3. ***Miscellaneous Income***
   Do you, or will you, have any moneys out on loan or deposited in accounts that will yield interest income during the period in question?

4. ***Sale of Long-Term Assets***
   If you are expecting to sell any of your fixed assets such as land, buildings, vehicles, machinery, equipment, etc., be sure to include only the cash you will receive during the current period.

Important: At this point in your worksheet, add up all sources of cash. If you do not have an amount equal to your projected needs, you will have to plan sources of cash covered under numbers 5 and 6.

5. ***Liabilities***
   This figure represents the amount you will be able to borrow from lending institutions such as banks, finance companies, the SBA, etc. Be reasonable about what you think you can borrow. If you have no collateral, have no business plan, or if you have a poor financial history, you will find it difficult, if not impossible, to find a lender. This source of cash requires preplanning.

6. ***Equity***
   Sources of equity come from owner investments, contributed capital, sale of stock, or venture capital. Do you anticipate the availability of personal funds? Does your business have the potential for growth that might interest a venture capitalist? Be sure to be realistic in this area. You cannot sell stock (or equity) to a nonexistent investor.

Sources of Cash Worksheet

Business Name: Genesis Multimedia

Time Period Covered: From January 1, 2000 to December 31, 2000

---

1. CASH ON HAND $20,000

2. SALES (REVENUES)

Product sales income*
Most of this sales revenue will not be received until Nov. or Dec.   90,000

Services income   22,000

Deposits on sales or services   0

Collections on accounts receivable   3,000

3. MISCELLANEOUS INCOME

Interest income   1,000

Payments to be received on loans   0

4. SALE OF LONG-TERM ASSETS   0

5. LIABILITIES   40,000

Loan funds (to be received during current period; from banks, through the SBA, or from other lending institutions)

6. EQUITY

Owner investments (sole proprietors/partners)   10,000

Contributed capital (corporation)

Sale of stock (corporation)

Venture capital   35,000

TOTAL CASH AVAILABLE

A. Without product sales =   **$131,000**

B. With product sales =   **$221,000**

Using the worksheets. Now that you have completed the two worksheets, you are ready to use that information. You have estimated how much cash will be needed for the year, and you now know what sources are available. In the next phase of cash flow planning, you will break the time period of one year into monthly segments and predict when the cash will be needed to make the financial year flow smoothly.

Project sales on a monthly basis based on payment of invoices, demand for your particular product or service, and ability to fill that demand. Figure the cost of goods, fixed and variable expenses in monthly increments. Most will vary. When do you plan to purchase the most inventory? What months will require the most advertising? Are you expecting a rent or insurance increase? When will commissions be due on expected sales. Determine your depreciable assets needs. How much will the payments be, and when will they begin? Fill in as much of the cash flow statement as you can using those projections and any others that you can comfortably determine.

To clarify the process of filling in a cash flow statement, we will walk you through January and February again using Genesis Multimedia as our example.

January Projections

1. Genesis Multimedia projects a beginning cash balance of $20,000.
2. Cash Receipts: Product manufacturing will not be completed until February, so there will be no sales. However, service income of $4,000 is projected.
3. Interest on the $20,000 will amount to about $100 at current rate.
4. There are no long-term assets to sell. Enter a zero.
5. Adding 1,2,3, and 4 the Total Cash Available will be $24,100.
6. Cash Payments: Product will be available from manufacturer in February, and payment will not be due until pickup. However, there will be prototype costs of $5,000.
7. Variable (Selling) Expenses: Estimated at $1,140.
8. Fixed (Administrative): Estimated at $1,215.
9. Interest Expense: No outstanding debts or loans. Enter zero.
10. Taxes: No profit for previous quarter. No estimated taxes would be due.
11. Payments on Long-Term Assets: Genesis plans to purchase office equipment to be paid in full at the time of purchase. Enter $1,139.
12. Loan Repayments: No loans have been received. Enter zero.
13. Owner Draws: Owner will need $2,000 for living expenses.
14. Total Cash Paid Out: Add 6 through 13. Total $10,494.
15. Cash Balance: Subtract Cash Paid Out from Total Cash Available $13,606.
16. Loans to be Received: Being aware of the $30,000 to be paid to the manufacturer in February, a loan of $40,000 is anticipated to increase Cash Available. (This requires advance planning.)
17. Equity Deposit: Owner plans to add $5,000 from personal C.D.
18. Ending Cash Balance: Adding 15, 16, and 17 the sum is $58,606.

February Projections

1. February Beginning Cash Balance: January Ending Cash Balance ($58,606).
2. Cash Receipts: Still no sales, but service income is $2,000.
3. Interest Income: Projected at about $120.
4. Sale of Long-Term Assets: None. Enter zero.
5. Total Cash Available: Add 1,2,3, and 4. The result is $60,726.
6. Cash Payments: $30,000 due to manufacturer, $400 due on packaging design.
7. Continue as in January. Don't forget to include payments on your loan.

Partial Cash Flow Statement
Genesis Multimedia

	Jan	Feb
BEGINNING CASH BALANCE	20,000	58,606
CASH RECEIPTS		
A. Sales/revenues	4,000	2,000
B. Receivables	0	0
C. Interest income	100	120
D. Sale of long-term assets	0	0
TOTAL CASH AVAILABLE	24,100	60,726
CASH PAYMENTS		
A. Cost of goods to be sold		
1. Purchases	0	30,000
2. Material	0	0
3. Labor	5,000	400
Total Cost of Goods	5,000	30,400
B. Variable Expenses (Selling)		
1. Advertising	300	
2. Freight	120	
3. Fulfillment of orders	0	
4. Packaging costs	270	
5. Sales/salaries	0	
6. Travel	285	
7. Miscellaneous selling expense	165	
Total Variable Expenses	1,140	
C. Fixed Expenses (Administrative)		CONTINUE
1. Financial administration	80	as in
2. Insurance	125	JANUARY
3. License/permits	200	
4. Office salaries	500	
5. Rent expenses	110	
6. Utilities	200	
7. Miscellaneous administrative expense	0	
Total Fixed Expenses	1,215	
D. Interest expense	0	
E. Federal income tax	0	
F. Other uses	0	
G. Long-term asset payments	1,139	
H. Loan payments	0	
I. Owner draws	2,000	
TOTAL CASH PAID OUT	10,494	
CASH BALANCE/DEFICIENCY	13,606	
Loans to be received	40,000	
Equity deposits	5,000	
ENDING CASH BALANCE	58,606	

Instructions for Completing
Your Pro Forma Cash Flow Statement

This page contains instructions for completing the cash flow statement on the next page. A blank form for your own projections can be found in Appendix III.

Vertical Columns are divided into 12 months and are followed by "6-month period" and "12-month period" columns.

Horizontal Positions on the statement contain all sources of cash and cash to be paid out. The figures are retrieved from the two previous worksheets and from individual budgets.

Figures are projected for each month, reflecting the flow of cash in and out of your business for a one-year period. Begin with the first month of your business cycle and proceed as follows:

1. Project the Beginning Cash Balance. Enter under "January."
2. Project the Cash Receipts for January. Apportion your total year's revenues throughout the 12 months. Try to weight revenues as closely as you can to a realistic selling cycle for your industry.
3. Add Beginning Cash Balance and Cash Receipts to determine Total Cash Available.
4. Project cash payments to be made for cost of goods to be sold (inventory that you will purchase or manufacture). Apportion your total inventory budget throughout the year, being sure you are providing for levels of inventory that will fulfill your needs for sales projected.
5. Customize your Variable and Fixed Expense categories to match your business.
6. Project Variable, Fixed, and Interest Expenses for January. Fill out any that you can for all 12 months.
7. Project cash to be paid out on Taxes, Long-Term Assets, Loan Repayments, and Owner Draws.
8. Calculate Total Cash Paid Out (Total of Cost of Goods to Be Sold, Variable, Fixed, Interest, Taxes, Long-Term Asset Payments, Loan Repayments, and Owner Draws).
9. Subtract Total Cash Paid Out from Total Cash Available. The result is entered under "Cash Balance/Deficiency." Be sure to bracket this figure if the result is a negative to avoid errors.
10. Look at Ending Cash Balance in each of the months and project Loans to be Received and Equity Deposits to be made. Add to Cash Balance/Deficiency to arrive at Ending Cash Balance for each month.
11. Ending Cash Balance for January is carried forward and becomes February's Beginning Cash Balance (as throughout the spreadsheet. Each month's ending balance is the next month's beginning balance).
12. Go to February and input any numbers that are still needed to complete that month. The process is repeated until December is completed.

To Complete the 6-Month and 12-Month Period Columns

1. The Beginning Cash Balance for January is entered in the first space of the 6-month and 12-month period column.
2. The monthly figures for each category (except Beginning Cash Balance, Total Cash Available, Cash Balance/Deficiency, and Ending Cash Balance) are added horizontally and the result entered in the corresponding Total category.
3. The 6- and 12-month period columns are then computed in the same manner as each of the individual months. If you have been accurate, your computations for the December Ending Cash Balance will be exactly the same as the Total Ending Cash Balance.

   Note: If your business is new, you will have to base your projections solely on market research and industry trends. If you have an established business, you will also use your financial statements from previous years.

Pro Forma Cash Flow Statement
Genesis Multimedia

Year: 2000

	Jan	Feb	Mar	Apr	May	Jun	6-MONTH PERIOD	Jul	Aug	Sep	Oct	Nov	Dec	12-MONTH PERIOD
BEGINNING CASH BALANCE	10,360	72,840	54,488	60,346	65,125	79,253	10,360	81,341	71,401	68,974	55,974	54,718	59,032	10,360
CASH RECEIPTS														
A. Sales/revenues	14,000	9,500	9,500	15,000	18,000	12,000	78,000	9,000	8,000	9,500	16,000	28,000	43,000	191,500
B. Receivables	400	400	300	500	450	425	2,475	500	750	650	600	1,250	8,000	14,225
C. Interest income	234	240	260	158	172	195	1,259	213	303	300	417	406	413	3,311
D. Sale of long-term assets	2,000	0	4,000	0	0	0	6,000	0	0	0	0	0	0	6,000
TOTAL CASH AVAILABLE	26,994	82,980	68,548	76,004	83,747	91,873	98,094	91,054	80,454	79,424	72,991	84,374	110,445	225,396
CASH PAYMENTS														
A. Cost of goods to be sold														
1. Purchases	800	16,500	3,700	200	200	300	21,700	9,000	430	540	6,700	14,000	12,000	64,370
2. Material	2,000	1,430	200	300	250	200	4,380	359	750	5,000	400	300	350	11,539
3. Labor	4,000	2,800	400	600	500	450	8,750	600	1,500	8,000	750	500	540	20,640
Total cost of goods	6,800	20,730	4,300	1,100	950	950	34,830	9,959	2,680	13,540	7,850	14,800	12,890	96,549
B. Variable expenses														
1. Advertising	900	300	900	250	300	700	3,350	350	300	640	1,300	1,200	1,400	8,540
2. Freight	75	75	75	75	180	70	550	75	75	90	180	300	560	1,830
3. Fulfillment of orders	300	300	300	400	350	300	1,950	300	280	325	450	600	975	4,880
4. Packaging costs	2,100	0	0	0	600	0	2,700	0	200	230	0	0	0	3,130
5. Sales/salaries	1,400	900	1,300	1,400	1,100	900	7,000	1,400	1,400	1,400	1,400	1,400	1,400	15,400
6. Travel	0	500	700	0	0	400	1,600	0	540	25	80	0	0	2,245
7. Misc. variable expense	100	100	100	100	100	100	600	100	100	100	100	100	100	1,200
Total variable expenses	4,875	2,175	3,375	2,225	2,630	2,470	17,750	2,225	2,895	2,810	3,510	3,600	4,435	37,225
C. Fixed expenses														
1. Financial administration	75	75	75	475	75	75	850	75	75	75	75	75	75	1,300
2. Insurance	1,564	0	0	0	0	0	1,564	1,563	0	0	0	0	0	3,127
3. License/permits	240	0	0	0	0	0	240	0	0	0	0	0	125	365
4. Office salaries	1,400	1,400	1,400	1,400	1,400	1,400	8,400	1,400	1,400	1,400	1,400	1,400	1,400	16,800
5. Rent expenses	700	700	700	700	700	700	4,200	700	700	700	700	700	700	8,400
6. Utilities	200	200	140	120	80	80	820	75	75	75	90	120	155	1,410
7. Misc. fixed expense	100	100	100	100	100	100	600	100	100	100	100	100	100	1,200
Total fixed expenses	4,279	2,475	2,415	2,795	2,355	2,355	16,674	3,913	2,350	2,350	2,365	2,395	2,555	32,602
D. Interest expense	0	0	0	234	233	232	699	231	230	225	223	222	220	2,050
E. Federal income tax	1,200	1	1	1,200	1	1,200	3,603	0	0	1,200	0	0	0	4,803
F. Other uses	0	0	0	0	0	0	0	0	0	0	0	0	0	0
G. Long-term asset payments	0	0	0	214	214	214	642	214	214	214	214	214	214	1,926
H. Loan payments	0	1,111	1,111	1,111	1,111	1,111	5,555	1,111	1,111	1,111	1,111	1,111	1,111	12,221
I. Owner draws	2,000	2,000	2,000	2,000	2,000	2,000	12,000	2,000	2,000	2,000	3,000	3,000	3,000	27,000
TOTAL CASH PAID OUT	19,154	28,492	13,202	10,879	9,494	10,532	91,753	19,653	11,480	23,450	18,273	25,342	24,425	214,376
CASH BALANCE/DEFICIENCY	7,840	54,488	55,346	65,125	74,253	81,341	6,341	71,401	68,974	55,974	54,718	59,032	86,020	11,020
LOANS TO BE RECEIVED	65,000	0	0	0	0	0	65,000	0	0	0	0	0	0	65,000
EQUITY DEPOSITS	0	0	5,000	0	5,000	0	10,000	0	0	0	0	0	0	10,000
ENDING CASH BALANCE	72,840	54,488	60,346	65,125	79,253	81,341	81,341	71,401	68,974	55,974	54,718	59,032	86,020	86,020

Quarterly Budget Analysis

Your Pro Forma Cash Flow Statement (Yearly Budget) is of no value to you as a business owner unless there is some means to evaluate the actual performance of your company and measure it against your projections.

What Is a Quarterly Budget Analysis?

A quarterly budget analysis is the financial analysis tool that is used to compare your projected cash flow statement with your business' actual performance. Its purpose is to let you know whether or not you are operating within your projections and to help you maintain control of all phases of your business operations. When your analysis shows that you are over or under budget in any area, it will be necessary to determine the reason for the deviation and implement changes for the future that will enable you to get back on track.

For example, if you have budgeted $1,000 in advertising funds for the first quarter and you find that you have actually spent $1,600, the first thing you should do is look at the sales that have occurred as a result of increased advertising. If they are over projections by an amount equal to or more than the $600, your budget will still be in good shape. If not, you will have to find expenses in your budget that can be revised to make up the deficit. You might be able to take a smaller draw for yourself or spend less on travel. You might even be able to increase your profits by adding a new product or service.

It should be clear at this point that the correct process to keep you from running out of operating capital in the middle of the year is to make yearly projections, analyze at the end of each quarter, and then revise your budget based on that analysis and current industry trends.

How to Develop a Quarterly Budget Analysis

The Quarterly Budget Analysis needs the following seven columns:
1. **Budget Item:** The list of budget items is taken from headings on the Pro Forma Cash Flow Statement. All items in your budget should be listed.
2. **Budget This Quarter:** Fill in the amount budgeted for current quarter from your Pro Forma Cash Flow Statement.
3. **Actual This Quarter:** Fill in actual receipts and expenditures for quarter.
4. **Variation This Quarter:** Subtract the amount spent or received from the amount budgeted for the current quarter. This will be the amount spent or received over or under budget.
5. **Year-to-Date Budget:** Amount budgeted from beginning of year through and including current quarter (from cash flow statement).
6. **Actual Year-to-Date:** Actual amount spent or received from beginning of year through current quarter.
7. **Variation Year-to-Date:** Subtract the amount spent or received from the amount budgeted from the start of the year through the current quarter.

 Note: You will not have any information to input into columns no. 3, 4, 5, 6, and 7 until you have been in business for at least one quarter.

All items contained in the Budget are listed on this form. The second column is the amount budgeted for the current quarter. By subtracting the amount actually spent, you will arrive at the variation for the quarter. The last three columns are for year-to-date-figures. If you analyze at the end of the 3rd quarter, figures will represent the first nine months of your tax year.

Making Calculations: When you calculate variations, the amounts are preceded by either a plus (+) or a minus (–), depending on whether the category is a revenue or an expense. If the actual amount is greater than the amount budgeted, (1) Revenue categories will represent the variation as a positive (+). (2) Expense categories will represent the variation as a negative (–).

Quarterly Budget Analysis

Business Name: Genesis Multimedia   **For the Quarter Ending: September 30, 2000**

BUDGET ITEM	THIS QUARTER			YEAR-TO-DATE		
	Budget	Actual	Variation	Budget	Actual	Variation
SALES REVENUES	145,000	150,000	5,000	400,000	410,000	10,000
Less cost of goods	80,000	82,500	(2,500)	240,000	243,000	(3,000)
GROSS PROFITS	65,000	67,500	2,500	160,000	167,000	7,000
VARIABLE EXPENSES						
1. Advertising/marketing	3,000	3,400	(400)	6,000	6,200	(200)
2. Freight	6,500	5,750	750	16,500	16,350	150
3. Fulfillment of orders	1,400	950	450	3,800	4,100	(300)
4. Packaging	750	990	(240)	2,200	2,300	(100)
5. Salaries/commissions	6,250	6,250	0	18,750	18,750	0
6. Travel	500	160	340	1,500	1,230	270
7. Miscellaneous	0	475	(475)	0	675	(675)
FIXED EXPENSES						
1. Financial/administrative	1,500	1,500	0	4,500	4,700	(200)
2. Insurance	2,250	2,250	0	6,750	6,750	0
3. Licenses/permits	1,000	600	400	3,500	3,400	100
4. Office salaries	1,500	1,500	0	4,500	4,500	0
5. Rent	3,500	3,500	0	10,500	10,500	0
6. Utilities	750	990	(240)	2,250	2,570	(320)
7. Miscellaneous	0	60	(60)	0	80	(80)
NET INCOME FROM OPERATIONS	36,100	39,125	3,025	79,250	84,895	5,645
INTEREST INCOME	1,250	1,125	(125)	3,750	3,700	(50)
INTEREST EXPENSE	1,500	1,425	75	4,500	4,500	0
NET PROFIT (Pretax)	35,850	38,825	2,975	78,500	84,095	5,595
TAXES	8,500	9,500	(1,000)	25,500	28,500	(3,000)
NET PROFIT (After Tax)	27,350	29,325	1,975	53,000	55,595	2,595

NON-INCOME STATEMENT ITEMS

1. Long-term asset repayments	2,400	3,400	(1,000)	7,200	8,200	(1,000)
2. Loan repayments	3,400	3,400	0	8,800	8,800	0
3. Owner draws	6,000	6,900	(900)	18,000	18,900	(900)

BUDGET DEVIATIONS

	This Quarter	Year-to-Date
1. Income statement items:	$1,975	$2,595
2. Non-income statement items:	($1,900)	($1,900)
3. Total deviation	$75	$695

Three-Year Income Projection

What Is a Three-Year Income Projection?

A three-year income projection is a pro forma income (or profit & loss) statement. This statement differs from a cash flow statement in that it includes only projected income and deductible expenses. This difference is illustrated as follows: Your company will make payments of $9,000 on a vehicle in 1996. $3,000 of that amount is interest. The full amount ($9,000) will be recorded on a cash flow statement; only the interest ($3,000) will be recorded on a projected income statement. Principal paid on your loan ($6,000) is not a deductible expense.

Variation in Period Covered

There is some difference of opinion as to the period of time that should be covered and whether or not it should be on an annual or month-by-month basis. If you are seeking funds, talk to the lender or investor about his or her specific requirements. If not, we suggest a three-year projection with annual rather than monthly projections. With the rapidly changing economy, it is difficult to make accurate detailed projections.

Account for Increases and Decreases

Increases in income and expenses are only realistic and should be reflected in your projections. Industry trends can also cause decreases in both income and expenses. An example of this might be in the computer industry where heavy competition and standardization of components has caused a decrease in both cost and sale price of both hardware and software. The state of the economy will also be a contributing factor in the outlook for your business.

Sources of Information

Information for a three-year projection can be developed from your pro forma cash flow statement and your business and marketing analysis. The first year's figures can be transferred from the totals of income and expense items. The second and third years' figures are derived by combining these totals with projected trends in your particular industry. Also, remember that certain expenses from your first year may not be repeated in future years. You may also have new expenses to take into account. For instance, you may have a new product or service, you may begin importing or exporting internationally and have customs and freight, or you may begin offering merchant credit card services and have associated fees. Again, if you are an established business, you will also be able to use past financial statements to help you determine what you project for the future of your business. Be sure to take into account fluctuations anticipated in costs, efficiency of operation, changes in your market, etc.

A filled-in example of a Three-Year Income Projection form is provided on the next page. A blank form for your use is located in Appendix III.

Three-Year Income Projection

Business Name: **Updated: September 26, 1999**

Genesis Multimedia	YEAR 1 2000	YEAR 2 2001	YEAR 3 2002	TOTAL 3 YEARS
INCOME				
1. Sales revenues	500,000	540,000	595,000	1,635,000
2. Cost of goods sold (c – d)	312,000	330,000	365,000	1,007,000
a. Beginning inventory	147,000	155,000	175,000	147,000
b. Purchases	320,000	350,000	375,000	1,045,000
c. C.O.G. available Sale (a + b)	467,000	505,000	550,000	1,192,000
d. Less ending inventory (12/31)	155,000	175,000	185,000	185,000
3. GROSS PROFIT ON SALES (1 – 2)	188,000	210,000	230,000	628,000
EXPENSES				
1. Variable (selling) (a thru h)	67,390	84,300	89,400	241,090
a. Advertising/marketing	22,000	24,500	26,400	72,900
b. Freight	9,000	12,000	13,000	34,000
c. Fulfillment of orders	2,000	3,500	4,000	9,500
d. Packaging costs	3,000	4,000	3,500	10,500
e. Salaries/wages/commissions	25,000	34,000	36,000	95,000
f. Travel	1,000	1,300	1,500	3,800
g. Miscellaneous selling expense	390	0	0	390
h. Depreciation (prod/serv assets)	5,000	5,000	5,000	15,000
2. Fixed (administrative) (a thru h)	51,610	53,500	55,800	160,910
a. Financial administration	1,000	1,200	1,200	3,400
b. Insurance	3,800	4,000	4,200	12,000
c. Licenses and permits	2,710	1,400	1,500	5,610
d. Office salaries	14,000	17,500	20,000	51,500
e. Rent expense	22,500	22,500	22,500	67,500
f. Utilities	3,000	3,500	3,600	10,100
g. Miscellaneous fixed expense	0	0	0	0
h. Depreciation (office equipment)	4,600	3,400	2,800	10,800
TOTAL OPERATING EXPENSES (1 + 2)	119,000	137,800	145,200	402,000
NET INCOME OPERATIONS (GP – Exp)	69,000	72,200	84,800	226,000
OTHER INCOME (Interest income)	5,000	5,000	5,000	15,000
OTHER EXPENSE (Interest expense)	7,000	5,000	4,000	16,000
NET PROFIT (LOSS) BEFORE TAXES	67,000	72,200	85,800	225,000
TAXES 1. Federal, self-employment	21,700	24,200	28,500	74,400
2. State	4,300	4,800	5,700	14,800
3. Local	0	0	0	0
NET PROFIT (LOSS) AFTER TAXES	41,000	43,200	51,600	135,800

At the end of each year, you can compare your company's projections against its actual performance. You may be required by some lenders or investors to extend your projection to five years. The process will be the same.

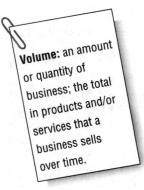

Volume: an amount or quantity of business; the total in products and/or services that a business sells over time.

Break-Even Analysis
What Is a Break-Even Point?

This is the point at which a company's costs exactly match the sales volume and at which the business has neither made a profit nor incurred a loss. The break-even point can be determined by mathematical calculation or by development of a graph. It can be expressed in:

1. **Total Dollars of Revenue** (exactly offset by total costs).
2. **Total Units of Production** (cost of which exactly equals the income derived by their sale).

To apply a Break-Even Analysis to an operation, you will need three projections:

1. **Fixed Costs:** (Administrative Overhead + Interest) Many of these costs remain constant even during slow periods. Interest expense must be added to fixed costs for a break-even analysis.
2. **Variable Costs:** (Cost of Goods + Selling Expenses) Usually varies with volume of business. The greater the sales volume, the higher the costs.
3. **Total Sales Volume:** (Projected sales of your products or services for same period).

Source of Information

All of your figures can be derived from your Three-Year Projection. Since break-even is not reached until your total revenues match your total expenses, the calculation of your break-even point will require that you add enough years revenues and expenses together until you see that the total revenues are greater than the total expenses. Retrieve the figures and plug them into the following mathematical formula.

Mathematically

A firm's sales at break-even point can be computed by using this formula:

B-E Point (Sales) = Fixed Costs + [(Variable Costs/Est. Revenues) x Sales]

Terms Used:
    a. Sales = volume of sales at Break-Even Point
    b. Fixed Costs = administrative expense, depreciation, interest
    c. Variable Costs = cost of goods and selling expenses
    d. Estimated Revenues = income (from sales of goods/services)

Example:
    a. S (Sales at B-E Point) = the unknown
    b. FC (Fixed Costs) = $25,000
    c. VC (Variable Costs) = $45,000
    d. R (Estimated Revenues) = $90,000

Using the formula, the computation would appear as follows:
    S (at B-E Point) = $25,000 + [($45,000/$90,000) x S]
    S = $25,000 + (1/2 x S)
    S – 1/2 S = $25,000
    1/2S = $25,000
    S = $50,000 (B-E Point in terms of dollars of revenue exactly offset by total costs)

Note: Figures shown in 10's of thousands of dollars (Ex: 2 = $20,000)
    B-Even Point (Sales) = Fixed Costs + [(Variable Costs/Est. Revenues) x Sales]
    Break-Even Point (Sales) = $25,000 = [($45,000/$90,000) x Sales]

Graphically

Break-even point in graph form for the same business would be plotted as illustrated below. There is a blank form for your use in the Sample Worksheet section.

Break-Even Analysis Graph

Business Name: Genesis Multimedia   **Date of Analysis: Sept 31, 1999**

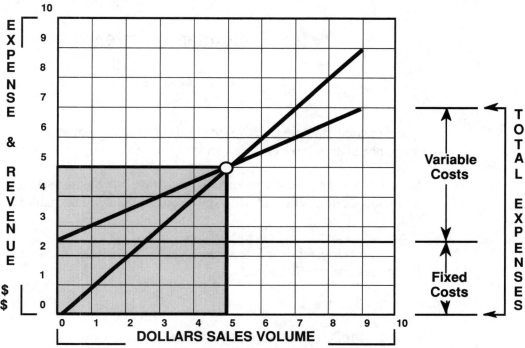

NOTE: Figures shown in 10's of thousands of dollars (Ex: 2 = $ 20,000)

To Complete The Graph: Determine the following projections:
1. **Fixed Costs for Period:** Those costs that usually remain constant and must be met regardless of your sales volume (administrative, rent, insurance, depreciation, salaries, etc.). Also add interest expenses. Ex: $25,000
2. **Variable Costs:** Cost associated with the production and selling of your products or services. If you have a product, you will include cost of goods (inventory purchases, labor, materials) with your variable costs (freight, packaging, sales commissions, advertising, etc.). If you wish, these costs may be expressed by multiplying the unit cost by the units to be sold for a product. Ex.: $1.50 per unit x 30,000 units = $45,000. For a service having no cost of goods, use total of projected selling expenses (variable).
3. **Total Sales Volume:** This is the figure representing your total projected revenues. You may also calculate revenues by multiplying projected units of product to be sold by sale price per unit. Ex.: 30,000 units @ $3.00 = $90,000. For a service, you can multiply your projected billable hours by your hourly rate. Ex.: 900 hours x $100 = $90,000

To Draw Graph Lines:
1. **Draw Horizontal Line** at point representing Fixed Costs (25).
2. **Draw Variable Cost Line** from left end of Fixed Cost Line sloping upward to point where Total Costs (Fixed + Variable) on vertical scale (7) meet Total Revenues on the horizontal scale (9).
3. **Draw Total Revenues Line** from zero through point describing Total Revenues on both scales (where 9 meets 9).

Break-Even Point. That point on the graph where the Variable Cost Line intersects the Total Revenue Line. This business estimates that it will break even at the time sales volume reaches $50,000. The triangular area below and to the left of that point represents company losses. The triangular area above and to the right of the point represents potential profit.

Actual Performance Statements

◈ ◈ ◈ ◈

The financial statements covered on the following pages are actual performance statements. They reflect the past activity of your business.

If you are a new business owner, you have no business history. Your financial section will end with the projected statements and a Personal Financial History.

If you are an established business, you will include the actual performance statements listed below:

☑ **Balance Sheet**

☑ **Profit & Loss (Income) Statement**

☑ **Business Financial History or Loan Application**

Balance Sheet

What Is a Balance Sheet?

The Balance Sheet is a financial statement that shows the financial position of the business as of a fixed date. It is usually done at the close of an accounting period. The Balance Sheet can be compared to a still photograph. It is a picture of what your business owns and owes at a particular given moment and will show you whether your financial position is strong or weak. By regularly preparing this statement, you will be able to identify and analyze trends in the financial strength of your business and thus implement timely modifications.

Assets, Liabilities, and Net Worth

All balance sheets are divided into three categories. The three are related in that, at any given time, a business's assets equal the total contributions by its creditors and owners. They are defined as follows:

Assets = Anything your business owns that has monetary value

Liabilities = Debts owed by the business to any of its creditors

Net Worth (Capital) = An amount equal to the owner's equity

The relationship between the three is simply illustrated in the following mathematical formula.

Assets – Liabilities = Net Worth

Examined as such, it becomes apparent that if a business possesses more assets than it owes to creditors, its net worth will be a positive. Conversely, if the business owes more money to creditors than it possesses in assets, the net worth will be a negative.

Projected Balance Sheets

If you are seeking financing, your lenders or investors may require that you provide them with projected balance sheets for "day-1," "after capital infusion," or "end-of-year 1." The financial information for a projected balance sheet as of a fixed date is compiled by using figures from the same-date column of your pro forma cash flow statement and same-date status on inventory, capital assets, long-term loans, and current liabilities. An example of an "end-of-year 1" projected balance sheet can be seen in the sample business plan for Marine Art of California in Appendix I. The form is the same for projected or actual balance sheets.

Categories and Format

The Balance Sheet must follow an accepted accounting format and contain the previously mentioned categories. By following this format, anyone reading the Balance Sheet can readily interpret it.

> A sample filled-in Balance Sheet and Explanation of Balance Sheet Categories are provided for you on the next two pages. There is a blank form for your own use in Appendix III.

Explanation of Categories for the Balance Sheet

ASSETS. Everything owned by or owed to your business that has cash value.

1. **Current assets:** Assets that can be converted into cash within one year of the date on the Balance Sheet.
   a. **Cash:** Money you have on hand. Include moneys not yet deposited.
   b. **Petty cash:** Money deposited to Petty Cash and not yet expended.
   c. **Accounts receivable:** Money owed to you for sale of goods and/or services.
   d. **Inventory**: Raw materials, work in process, and goods manufactured or purchased for resale.
   e. **Short-term investments:** Expected to be converted to cash within one year—stocks, bonds, CDs. List at lesser of cost or market value.
   f. **Prepaid expenses:** Goods or services purchased or rented prior to use (ex: rent, insurance, prepaid inventory purchases, etc.).

2. **Long-Term investments:** Stocks, bonds, and special savings accounts to be kept for at least one year.

3. **Fixed assets:** Resources a business owns and does not intend for resale.
   a. **Land:** List at original purchase price.
   b. **Buildings:** List at cost less depreciation.
   c. **Equipment, furniture, autos/vehicles:** List at cost less depreciation. *Kelley Blue Book* can be used to determine current value of vehicles.

LIABILITIES. What your business owes; claims by creditors on your assets.

1. **Current liabilities:** Those obligations payable within one operating cycle.
   a. **Accounts payable:** Obligations payable within one operating cycle.
   b. **Notes payable:** Short-term notes; list the balance of principal due. Separately list the current portion of long-term debts.
   c. **Interest payable:** Interest accrued on loans and credit.
   d. **Taxes payable:** Amounts estimated to have been incurred during the accounting period.
   e. **Payroll accrual:** Current Liabilities on salaries and wages.

2. **Long-Term liabilities:** Outstanding balance less the current portion due (business loans, mortgages, vehicle, etc.).

NET WORTH (Also called "Owner Equity"). The claims of the owner or owners on the assets of the business (document according to the legal structure of your business).

1. **Proprietorship or partnership:** Each owner's original investment plus earnings after withdrawals.

2. **Corporation:** The sum of contributions by owners or stockholders plus earnings retained after paying dividends.

Balance Sheet

Business Name: **Genesis Multimedia**   Date: September 30, 1999

ASSETS

Current assets

Cash	$	8,742
Petty cash	$	167
Accounts receivable	$	5,400
Inventory	$	101,800
Short-term investments	$	0
Prepaid expenses	$	1,967

Long-Term investments $ 0

Fixed assets

Land (valued at cost)		$ 185,000
Buildings		$ 143,000
1. Cost	171,600	
2. Less acc. depr.	28,600	
Improvements		$ 0
1. Cost		
2. Less acc. depr.		
Equipment		$ 5,760
1. Cost	7,200	
2. Less acc. depr.	1,440	
Furniture		$ 2,150
1. Cost	2,150	
2. Less acc. depr.	0	
Autos/vehicles		$ 16,432
1. Cost	19,700	
2. Less acc. depr.	3,268	

Other assets

1.	$	
2.	$	

TOTAL ASSETS $ 470,418

LIABILITIES

Current liabilities

Accounts payable	$	2,893
Notes payable	$	0
Interest payable	$	1,842
Taxes payable		
Federal income tax	$	5,200
Self-employment tax	$	1,025
State income tax	$	800
Sales tax accrual	$	2,130
Property tax	$	0
Payroll accrual	$	4,700

Long-term liabilities

Notes payable	$	196,700

TOTAL LIABILITIES $ 215,290

NET WORTH (EQUITY)

Proprietorship	$	
or		
Partnership		
John Smith, 60% equity	$	153,077
Mary Blake, 40% equity	$	102,051
or		
Corporation		
Capital stock	$	
Surplus paid in	$	
Retained earnings	$	

TOTAL NET WORTH $ 255,128

Assets – Liabilities = Net Worth
and
Liabilities + Equity = Total Assets

Profit & Loss (Income) Statement

What Is a Profit & Loss (Income) Statement?

This statement shows your business financial activity over a period of time, usually your tax year. In contrast to the Balance Sheet, which shows a picture of your business at a given moment, the Profit & Loss Statement (P&L) can be likened to a video (moving picture)—showing what has happened in your business over a period of time. It is an excellent tool for assessing your business. You will be able to pick out weaknesses in your operation and plan ways to run your business more effectively, thereby increasing your profits. For example, you may find that some heavy advertising that you did in March did not effectively increase your sales. In following years, you may decide to utilize your advertising funds more effectively by using them at a time when there is increased customer spending taking place. In the same way, you might examine your Profit & Loss Statement to see what months have the heaviest sales volume and plan your inventory accordingly. Comparison of your P&Ls from several years will give you an even better picture of the trends in your business. Do not underestimate the value of this particular tool when planning your tactics.

How to Develop a Profit and Loss Statement

The Profit & Loss Statement (Income Statement) is compiled from actual business transactions, in contrast to pro forma statements, which are projections for future business periods. The P&L shows where your money has come from and where it was spent over a specific period of time. It should be prepared not only at the end of the fiscal year, but at the close of each business month. It is one of the two principal financial statements prepared from the ledgers and the records of a business. Income and expense account balances are used in the Profit & Loss Statement. The remaining asset, liability, and capital information provides the figures for the Balance Sheet covered on the last three pages.

At the end of each month, the accounts in the General Ledger are balanced and closed. Balances from the revenue accounts (numbered 400-499) and the expense accounts (numbered 500-599) must be transferred to your Profit & Loss Statement.

If you use an accounting professional or have a good in-house software program, either should generate a profit & loss statement and balance sheet for you at the end of every month as well as at the end of your tax year. Many small business owners do their bookkeeping manually. If your general records are set up properly, the transfer of information should still be fairly simple as long as you understand what information is needed and which general records are to be used as sources.

Format and Sources of Information

The Profit & Loss (or Income) Statement must also follow an accepted accounting format and contain certain categories. On the next page, you will see the correct format and a brief explanation of the items to be included or computations to be made in each category in order to arrive at "The Bottom Line" or owner's share of the profit for the period.

Income

1. **Net sales (Gross sales less Returns and Allowances):** What were your cash receipts for the period? If your accounting is on an accrual basis, what amount did you invoice out during the period? You may wish to have subcategories for different types of sales.

2. **Cost of goods sold:** The cost of manufacturing or purchase of products sold for the period. The Cost of Goods is calculated using a, b, and c below. (a + b - c = COG).

   a. **Beginning inventory:** Product on hand at beginning of accounting period.

   b. **Purchases:** Material, labor, or cost on inventory purchased during accounting period.

   c. **Ending inventory:** Product on hand at the end of the accounting period.

3. **Gross profit:** Computed by subtracting Cost of Goods Sold from Net Sales (1 – 2).

> **Note:** If you are in a service business and do not sell any products you *will not* have any cost of goods to compute. Net sales and gross profit will be the same.

Expenses

1. **Variable expenses (selling):** What expenses did you have that were directly related to your product or service? (e.g., advertising/marketing, freight, fulfillment of orders, sales salaries/commissions, trade shows, travel, vehicles, depreciation (production equip), etc.? These expenses vary and are usually directly proportional to your volume of business. Divide into sub-categories customized to your business.

2. **Fixed expenses (administrative):** What expenses did you have during the period on office overhead (accounting/legal, insurance, office supplies, office salaries, rent, utilities, depreciation of office equipment, etc.)? These expenses are often fixed and remain the same regardless of your volume of business. They should also be divided into subcategories customized to your business.

Net income from operations. Gross Profit (3) minus Total Fixed (Selling) Expenses and Variable (Administrative) Expenses (Expense nos. 1 and 2)

Other income: Interest received during the period

Other expense: Interest paid out during the period

Net profit (loss) before income taxes. The Net Income from Operations plus Interest Income minus Interest Expense. The amount of profit prior to income taxes.

Income taxes: List taxes paid out during the period (federal, state, local, self-employment)

Net profit (loss) after income taxes. Subtract all income taxes paid out from the net profit (or loss) before income taxes. This is what is known as "the bottom line."

Sample Forms

The next two pages contain two Profit & Loss Statement forms. As you will see in the Example 12-Month Profit & Loss Statement, the spreadsheet is divided into columns representing each of the 12 months plus 6-month and annual total columns. At the end of your tax year, you will have filled in all monthly columns. After calculating your annual totals, your P&L will be complete. At the end of the year, this form will provide an accurate moving picture of the year's financial activity. The second one is a single form to be used for either a monthly, quarterly, or annual profit & loss statement. Blank forms for your own use are provided in Appendix III.

Profit & Loss (Income) Statement
Genesis Multimedia

For the Year: 1999

	Jan	Feb	Mar	Apr	May	Jun	6-MONTH TOTALS	Jul	Aug	Sep	Oct	Nov	Dec	12-MONTH TOTALS
INCOME														
1. Net sales (Gr - R&A)	14,400	10,140	10,060	15,658	18,622	12,620	81,500	11,500	9,850	10,150	16,600	29,250	51,000	209,850
2. Cost of goods to be sold	2,800	2,900	4,200	7,700	7,350	2,750	27,700	2,959	2,580	2,740	6,250	13,400	23,290	78,919
a. Beginning inventory	27,000	31,000	48,500	48,600	42,000	35,600	27,000	33,800	40,800	40,900	51,700	53,300	54,700	27,000
b. Purchases	6,800	20,400	4,300	1,100	950	950	34,500	9,959	2,680	13,540	7,850	14,800	12,890	96,219
c. C.O.G. available for sale	33,800	51,400	52,800	49,700	42,950	36,550	61,500	43,759	43,480	54,440	59,550	68,100	67,590	123,219
d. Less ending inventory	31,000	48,500	48,600	42,000	35,600	33,800	33,800	40,800	40,900	51,700	53,300	54,700	44,300	44,300
3. Gross profit	11,600	7,240	5,860	7,958	11,272	9,870	53,800	8,541	7,270	7,410	10,350	15,850	27,710	130,931
EXPENSES														
1. Variable (selling) expenses														
a. Advertising	900	300	900	250	300	300	2,950	350	300	640	1,300	1,200	1,400	8,140
b. Freight	75	75	75	75	180	70	550	75	75	90	180	300	560	1,830
c. Fulfillment of orders	300	300	300	400	350	300	1,950	300	280	325	450	600	975	4,880
d. Packaging costs	2,100	0	0	0	600	0	2,700	0	200	230	0	0	0	3,130
e. Sales salaries/commissions	1,400	900	1,300	1,400	1,100	900	7,000	1,400	1,400	1,400	1,400	1,400	1,400	15,400
f. Travel	0	500	700	0	0	400	1,600	0	540	25	80	0	0	2,245
g. Misc. variable expense	50	47	73	40	28	62	300	90	73	46	39	74	87	709
h. Depreciation	0	0	0	0	0	0	0	0	0	0	0	0	2,660	2,660
Total variable expenses	4,825	2,122	3,348	2,165	2,558	2,032	17,050	2,215	2,868	2,756	3,449	3,574	7,082	38,994
1. Fixed (admin) expenses														
a. Financial administration	75	75	75	475	75	75	850	75	75	75	75	75	75	1,300
b. Insurance	1,564	0	0	0	0	0	1,564	1,563	0	0	0	0	0	3,127
c. Licenses/permits	240	0	0	0	0	0	240	0	0	0	0	0	125	365
d. Office salaries	1,400	1,400	1,400	1,400	1,400	1,400	8,400	1,400	1,400	1,400	1,400	1,400	1,400	16,800
e. Rent expenses	700	700	700	700	700	700	4,200	700	700	700	700	700	700	8,400
f. Utilities	200	200	140	120	80	80	820	75	75	75	90	120	155	1,410
g. Misc. fixed expense	54	38	42	57	28	64	283	60	72	31	48	45	89	628
h. Depreciation	0	0	0	0	0	2,660	2,660	0	0	0	0	0	2,660	5,320
Total fixed expenses	4,233	2,413	2,357	2,752	2,283	4,979	19,017	3,873	2,322	2,281	2,313	2,340	5,204	37,350
Total operating expense	9,058	4,535	5,705	4,917	4,841	7,011	36,067	6,088	5,190	5,037	5,762	5,914	12,286	76,344
Net Income From Operations	2,542	2,705	155	3,041	6,431	2,859	17,733	2,453	2,080	2,373	4,588	9,936	15,424	54,587
Other Income (interest)	234	240	260	158	172	195	1,259	213	303	300	417	406	413	3,311
Other Expense (interest)	0	0	0	234	233	232	699	231	230	225	223	222	220	2,050
Net Profit (Loss) Before Taxes	2,776	2,945	415	2,965	6,370	2,822	18,293	2,435	2,153	2,448	4,782	10,120	15,617	55,848
Taxes: a. Federal	1,950	0	0	1,950	0	1,950	5,850	0	0	1,950	0	0	0	7,800
b. State	350	0	0	350	0	350	1,050	0	0	350	0	0	0	1,400
c. Local	0	0	0	0	0	0	0	0	0	0	0	0	0	0
NET PROFIT (LOSS) AFTER TAXES	476	2,945	415	665	6,370	522	11,393	2,435	2,153	148	4,782	10,120	15,617	46,648

Profit & Loss (Income) Statement
Genesis Multimedia

Beginning: January 1, 1999   **Ending: December 31, 1999**

INCOME		
1. Sales revenues		$ 209,850
2. Cost of goods sold (c – d)		78,919
a. Beginning inventory (1/01)	27,000	
b. Purchases	96,219	
c. C.O.G. avail. sale (a + b)	123,219	
d. Less ending inventory (12/31)	44,300	
3. Gross profit on sales (1 – 2)		$ 130,931
EXPENSES		
1. Variable (selling) (a thru h)		38,994
a. Advertising/marketing	8,140	
b. Freight	1,830	
c. Fulfillment of orders	4,880	
d. Packaging costs	3,130	
e. Salaries/wages/commissions	15,400	
f. Travel	2,245	
g. Misc. variable (selling) expense	709	
h. Depreciation (prod/serv assets)	2,660	
2. Fixed (administrative) (a thru h)		37,350
a. Financial administration	1,300	
b. Insurance	3,127	
c. Licenses and permits	365	
d. Office salaries	16,800	
e. Rent expense	8,400	
f. Utilities	1,410	
g. Misc. fixed (administrative) expense	628	
h. Depreciation (office equipment)	5,320	
Total operating expenses (1 + 2)		76,344
Net Income from operations (GP – Exp)		$ 54,587
Other income (interest income)		3,311
Other expense (interest expense)		2,050
Net profit (loss) before taxes		$ 55,848
Taxes		
a. Federal	7,800	
b. State	1,400	9,200
c. Local	0	
NET PROFIT (LOSS) AFTER TAXES		$ 46,648

Business Financial History

The business financial history is the last of the financial statements required in your business plan. It is a summary of financial information about your company from its start to the present.

If Yours Is a New Business

You will have only projections for your business. If you are applying for a loan, the lender will require a Personal Financial History. This will be of benefit in that it will show the manner in which you have conducted your personal business, an indicator of the probability of your succeeding in your business.

If Yours Is an Established Business

The loan application and your Business Financial History are the same. When you indicate that you are interested in obtaining a business loan, the institution considering the loan will supply you with an application. The format may vary slightly. When you receive your loan application, be sure to review it and think about how you are going to answer each item. Answer all questions and, by all means, be certain your information is accurate and that it can be easily verified.

Information Needed and Sources

As you fill out your Business Financial History (loan application), it should become immediately apparent why this is the last financial document to be completed. All of the information needed will have been compiled previously in earlier parts of your plan and in the financial statements you have already completed. To help you with your financial history, the following is a list of information most frequently required. We have also listed some of the sources you can refer to for that information:

Net worth: determined by deducting the amount of all personal liabilities fro the total of all personal assets.

Cosigners: joint signers of a loan agreement, pledging to meet the obligations in case of default.

1. **Assets, liabilities, net worth:** You should recognize these three as balance sheet terms. You have already completed the Balance Sheet for your company and need only to go back to that record and bring the dollar amounts forward.

2. **Contingent liabilities:** These are debts you may come to owe in the future (for example: default on a cosigned note or settlement of a pending lawsuit).

3. **Inventory details:** Information is derived from your Inventory Record. Also, in the Organizational Plan you should already have a summary of your current policies and methods of evaluation.

4. **Profit & loss statement:** This is revenue and expense information. You will transfer the information from your Annual Profit & Loss (last statement completed) or from compilation of several if required by the lender.

5. **Real estate holdings, stocks, and bonds:** Refer back to your Organizational Plan. You may also have to go through your investment records for more comprehensive information

6. **Legal structure information (sole proprietorship, partnership, or corporation):** There are generally three separate schedules on the financial history, one for each form of legal structure. You will be required to fill out the one that is appropriate to your business. In the Organizational section, you will have covered two areas that will serve as the source of this information—Legal Structure and Management. Supporting Documents may also contain some of the information that you will need.

7. **Audit information:** Refer back to the Organizational Plan under Recordkeeping. You may also be asked questions about other prospective lenders, whether you are seeking credit, who audits your books, and when they were last audited.

8. **Insurance coverage:** You will be asked to provide detailed information such as items covered and type and value of coverage. Your Organizational Plan should contain information on coverage that can be brought forth to the financial history.

Business Financial History form. You will find an example of a Business Financial History that might be required by a potential lender or investor on pages 94 and 95.

Personal Financial Statement form. If you are a new business and need your Personal Financial Statement for this section, you will find a sample form in Chapter 7, "Supporting Documents."

Business Financial History

FINANCIAL STATEMENT
INDIVIDUAL, PARTNERSHIP, OR CORPORATION

FINANCIAL STATEMENT OF_____

RECEIVED AT_____BRANCH

NAME_____

BUSINESS_____

ADDRESS_____

AT CLOSE OF BUSINESS_____19____

To

The undersigned, for the purpose of procuring and establishing credit from time to time with you and to induce you to permit the undersigned to become indebted to you on notes, endorsements, guarantees, overdrafts or otherwise, furnishes the following (or in lieu thereof the attached, which is the most recent statement prepared by or for the undersigned) as being a full, true and correct statement of the financial condition of the undersigned on the date indicated, and agrees to notify you immediately of the extent and character of any material change in said financial condition, and also agrees that if the undersigned, or any endorser or guarantor of any of the obligations of the undersigned, at any time fails in business or becomes insolvent, or commits an act of bankruptcy, or if any deposit account of the undersigned with you, or any other property of the undersigned held by you, be attempted to be obtained or held by writ of execution, garnishment, attachment or other legal process, or if any of the representations made below prove to be untrue, or if the undersigned fails to notify you of any material change as above agreed, or if the business, or any interest therein, of the undersigned is sold, then and in such case, at your option, all of the obligations of the undersigned to you, or held by you, shall immediately become due and payable, without demand or notice. This statement shall be construed by you to be a continuing statement of the condition of the undersigned, and a new and original statement of all assets and liabilities upon each and every transaction in and by which the undersigned hereafter becomes indebted to you, until the undersigned advises in writing to the contrary.

ASSETS	DOLLARS	CENTS	LIABILITIES	DOLLARS	CENTS
Cash In_____ (NAME OF BANK)			Notes Payable to Banks_____		
Cash on Hand_____			Notes Payable and Trade Acceptances for Merchandise_____		
Notes Receivable and Trade Acceptance (Includes $_____ Past Due)			Notes Payable to Others_____		
Accounts Receivable—$_____ Less Reserves $_____			Accounts Payable (Includes $_____Past Due)_____		
Customer's . . . (Includes $_____ Past Due)			Due to Partners, Employes, Relatives, Officers, Stockholders or Allied Companies_____		
Merchandise—Finished—How Valued_____			Chattel Mortgages and Contracts Payable (Describe Monthly Payments) . . . . $_____		
Merchandise—Unfinished—How Valued_____			Federal and State Income Tax_____		
Merchandise—Raw Material—How Valued_____			Accrued Liabilities (Interest, Wages, Taxes, Etc.)_____		
Supplies on Hand_____			Portion of Long Term Debt Due Within One Year_____		
Stocks and Bonds—Listed (See Schedule B)_____					
TOTAL CURRENT ASSETS			**TOTAL CURRENT LIABILITIES**		
Real Estate—Less Depreciation of: $_____ Net (See Schedule A)			Liens on Real Estate (See Schedule A) $_____		
Machinery and Fixtures— Less Depreciation of: $_____ Net			Less Current Portion Included Above $_____ Net		
Automobiles and Trucks— Less Depreciation of: $_____ Net			Capital Stock—Preferred_____		
Stocks and Bonds—Unlisted (See Schedule B)_____			Capital Stock—Common_____		
Due from Partners, Employes, Relatives, Officers, Stockholders or Allied Companies_____			Surplus—Paid In_____		
Cash Value Life Insurance_____			Surplus—Earned and Undivided Profits_____		
Other Assets (Describe)_____			Net Worth (If Not Incorporated)_____		
TOTAL			**TOTAL**		

PROFIT AND LOSS STATEMENT FOR THE PERIOD FROM_____ TO_____

CONTINGENT LIABILITIES (NOT INCLUDED ABOVE)

				DOLLARS	CENTS
Net Sales (After Returned Sales and Allowances)_____			As Guarantor or Endorser_____		
Cost of Sales:			Accounts, Notes, or Trade Acceptances Discounted or Pledged_____		
Beginning Inventory			Surety On Bonds or Other Continent Liability_____		
Purchases (or cost of goods mfd.)			Letters of Credit_____		
TOTAL			Judgments Unsatisfied or Suits Pending_____		
Less: Closing Inventory			Merchandise Commitments and Unfinished Contracts_____		
Gross Profit on Sales			Merchandise Held On Consignment From Others_____		
			Unsatisfied Tax Liens or Notices From the Federal or State Governments of Intention to Assess Such Liens_____		

RECONCILEMENT OF NET WORTH OR EARNED SURPLUS

Operating Expenses:					
Salaries—Officers or Partners			Net Worth or Earned Surplus at Beginning of Period_____		
Salaries and Wages—Other			Add Net Profit or Deduct Net Loss_____		
Rent			Total_____		
Depreciation			Other Additions (Describe)_____		
Bad Debts			Total		
Advertising					
Interest			Less: Withdrawals or Dividends_____		
Taxes—Other Than Income			Other Deductions (Explain)_____		
Insurance			Total Deductions_____		
Other Expenses			Net Worth or Capital Funds on This Financial Statement_____		
Net Profit from Operations					

DETAIL OF INVENTORY

Other Income					
Less Other Expense			Is Inventory Figure Actual or Estimated?_____		
Net Profit Before Income Tax			By Whom Taken or Estimated_____ When?_____		
Federal and State Income Tax			Buy Principally From_____		
Net Profit or Loss			Average Terms of Purchase_____ Sale_____		
(To Net Worth or Earned Surplus)			Time of Year Inventory Maximum_____ Minimum_____		

FINANCIAL STATEMENT—FIRM OR CORPORATION—WOLCOTTS FORM 2001 (price class 6-2)

Business Financial History

SCHEDULE A   LIST OF REAL ESTATE AND IMPROVEMENTS WITH ENCUMBRANCES THEREON

DESCRIPTION, STREET NUMBER, LOCATION	TITLE IN NAMES OF	BOOK VALUE		MORTGAGES OR LIENS		TERMS OF PAYMENT	HOLDER OF LIEN
		LAND	IMPROVEMENTS	MATURITY	AMOUNT		
		$	$		$	$	
TOTALS		$	$		$	$	

SCHEDULE B   STOCKS & BONDS: Describe Fully. Use Supplemental Sheet if Necessary. Indicate if Stocks Are Common or Preferred. Give Interest Rate and Maturity of Bonds.

NO. OF SHARES AMT. OF BONDS	NAME AND ISSUE (DESCRIBE FULLY)	BOOK VALUE		MARKET VALUE	
		LISTED	UNLISTED	PRICE	VALUE
		$	$		$
	TOTALS	$	$		$

SCHEDULE C   Complete if Statement is for an Individual or Sole Proprietorship

Age _____ Number of Years in Present Business _____   Date of Filing Fictitious Trade Style _____

What Property Listed in This Statement is in Joint Tenancy? _____   Name of Other Party _____

What Property Listed in This Statement is Community Property? _____   Name of Other Party _____

With What Other Business Are You Connected? _____   Have You Filed Homestead? _____

Do You Deal With or Carry Accounts With Stockbrokers? _____ Amount $ _____   Name of Firm _____

SCHEDULE D   Complete if Statement is of a Partnership

NAME OF PARTNERS (INDICATE SPECIAL PARTNERS)	AGE	AMOUNT CONTRIBUTED	OUTSIDE NET WORTH	OTHER BUSINESS CONNECTIONS
		$	$	

Date of Organization _____   Limited or General? _____   Terminates _____
If Operating Under Fictitious Trade Style, Give Date of Filing _____

SCHEDULE E   Complete if Statement is of a Corporation

	AUTHORIZED	PAR VALUE	OUTSTANDING		ISSUED FOR	
			SHARES	AMOUNT	CASH	OTHER (DESCRIBE)
Common Stock	$	$		$	$	
Preferred Stock	$	$		$	$	

Bonds—Total Issue $ _____   Outstanding $ _____   Due _____   Interest Rate _____

Date Incorporated _____   Under Laws of State of _____

OFFICERS	AGE	SHARES OWNED		DIRECTORS AND PRINCIPAL STOCKHOLDERS	SHARES OWNED	
		COMMON	PREFERRED		COMMON	PREFERRED
President				Director		
Vice President				Director		
Secretary				Director		
Treasurer						

SCHEDULE F   Complete in ALL Cases   INSURANCE

Are Your Books Audited by Outside Accountants? _____ Name _____
Date of Last Audit _____ To What Date Has the U.S. Internal Revenue Department Examined Your Books? _____
Are You Borrowing From Any Other Branch of This Bank? _____ Which? _____
Are You Applying for Credit At Any Other Source? _____ Where? _____
Have You Ever Failed in Business? _____ If So, Attach a Complete Explanation and State Basis of Settlement With Creditors _____
Lease Has _____ Years to Run, With Monthly Rental of $ _____

Merchandise _____ $ _____
Machinery & Fixtures _____ $ _____
Buildings _____ $ _____
Earthquake _____ $ _____
Is Extended Coverage Endorsement Included? _____
Do You Carry Workmen's Compensation Insurance? _____

Automobiles and Trucks:
Public Liability $ _____ M/$ _____ M
Collision _____ $ _____
Property Damage _____ $ _____
Life Insurance _____ $ _____
Name of Beneficiary _____

STATEMENT OF BANK OFFICER:
Insofar as our records reveal, this Financial Statement is accurate and true. The foregoing statement is (a copy of) the original signed by the maker, in the credit files of this Bank.

The undersigned solemnly declares and certifies that the above statement (or in lieu thereof, the attached statement, as the case may be) and supporting schedules, both printed and written, give a full, true, and correct statement of the financial condition of the undersigned as of the date indicated.

Signature _____

_____   By _____
ASSISTANT CASHIER-MANAGER

(TITLE, IF CORPORATION)

Financial Statement Analysis: The Final Tool

The Financial Documents we have presented will most probably be sufficient for both your own use and that of potential lenders. Some of the documents may not be required. You should also note that we may have omitted forms required by some lenders. The important thing for you to be aware of when compiling financial statements is that the information must be correct, it must reflect the assumptions developed in the Organizational and Marketing Plans, and you must have supportive records that back up your numbers.

By now you will have completed all of the pro forma and actual financial statements required for your business. There is an additional financial tool, however, that will help you and your lenders and/or investors to look at your business, analyze it according to industry standards, and make decisions that will increase profitability. That tool is financial statement analysis. It is accomplished by applying a set of formulas to the information on your profit & loss (income) statements and balance sheets.

How to Analyze Financial Statements

In the last six pages of this section, we will explain financial statement analysis and give you examples of how you can use it to look at your business. Doing a financial statement analysis of your business is like all of the other tasks you have already completed. There is a definite process and if you follow it step-by-step, you will have added a valuable component to your business plan.

Read the next six pages. When you are finished reading, go to the sample business plan in Appendix I and see how the analysis was done for Marine Art of California. You will notice that there are five pages of spreadsheets preceded by a one-page summary. Apply the formulas to your income statements and balance sheets to figure the ratios for your business. You can also complete a vertical analysis using the same income statements and balance sheets. A horizontal analysis can only be completed if you have been in business for two or more years.

Analysis summary. Once you have figured the ratios and completed your vertical and/or horizontal analyses, be sure to develop a summary sheet for your business plan. The summary sheet allows you and/or your lenders and investors to get a quick overview of your business and how it compares to industry standards. The summary should contain: (1) a list of your projected ratios, (2) a list of actual ratios, if you are a current business, (3) a list of standard ratios for your industry. After you list the ratios, you should finish your summary with your interpretation of what they indicate for the future of the company.

Remember

The information in your Business Plan is not only to aid you in dealing with a lender or investor. More important, it is for your own use on an ongoing basis. We realize that the completion of your financial documents and a financial statement analysis is a difficult job. However, if you have done your homework, the financial section of your business plan will be invaluable to you in the assessment of your operation and may very well be the deciding factor between success and failure.

Financial Statement Analysis

◆ ◆ ◆ ◆

Putting Your Financial Statements to Work

To better utilize the financial section of your business plan as a working tool, you will use the financial statements that you have prepared to analyze your business. The following pages are devoted to giving you the basics about financial statement analysis. After you have read the material and understand how to apply the formulas to develop ratios, you can do an analysis of your own business and append it to the end of your financial section. If you are a new business, your analysis will be based on projections only. If you are a current business, you will use your historical profit & loss (income) statements and balance sheets.

Ratios: the relationship of one thing to another; a shortcut way of comparing things that can be expressed as numbers or degrees.

Your financial statements contain the information you need to help make decisions regarding your business. Many small business owners think of their financial statements as requirements for creditors, bankers, or tax preparers only, but they are much more than that. When analyzed, your financial statements can give you key information needed on the financial condition and the operations of your business.

Financial statement analysis requires measures to be expressed as ratios or percentages. For example, consider the situation where total assets on your balance sheet are $10,000. Cash is $2,000; Accounts Receivable are $3,000; and Fixed Assets are $5,000. The relationships of each of the three to total assets would be expressed as follows:

	Ratio	Relationship	Percentages
Cash	.2	.2:1	20%
Accounts Receivable	.3	.3:1	30%
Fixed Assets	.5	.5:1	50%

Financial statement analysis involves the studying of relationships and comparisons of (1) items in a single year's financial statement, (2) comparative financial statements for a period of time, and (3) your statements with those of other businesses.

Note: A Financial Statement Analysis Form is provided in Appendix III for your use. The form has all the formulas for figuring your ratios. Input the appropriate figures from your income statements and balance sheets and calculate according to the formulas. This will give you the information for your analysis summary.

Analyzing Your P&L (Income) Statements and Balance Sheets

Many analytic tools are available, but we will focus on the following measures, using your profit & loss (income) statements and balance sheets, that are of most importance to a small business owner in the business planning process:

✦ **Liquidity Analysis**	✦ **Measures of Investment**
✦ **Profitability Analysis**	✦ **Vertical Financial Statement Analysis**
✦ **Measures of Debit**	✦ **Horizontal Financial Statement Analysis**

Liquidity Analysis

The liquidity of a business is the ability it has to meet financial obligations. The analysis focuses on the **balance sheet** relationships for the current assets and current liabilities. The three main measures of liquidity and their formulas are as follows:

> Liquidity ratios can be used to see if your business is in any risk of insolvency. You will also be able to assess your ability to increase or decrease current assets for your business strategy. How would these moves affect your liquidity?
>
> Your creditors will use these ratios to determine whether or not to extend credit to you. They will compare the ratios for previous periods and with those of similar businesses.

1. **Net working capital:** The excess of current assets over current liabilities is net working capital. The more net working capital a business has, the less risky it is, as it has the ability to cover current liabilities as they come due.

$$\textbf{Current assets} - \textbf{Current liabilities} = \textbf{Net working capital}$$

2. **Current ratio:** The current ratio is a more dependable indication of liquidity than the net working capital. The current ratio is computed with the following formula:

$$\textbf{Current ratio} = \frac{\textbf{Current assets}}{\textbf{Current liabilities}}$$

There is no set criteria for the normal current ratio, as that is dependent on the business you are in. If you have predictable cash flows, you can operate with a lower current ratio.

A higher ratio means a more liquid position. A ratio of 2.0 is considered acceptable for most businesses. This would allow a company to lose 50 percent of its current assets and still be able to cover current liabilities. For most businesses, this is an adequate margin of safety.

3. **Quick ratio:** Since inventory is the most difficult current asset to dispose of quickly, it is subtracted from the current assets in the quick ratio to give a tougher list of liquidity. A

quick ratio of 1.00 or greater is usually recommended, but that is dependent upon the business you are in. The quick ratio is computed as follows:

$$\text{Quick ratio} = \frac{\text{Current assets} - \text{Inventory}}{\text{Current liabilities}}$$

Profitability Analysis

A Profitability Analysis will measure the ability of a business to make a profit. This type of analysis will utilize your **profit & loss (income) statements.** Three of these measures and their formulas are as follows:

> The higher the gross profit margin, the better. The normal rate is dependent on the business you are in. The Gross Profit Margin is the actual mark-up you have on the goods sold.

1. **Gross profit margin:** The gross profit margin indicates the percentage of each sales dollar remaining after a business has paid for its goods.

$$\text{Gross profit margin} = \frac{\text{Gross profit}}{\text{Sales}}$$

2. **Operating profit margin:** This ratio represents the pure operations profits, ignoring interest and taxes. In other words, this is the percentage of each sales dollar remaining after a business has paid for its goods and paid for its variable and fixed expenses. Naturally, a high operating profit margin is preferred.

$$\text{Operating profit margin} = \frac{\text{Income from operations}}{\text{Sales}}$$

3. **Net profit margin:** The net profit margin is clearly the measure of a business success with respect to earnings on sales.

$$\text{Net profit margin} = \frac{\text{Net profit}}{\text{Sales}}$$

A higher margin means the firm is more profitable. The net profit margin will differ according to your specific type of business. A 1 percent margin for a grocery store is not unusual due to the large quantity of items handled; while a 10 percent margin for a jewelry store would be considered low.

As a business owner, you can see just how profitable your business is. If the ratios are too low, you will want to analyze why.

> Your creditors will look at these ratios to see just how profitable your business is. Without profits, a business can't attract outside financing.

> ◈ **Do you have a high enough mark-up on your products? Check your gross profit margin.**

✦ **Are your operating expenses too high? Check your operating profit margin.**

✦ **Are your interest expenses too high? Check your net profit margin.**

Debt Measures

The debt position of a business indicates the amount of other people's money that is being used to generate profits.

Many new businesses assume too much debt too soon in an attempt to grow too quickly. The measures of debt use the **balance sheet** to tell how indebted your business is and how able it is to service the debts. The more indebtedness you have, the greater will be your risk of failure.

> The acceptable ratio is dependent upon the policies of your creditors and bankers. If, for instance, you had rates of 79 percent and 74 percent for two consecutive years, these would be excessively high and show a very high risk of failure. Clearly ¾ of the company is being financed by other people's money, and it does not put the business in a good position for acquiring new debt.

1. **Debt to assets ratio:** This is a key financial ratio used by creditors. It shows what you owe in relationship to what you own. The higher this ratio, the more risk of failure.

$$\text{Debt to assets ratio} = \frac{\text{Total liabilities}}{\text{Total assets}}$$

2. **Debt to equity ratio:** This is a key financial ratio used by creditors. It shows what is owed in relationship to the owners' equity in the company. Again, the higher this ratio, the more risk of failure.

$$\text{Debt to equity ratio} = \frac{\text{Total liabilities}}{\text{Total equity (net worth)}}$$

If your business plan includes the addition of long-term debt at a future point, you will want to monitor your debt ratio. If you are seeking a lender, is it within the limits acceptable to your banker?

Investment Measures

As a small business owner, you have invested money to acquire assets, and you should be getting a return on these assets. Even if the owner is taking a salary from the business, he/she also should be earning an additional amount from the investment in the company.

> The higher the ROI, the better. The business owner should get a target for the ROI. What do you want your investment to earn? Many small business owners have successfully created jobs for themselves, but still don't earn a fair return on their investment. Set your target for ROI, and work towards it.

1. **Return on investment (ROI):** The Return on Investment uses your balance sheet and measures the effectiveness of you, as the business owner, to generate profits from the available assets.

$$\text{ROI} = \frac{\text{Net profits}}{\text{Total assets}}$$

Vertical Financial Statement Analysis

Percentage analysis is used to show the relationship of the components in a single financial statement.

1. *For a balance sheet:*
   Each asset on the balance sheet is stated as a percent of the total assets, and each liability and equity item is stated as a percent of the total liabilities and owner equity (or net worth).

2. *For an income statement:*
   In vertical analysis of the income statement, each item is stated as a percent of the total net sales.

An evaluation of the components on single financial statements from one or more years can show you changes that may alert you to investigate your current expenditures. For example, a high percentage increase in cost of goods sold should be cause for investigation—or a decrease in gross profit from one year to the next might trigger the owner to look at the mark-up.

You can also evaluate your percentages against those of competitors or against industry standards for your trade to help you make judgments that can help your business be more profitable in the future. If your competitor is making a gross profit of 47 percent and yours is only 32 percent, you will want to know the reason why. Does he have a better source for purchasing product? Is his manufacturing process more efficient?

Horizontal Financial Statement Analysis

Horizontal analysis is a percentage analysis of the increases and decreases in the items on comparative financial statements.

The increase or decrease of the item is listed, and the earlier statement is used as the base. The percentage of increase or decrease is listed in the last column.

1. *For a balance sheet:*
   Assets, Liabilities, and Owners' Equity of one year are measured against a second year. The increase or decrease of the item is listed followed by the percentage of increase or decrease.

2. *For an income statement:*
   In horizontal analysis of the income statement, Income and Expense items of one year are measured against a second year. The increase or decrease of the item is listed followed by the percentage of increase or decrease.

The horizontal financial statement analysis can also alert to you to potential or current problems that can decrease your profitability. As an example, if you have an increase in sales, but a decrease in gross profit, you might look at your mark-up. If you have a large increase in advertising expense, you will need to see if the expense was justified by increased sales.

Summary

Now, you can see how financial statement analysis can be a tool to help you manage your business.

Operating costs: expenditures arising out of current business activities. Costs incurred to do business: i.e.: salaries, electricity, rental, etc.

- ◆ If the analysis produces results that don't meet your expectation or if the business is in danger of failure, you must analyze your expenses and your use of assets. Your first stop should be to cut expenses and increase the productivity of your assets.

- ◆ If your return on investment is too low, examine how you could make your assets (equipment, machinery, fixtures, inventory, etc.) work better for your benefit.

- ◆ If your profit is low, be sure that your mark-up is adequate; analyze your operating expenses to see that they are not too high, and review your interest expenses.

- ◆ If your liquidity is low, you could have a risk of becoming insolvent. Examine the level and composition of current assets and current liabilities.

- ◆ The vertical and horizontal financial statement analysis will reveal trends and compositions that signify trouble. Using your management skills, you can take corrective action.

Note: For a more detailed discussion of Financial Statement Analysis, see our basic recordkeeping and accounting small business book, *Keeping the Books* (Chicago: Dearborn, 1998). For an example, see the sample business plan for Marine Art of California in Appendix I and Dayne Landscaping, Inc.'s plan in Appendix II.

Supporting Documents

· ·

Now that you have completed the main body of your business plan, it is time to consider any additional records that pertain to your business and that should be included in your business plan.

Supporting Documents are the records that back up the statements and decisions made in the three main parts of your business plan. This file covers most of the documents which you will want to include. They will be discussed in the following order:

☑ **Personal Resumes**

☑ **Owner's Financial Statement**

☑ **Credit Reports**

☑ **Copies of Leases**

☑ **Letters of Reference**

☑ **Contracts**

☑ **Legal Documents**

☑ **Miscellaneous Documents**

After completing the main body of your business plan, you are now ready to consider the Supporting Documents that should be included. These are the records that back up the statements and decisions made in the three main parts of your business plan. As you are compiling the first three sections, it is a good idea to keep a separate list of the Supporting Documents that you mention or that come to mind. Many of these documents will actually be needed as you write your plan so that you will have solid financial information to use in your projections.

For instance, discussion of your business location might indicate a need for demographic studies, location maps, area studies, leases, etc. The information in the lease agreement will state the financial terms. Once you have the location, you will also know the square footage of your facility and you will be able to project other associated costs, such as utilities, improvements, etc.

If you are considering applying for a loan to purchase equipment, your supporting documents might be existing equipment purchase agreements or lease contracts. If you are planning a major advertising campaign, include advertising rate sheets from your targeted advertiser.

If you are doing business internationally, you may wish to include customs documents, trade agreements, shipping agreements. If you are exporting a product or providing a service in a foreign country, it might be beneficial to include demographics on your target market, competition evaluations, and anything else that is pertinent to your business.

By listing these items as you think of them and gathering them as you are working on your business plan, you will have a fairly complete set of all of your supporting documents by the time you finish writing your organizational, marketing, and financial sections. You can sort them into a logical sequence, add them to your working copy, and be ready to add any new ones that become pertinent during the lifetime of your business.

 Note: All supporting documents need not be included in every copy of your business plan. Include only that information you think will be needed by the potential lender or investor. The rest should be kept with your copy of the plan and be easily accessible should they be requested by the lender, investor, or anyone else with whom it would be beneficial to share the company's business plan.

The following pages will cover most of the documents you will normally need to include. At the end of the chapter, we have included examples of some of the types of supporting documents.

Personal Resumes

If you are a sole proprietor, include your own resume. If your business is a partnership, there should be a resume for each partner. If you have formed a corporation, include resumes for all officers of the corporation.

It is also a good idea to include resumes for your management and any other key personnel that will be involved in making decisions and affecting the profitability of the company, showing why they were chosen, what their skills are, and how the company will benefit from their management.

A resume need not and should not be a lengthy document. Preferably, it should be contained on one page for easy reading. Include the following categories and information:

- ◆ **Work history:** Name of business with dates of employment. Begin with most recent. Include duties, responsibilities, and related accomplishments.
- ◆ **Educational background:** Schools and dates you attended, degrees earned, fields of concentration.
- ◆ **Professional affiliations and honors:** List organizations to which you belong that will add to your credibility. Tell about any awards that you or your business have received that set you apart from others in your field.
- ◆ **Special skills:** For example: relates well to others, able to organize, not afraid to take risks, etc.

If you find it difficult to write your own resume, there are professionals who will do it for you for a nominal fee. A well-written resume will be a useful tool and should always be kept up-to-date. Once written, it is a simple task to update your information, adding new items and eliminating those that will not benefit you in your current endeavors. An example of of a resume is located on p. 110.

Owner's Financial Statement

This is a statement of the owner/owners personal assets and liabilities. Information can be compiled in the same manner as a Balance Sheet (see "Balance Sheet" in Chapter 6). Use the same format and list all assets and liabilities to determine net worth. If you are a new business owner, your personal financial statement will be included as a part of the Financial Documents section and may be a standard form supplied by the potential lender. See the example on pp.108–109.

Credit Reports

Credit ratings are of two types, business and personal. If you are already in business, you may have a Dun & Bradstreet rating. You can also ask your suppliers or wholesalers to supply you with letters of credit. Personal credit ratings can be obtained upon request through credit bureaus, banks, and companies with whom you have dealt on a basis other than cash.

Copies of Leases

Include all lease agreements currently in force between your company and a leasing agency. Some examples are the lease agreement for your business premises, equipment, automobiles, etc. These agreements will provide solid back-up for the financial information that you have projected regarding the lease of property and assets. It is important to note here that all lease agreements should be carefully entered into. In many instances they will contain clauses (especially in the case of site locations) that can eat heavily into a company's profits.

Letters of Reference

These are letters recommending you as being a reputable and reliable business person worthy of being considered a good risk. There are two types of letters of reference:

1. **Business references:** Written by business associates, suppliers, and customers.

2. **Personal references:** Written by nonbusiness associates who can assess your business skills (not by friends or relatives). The new business owner will have to utilize personal references.

Contracts

Include all business contracts, both completed and currently in force. Some examples are:

- ✦ **Current loan contracts**
- ✦ **Papers on prior business loans**
- ✦ **Purchase agreements on large equipment**
- ✦ **Vehicle purchase contracts**
- ✦ **Service contracts**
- ✦ **Maintenance agreements**
- ✦ **Miscellaneous contracts**

Legal Documents

Include all legal documents pertaining to your business. Examples are:

- ◆ **Articles of Incorporation**
- ◆ **Partnership Agreements**
- ◆ **Limited Partnership Agreements**
- ◆ **Strategic Alliance Agreements**
- ◆ **Due Diligence Reports**
- ◆ **Business Licenses and DBAs**
- ◆ **Copyright, trademark, and patent registrations**
- ◆ **Trade agreements**
- ◆ **Licensing agreements**
- ◆ **Insurance policies, agreements, etc.**
- ◆ **Property and vehicle titles**

Miscellaneous Documents

These are all the documents (other than the above) which are referred to, but not included, in the Organizational and Marketing sections of your business plan.

A good example of what we mean should be those records related to selecting your location in the Organizational or Marketing Plan. Your location might be finalized as the result of the development of a Location Plan. You can refer to this section in your Table of Contents. The potential lender or investor can then turn to this portion of your plan and examine that Location Plan that includes:

- ◆ **Demographic and psychographic studies**
- ◆ **Map of selected location**
- ◆ **Area studies (crime rate, income, etc.)**

To Help You

The next four pages contain samples of a personal financial statement, a resume, and a trade offering. You will also find examples of several other types of supporting documents in Appendix I: Marine Arts of California Business Plan and Appendix II: Dayne Landscaping, Inc. Business Plan.

Personal Financial History

PERSONAL FINANCIAL STATEMENT
(DO NOT USE FOR BUSINESS)

As of _____ _____ 19 _____

Received at _____ Branch

Name _____

Employed by _____ Years _____

Address _____

Position _____ Age _____ Name of Spouse _____

If Employed Less Than
1 Year, Previous Employer _____

The undersigned, for the purpose of procuring and establishing credit from time to time with you and to induce you to permit the undersigned to become indebted to you on notes, endorsements, guarantees, overdrafts or otherwise, furnishes the following (or in lieu thereof the attached) which is the most recent statement prepared by or for the undersigned as being a full, true and correct statement of the financial condition of the undersigned on the date indicated, and agrees to notify you immediately of the extent and character of any material change in said financial condition, and also agrees that if the undersigned, or any endorser or guarantor of any of the obligations of the undersigned, at any time fails in business or becomes insolvent, or commits an act of bankruptcy, or dies, or if a writ of attachment, garnishment, execution or other legal process be issued against property of the undersigned or if any assessment for taxes against the undersigned, other than taxes on real property, is made by the federal or state government or any department thereof, or if any of the representations made below prove to be untrue, or if the undersigned fails to notify you of any material change as above agreed, or if such change occurs, or if the business, or any interest therein, of the undersigned is sold, then and in such case, all of the obligations of the undersigned to you or held by you shall immediately be due and payable, without demand or notice. This statement shall be construed by you to be a continuing statement of the condition of the undersigned, and a new and original statement of all assets and liabilities upon each and every transaction in and by which the undersigned hereafter becomes indebted to you, until the undersigned advises in writing to the contrary.

ASSETS	DOLLARS	cents	LIABILITIES	DOLLARS	cents
Cash in B of _____ (Branch)			Notes payable B of _____ (Branch)		
Cash in _____ (Other - give name)			Notes payable _____ (Other)		
Accounts Receivable-Good _____			Accounts payable _____		
Stocks and Bonds (Schedule B) _____			Taxes payable _____		
Notes Receivable-Good _____			Contracts payable _____ (To whom)		
Cash Surrender Value Life Insurance _____			Contracts payable _____ (To whom)		
Autos _____ (Year-Make) _____ (Year-Make)			Real Estate indebtedness (Schedule A) _____		
Real Estate (Schedule A) _____			Other Liabilities (describe)		
Other Assets (describe)			1. _____		
1. _____			2. _____		
2. _____			3. _____		
3. _____			4. _____		
4. _____			TOTAL LIABILITIES		
5. _____			NET WORTH		
TOTAL ASSETS			**TOTAL**		

ANNUAL INCOME		and	ANNUAL EXPENDITURES (Excluding Ordinary living expenses)		
Salary _____			Real Estate payment (s) _____		
Salary (wife or husband) _____			Rent _____		
Securities Income _____			Income Taxes _____		
Rentals _____			Insurance Premiums _____		
Other (describe)			Property Taxes _____		
1. _____			Other (describe-include instalment payments other than real estate)		
2. _____			1. _____		
3. _____			2. _____		
4. _____			3. _____		
5. _____					
TOTAL INCOME			**TOTAL EXPENDITURES**		

LESS-TOTAL EXPENDITURES

NET CASH INCOME
(exclusive of ordinary living expenses) _____

Personal Financial History

What assets in this statement are in joint tenancy? _____ Name of other Party _____

Have you filed homestead? _____

Are you a guarantor on anyone's debt? _____ If so, give details _____

Are any encumbered assets or debts secured except as indicated? _____ If so, please itemize by debt and security _____

_____

Do you have any other business connections? _____ If so, give details _____

Are there any suits or judgments against you? _____ Any pending? _____

Have you gone through bankruptcy or compromised a debt? _____

Have you made a will? _____ Number of dependents _____

SCHEDULE A—REAL ESTATE

Location and type of Improvement	Title in Name of	Estimated Value	Amount Owing	To Whom Payable
		$	$	

SCHEDULE B—STOCKS AND BONDS

Number of Shares Amount of Bonds	Description	Current Market on Listed	Estimated Value on Unlisted
		$	$

If additional space is needed for Schedule A and/or Schedule B, list on separate sheet and attach.

INSURANCE

Life Insurance $ _____ Name of Company _____ Beneficiary _____

Automobile Insurance:
Public Liability — yes ☐ no ☐   Property Damage — yes ☐   no ☐
Comprehensive personal Liability-yes ☐   no ☐

STATEMENT OF BANK OFFICER:

Insofar as our records reveal, this Financial Statement is accurate and true. The foregoing statement is (a copy of) the original signed by the maker, in the credit files of this bank.

_____ Assistant Cashier Manager

The undersigned certifies that the above statement (or in lieu thereof, the attached statement, as the case may be) and supporting schedules, both printed and written, give a full, true, and correct statement of the financial condition of the undersigned as of the date indicated.

_____   _____
Date signed   Signature

Sample Resume

JOHN SMITH
742 South Street
Jamestown, NY 10081
(555) 555-0221

WORK EXPERIENCE

1995–Present   **Aerotech, Inc.**
Burke, New York
Corporate President: Overall management responsibility for tool and die manufacture providing specialized parts to the aerospace industry. Specific management of Research and Development Department.

1990–1995   **ABC Components**
Jamestown, New York
Sole Proprietor and General Manager: Sole responsibility for research and development of specialty aircraft parts. Long-term goal of expanding to incorporate and provide specialty parts to aerospace industry.

1980–1990   **Jackson Aircraft Co.**
Burke, New York
Quality Control Supervisor: Responsibility for the development and implementation of a quality control program for automated aircraft assembly facility. Implemented quality control program resulting in $4.3 million in increased profits to the company.

EDUCATION

University of California, Berkeley—Master of Business Administration, emphasis on Marketing, 1989.
Stanford University, Palo Alto, CA—Bachelor of Civil Engineering, 1980.

PROFESSIONAL AFFILIATIONS

American Society of Professional Engineers
New York City Industrial League
Burke Chamber of Commerce

SPECIAL RECOGNITION

New York Businessman of the Year, 1998
New York Council on Small Business, 1994—present
Director, Burke Chamber of Commerce

SPECIAL SKILLS

Resourceful and well-organized; Relate well to employees;
Self-motivated and not afraid to take risks.

Sample Trading Offer

CAPITAL, INC.
PRESENTS

GENESIS MULTIMEDIA, INC.

248,000 SHARES OF COMMON STOCK

RESALE OF SECURITIES
UNDER
REGULATIONS

TRADING OFFER

CAPITAL, INC.

Capital, Inc. hereby introduces Genesis Multimedia, Inc. This company has been in operation since 1988 and currently has $7,000,000 in annual sales. The company is currently trading on the OTC Bulletin Board.

Listed below is the Bid and Ask price of Genesis Multimedia, Inc., trading symbol (GMMI), CUSIP no. 274106-12-5:

	BID	ASK
Current	34.25	35.5
Discount	5%	6%

RESTRICTED

Capital, Inc. has purchased these shares under an agreement that shares cannot come back into the United States before one year. As a consequence, the transfer agent will issue instructions that no shares being resold under this purchase can be transferred to any person in the United States before one year. Although Genesis Multimedia, Inc. is a fully reporting company for over one year, these shares can come back into United States pursuant to an exemption from registration or a filing of a registration before 41 days. After 41 days, any sales of these securities can be sold to any U.S. person or to an account of any U.S. person who is outside the United States.

INVESTOR'S QUALIFICATIONS

The shares may be freely traded outside the United States and can be sold or transferred to any non-U.S. person within 41 days and to any U.S. person after 41 days.

U.S. Tax Information

A basic understanding of the U.S. tax system is an absolute necessity if you are going to write a business plan for a business that will operate within or do business in the U.S. It has long been a premise of the majority of taxpayers that the system is unwieldy, complicated, unfair, and a plague to most Americans. If you will overlook that discontent for a moment, we will attempt to show you how a basic understanding of the tax system can be an invaluable aid to you during business planning.

We have also included some visual aids and lists that should help you with your business planning in relation to taxes.

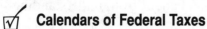 **Calendars of Federal Taxes**

☑ **Free IRS Publications**

☑ **Information Resources**

If You Are Doing Business Internationally

Business planning follows the same format throughout the world. With the spread of global trade, all countries are seeking common ground upon which to do business together and a business plan serves as an important link leading to successful international venturing. If you are in the United States and you participate in foreign trade, you will need to understand the legalities pertaining to the countries with which you are doing business. By the same token, those businesses outside the United States will need to familiarize themselves with the American legal and tax systems. In this chapter, we will deal only with cursory tax information pertaining to the United States. It should in no way be construed as legal or accounting advice by the reader.

Comparing Our Tax System and Small Business Accounting

Looking at the U.S. tax system and small business accounting is like studying the chicken and the egg. They cannot be separated. Many new business owners attempt to set up a recordkeeping system without examining and understanding the Internal Revenue Service's tax forms to be completed at the end of the year. This is a gross error for two reasons. The first is failure to account for financial information required by the IRS at tax time. More important, however, is the failure to utilize information and services that will help you to develop an effective recordkeeping system, which will, in turn, enable you to analyze your business and implement changes to keep it on the track to profitability.

In order that you can better comprehend the relationship between business planning and the tax system, we will introduce you to two tax forms and show you how you can benefit from understanding those forms.

Schedule C (Form 1040)

This form is entitled "Profit or (Loss) From Business or Profession" (required tax reporting form for all sole proprietors).

Information required. Gross receipts or sales, beginning and ending inventories, labor, materials, goods purchased, returns and allowances, deductions, and net profit or loss. The net profit is the figure upon which your income tax liability is based. If you understand how to read a profit & loss statement, you will quickly see that a Schedule C is simply a profit & loss statement for your tax year. Filling it out simply requires the transfer of P&L information from the annual total column of the P&L in your own accounting records.

Benefits of understanding. In order to provide the year-end information required on a Schedule C and to figure income tax liability, it will be necessary for you to set up a recordkeeping system that will generate a profit & loss statement and balance sheet. You will need a general ledger, petty cash record, payroll records, inventory records, a fixed asset log (depreciation record), accounts payable, and accounts receivable. If you are a new business, a quick examination of the standard categories of expenses listed on a Schedule C can help you to determine many of the fixed and variable expense categories to be used in your general ledger. Those same categories will provide a means to sort out and record petty cash expenditures so they can be used as tax deductible expenses.

Accounts payable: amounts owed by a business to its creditors on open accounts for goods purchased or services rendered.

In addition to the setting up of categories for keeping expenses in a general ledger, you will want to divide types of income as well. This will tell you which sources are the most profitable for your business. Year-end totals of income and expense items are used to develop profit & loss statements and subsequently your Schedule C. Fixed asset records, inventory records, and accounts receivable, accounts payable, etc. are used to develop balance sheets. These are the two most important of the financial statements used to analyze your business.

Note: Form 1065, "U.S. Partnership Return of Income" and Form 1120-A or Form 1120, "U.S. Corporation Income Tax Returns" are used for these legal structures.

Schedule SE (Form 1040)

This form is entitled "Computation of Social Security Self-Employment Tax."

Information required. This is a computation of the business owner's contribution to Social Security, which is based on the owner's draw or salary. As the business owner, taking a draw, you pay both the employer's and the employee's share of social security in the form of self-employment tax. This tax is paid as a part of your estimated tax (1040ES) each quarter. If, as a business owner, you elect to pay yourself a salary, your business will be liable for 50 percent of your social security tax obligation and you as the employee will be liable for the other 50 percent.

Benefits of understanding. Schedule SE will help you to compute your tax liability, which can be translated into your Cash Flow Statement. Failure to familiarize yourself with the requirements on how to compute this tax and know what percentage of your net income will be owed will result in a false picture as to the net profit of your business. Don't forget—the IRS is interested in your net profit before taxes. You are concerned with net profit *after* taxes.

Federal Taxes for Which You May Be Liable

Familiarize yourself with the federal taxes for which you may be liable and the times at which they will have to be paid. Your cash flow statement will have to reflect these payments. If you fail to include taxes to be paid, you will find yourself with an unbalanced budget and possibly a serious cash deficiency.

The legal structure of your business will determine reporting dates; they are not the same for sole proprietorships and partnerships as they are for S corporations and C corporations.

Calendars of Federal Taxes

The tax calendars we have developed and provided in this chapter should be of some help to you in meeting your tax reporting requirements. We have set them up according to the date of the liability. Paste a copy of the one pertaining to your legal structure on the wall as a visual reminder. Be sure to look ahead as the due dates are firm, and a penalty may be imposed for not reporting on time.

Free IRS Publications

As you can see from the above examples, examination of required tax forms and the understanding of allowable business deductions can lead to the discovery of many types of records that you will need and profit from in your business. That same examination will also lead a smart business owner with an inquiring mind to a thousand questions left unanswered.

- ◈ **How do I set up my records?**
- ◈ **What accounting method is required for my business?**
- ◈ **How do I determine what is and what is not deductible?**
- ◈ **Is inventory based on cost or sale price?**
- ◈ **What is an independent contractor?**
- ◈ **What are the rules pertaining to home-based businesses?**
- ◈ **What items are depreciable—and at what rate?**
- ◈ **How are automobile expenses figured?**
- ◈ **As a business owner, can I invest in tax-deferred savings?**
- ◈ **What is an S corporation?**
- ◈ **What is the basis for determination of the tax year?**
- ◈ **What travel expenses are allowable?**
- ◈ **Is it better to lease or purchase a vehicle?**

◆ **When do I start paying estimated taxes?**

◆ **What is the best legal structure for my business?**

What most of us don't know is that the United States government has spent a great deal of time and money to make free publications available for preparation of income taxes. Those same publications will answer all of your questions and some that have not yet occurred to you. They will also provide you with many samples of business statements and information on how to complete them.

Make It Your Business to Send for (or Download)
and Study These Publications!

We have many students with great ideas for a product or service, but no desire to concern themselves with paperwork and recordkeeping. Those businesses are doomed to failure. We cannot place too much emphasis on the importance of understanding your business recordkeeping and its interrelationship with tax accounting. Financial analysis will help to make your profits grow.

It is important that you set up a tax information file, and also that you keep it current. Make it your business to update your file with new publications. Study the revisions that take place in our tax laws. Remember that your business plan is an ongoing process requiring the implementation of many changes. You may rest assured that many of those changes will be a direct result of new tax laws.

To Help You Understand Taxes and Set Up a File of IRS Publications

In order to aid you in your business, we have devoted the remainder of this chapter to providing you with the following:

Calendars of federal taxes for which a sole proprietor, partnership, S corporation, or corporation may be liable. You will find four calendars. Choose the one that is appropriate to your legal structure.

A list of free publications available from the IRS which will be helpful to business owners. We strongly suggest that you send for all of them on a yearly basis. Keep them in a three-ring binder so that you can refer to them as the need arises. These publications are updated every November and can be ordered shortly thereafter.

An information page telling you where and how to send for free forms and publications. You can request them by mail, call a toll free number and ask for them by number, or download them via the Internet.

Sole Proprietor

Calendar of Federal Taxes for Which You May Be Liable

January	15	Estimated tax	Form 1040ES
	31	Social security (FICA) tax and the withholding of income tax. Note: See IRS rulings for deposit—Pub. 334	Forms 941, 941E, 942 and 943
	31	Providing information on social security (FICA) tax and the withholding of income tax	Form W-2 (to employee)
	31	Federal unemployment (FUTA) tax	Form 940-EZ or 940
	31	Federal unemployment (FUTA) tax (only if liability for unpaid taxes exceeds $100)	Form 8109 (to make deposits)
	31	Information returns to nonemployees and transactions with other persons	Form 1099 (to recipients)
February	28	Information returns to nonemployees and transactions with other persons	Form 1099 (to IRS)
	28	Providing information on social security (FICA) tax and the withholding income tax	Forms W-2 and W-3 (to Social Security Admin.)
April	15	Income tax	Schedule C (Form 1040)
	15	Self-employment tax	Schedule SE (Form 1040)
	15	Estimated tax	Form 1040ES
	30	Social security (FICA) tax and the withholding of income tax Note: See IRS rulings for deposit—Pub. 334	Forms 941, 941E, 942, and 943
	30	Federal unemployment (FUTA) tax (only if liability for unpaid taxes exceeds $100)	Form 8109 (to make deposits)
June	15	Estimated tax	Form 1040ES
July	31	Social security (FICA) tax and the withholding of income tax Note: See IRS rulings for deposit—Pub. 334	Forms 941, 941E, 942, and 943
	31	Federal unemployment (FUTA) tax (only if liability for unpaid taxes exceeds $100)	Form 8109 (to make deposits)
September	15	Estimated tax	Form 1040ES
October	31	Social security (FICA) tax and the withholding of income tax. Note: See IRS rulings for deposit—Pub. 334	Forms 941, 941E, 942, and 943
	31	Federal unemployment (FUTA) tax (only if liability for unpaid taxes exceeds $100)	Form 8109 (to make deposits)

If your tax year is not January 1st through December 31st:

✦ Schedule C (Form 1040) is due the 15th day of the 4th month after end of the tax year. Schedule SE is due same day as Form 1040.

✦ Estimated tax (1040ES) is due the 15th day of 4th, 6th, and 9th months of tax year, and the 15th day of 1st month after the end of tax year.

Partnership

Calendar of Federal Taxes for Which You May Be Liable

January	15	Estimated tax (individual who is a partner)	Form 1040ES
	31	Social security (FICA) tax and the withholding of income tax Note: See IRS rulings for deposit—Pub. 334	Forms 941, 941E, 942, and 943
	31	Providing information on social. security (FICA) tax and the withholding of income tax	Form W-2 (to employee)
	31	Federal unemployment (FUTA) tax	Form 940-EZ or 940
	31	Federal unemployment (FUTA) tax (only if liability for unpaid taxes exceeds $100)	Form 8109 (to make deposits)
	31	Information returns to nonemployees and transactions with other persons	Form 1099 (to recipients)
February	28	Information returns to nonemployees and transactions with other persons	Form 1099 (to IRS)
	28	Providing information on social security (FICA) tax and on withholding income tax	Forms W-2 and W-3 (to Social Security Admin.)
April	15	Income tax (individual who is a partner)	Schedule C (Form 1040)
	15	Annual return of income	Form 1065
	15	Self-employment tax (individual who is partner)	Schedule SE (Form 1040)
	15	Estimated tax (individual who is partner)	Form 1040ES
	30	Social security (FICA) tax and the withholding of income tax Note: See IRS rulings for deposit—Pub. 334	Forms 941, 941E, 942, and 943
	30	Federal unemployment (FUTA) tax (only if liability for unpaid taxes exceeds $100)	Form 8109 (to make deposits)
June	15	Estimated tax (individual who is a partner)	Form 1040ES
July	31	Social security (FICA) tax and the withholding of income tax Note: See IRS rulings for deposit—Pub. 334	Forms 941, 941E, 942, and 943
	31	Federal unemployment (FUTA) tax (only if liability for unpaid taxes exceeds $100)	Form 8109 (to make deposits)
September	15	Estimated tax (individual who is a partner)	Form 1040ES
October	31	Social security (FICA) tax and the withholding of income tax Note: See IRS rulings for deposit—Pub. 334	Forms 941, 941E, 942, and 943
	31	Federal unemployment (FUTA) tax (only if liability for unpaid taxes exceeds $100)	Form 8109 (to make deposits)

If your Tax Year is not January 1st through December 31st:

◈ Income tax is due the 15th day of the 4th month after end of tax year.

◈ Self-employment tax is due the same day as income tax (Form 1040).

◈ Estimated tax (1040ES) is due the 15th day of the 4th, 6th, and 9th month of the tax year and the 15th day of 1st month after end of the tax year.

S Corporation

Calendar of Federal Taxes for Which You May Be Liable

January	15	Estimated tax (individual S corp. shareholder)	Form 1040ES
	31	Social security (FICA) tax and the withholding of income tax Note: See IRS rulings for deposit—Pub. 334	Forms 941, 941E, 942, and 943
	31	Providing information on social security (FICA) tax and the withholding of income tax	Form W-2 (to employee)
	31	Federal unemployment (FUTA) tax	Form 940-EZ or 940
	31	Federal unemployment (FUTA) tax (only if liability for unpaid taxes exceeds $100)	Form 8109 (to make deposits)
	31	Information returns to nonemployees and transactions with other persons	Form 1099 (to recipients)
February	28	Information returns to nonemployees and transactions with other persons	Form 1099 (to IRS)
	28	Providing information on social security (FICA) tax and the withholding of income tax	Forms W-2 and W-3 (to Social Security Admin.)
March	15	Income tax	Form 1120S
April	15	Income tax (individual S corp. shareholder)	Form 1040
	15	Estimated tax (individual S corp. shareholder)	Form 1040ES
	30	Social security (FICA) tax and the withholding of income tax Note: See IRS rulings for deposit—Pub. 334	Forms 941, 941E, 942, and 943
	30	Federal unemployment (FUTA) tax (only if liability for unpaid taxes exceeds $100)	Form 8109 (to make deposits)
June	15	Estimated tax (individual S corp. shareholder)	Form 1040ES
July	31	Social security (FICA) tax and the withholding of income tax Note: See IRS rulings for deposit—Pub. 334	Forms 941, 941E, 942, and 943
	31	Federal unemployment (FUTA) tax (only if liability for unpaid taxes exceeds $100)	Form 8109 (to make deposits)
September	15	Estimated tax (individual S corp. shareholder)	Form 1040ES
October	31	Social security (FICA) tax and the withholding of income tax Note: See IRS rulings for deposit—Pub. 334	Forms 941, 941E, 942, and 943
	31	Federal unemployment (FUTA) tax (only if liability for unpaid taxes exceeds $100)	Form 8109 (to make deposits)

If your tax year is not January 1st through December 31st:

✦ S corporation income tax (1120S) and individual S corporation shareholder income tax (Form 1040) are due the 15th day of the 4th month after end of tax year.

✦ Estimated tax of individual shareholder (1040ES) is due 15th day of 4th, 6th, and 9th months of tax year, and 15th day of 1st month after end of tax year.

Corporation

Calendar of Federal Taxes for Which You May Be Liable

January	31	Social security (FICA) tax and the withholding of income tax Note: See IRS rulings for deposit—Pub. 334	Forms 941, 941E, 942, and 943
	31	Providing information on social security (FICA) tax and the withholding of income tax	Form W-2 (to employee)
	31	Federal unemployment (FUTA) tax	Form 940-EZ or 940
	31	Federal unemployment (FUTA) tax (only if liability for unpaid taxes exceeds $100)	Form 8109 (to make deposits)
	31	Information returns to nonemployees and transactions with other persons	Form 1099 (to recipients)
February	28	Information returns to nonemployees and transactions with other persons	Form 1099 (to IRS)
	28	Providing information on social security (FICA) tax and the withholding of income tax	Forms W-2 and W-3 (to Social Security Admin.)
March	15	Income tax	Form 1120 or 1120-A
April	15	Estimated tax	Form 1120-W
	30	Social security (FICA) tax and the withholding of income tax Note: See IRS rulings for deposit—Pub. 334	Forms 941, 941E, 942, and 943
	30	Federal unemployment (FUTA) tax (only if liability for unpaid taxes exceeds $100)	Form 8109 (to make deposits)
June	15	Estimated tax	Form 1120-W
July	31	Social security (FICA) tax and the withholding of income tax Note: See IRS rulings for deposit—Pub. 334	Forms 941, 941E, 942, and 943
	31	Federal unemployment (FUTA) tax (only if liability for unpaid taxes exceeds $100)	Form 8109 (to make deposits)
September	15	Estimated tax	Form 1120-W
October	31	Social security (FICA) tax and the withholding of income tax Note: See IRS rulings for deposit—Pub. 334	Forms 941, 941E, 942, and 943
	31	Federal unemployment (FUTA) tax (only if liability for unpaid taxes exceeds $100)	Form 8109 (to make deposits)
December	15	Estimated tax	Form 1120-W

If your tax year is not January 1st through December 31st:

◆ Income tax (Form 1120 or 1120-A) is due on the 15th day of the 3rd month after the end of the tax year.

◆ Estimated tax (1120-W) is due the 5th day of the 4th, 6th, 9th, and 12th months of the tax year.

Free Tax Publications Available from the IRS

The following is a list of IRS Publications that may prove helpful to you in the course of your business. Make it a point to keep a file of tax information. Send for these publications and update your file with new publications at least once a year. The United States government has spent a great deal of time and money to make this information available to you for preparation of income tax returns.

By phone or mail. You may call IRS toll free at **1-800-TAX-FORM (1-800-829-3676)** between 8 A.M. and 5 P.M. weekdays and 9 A.M. to 3 P.M. on Saturdays. If you wish to order publications or forms by mail, you will find an order form for the publications on page 124.

By computer and modem. If you subscribe to an online service, ask if IRS information is available and, if so, how to access it. The IRS offers the ability to download electronic print files of current tax forms, instructions, and taxpayer information publications (TIPs) in three different file formats. Internal Revenue Information Services (IRIS) is housed within FedWorld, known also as the Electronic Marketplace of U.S. Government information, a broadly accessible electronic bulletin board system. FedWorld offers direct dial-up access, as well as Internet connectivity, and provides "gateway" access to more than 140 different Government bulletin boards.

IRIS at FedWorld can be reached by:

1. Modem (dial-up) The Internal Revenue Information Services bulletin board at 703-321-8020
2. Telnet—iris.irs.ustreas.gov
3. File Transfer Protocol (FTP)—connect to ftp.irs.ustreas.gov, or
4. World Wide Web—www.irs.treas.gov

Tax Guide for Small Business

Begin by reading the Publication 334, *Tax Guide for Small Business*. It is a general guide to all areas of small business and will give you the most comprehensive information.

Listing of Publications for Small Business

If you are a small business owner, the following IRS publications are good to have on hand as reference material and will give you fairly detailed information on specific tax-related topics.

15 Circular E, *Employer's Tax Guide*

15A *Employers Supplemental Tax Guide*

Order Information for
IRS Forms and Publications

Where to Send Your Order for Free Forms and Publications

You can visit your local IRS office or order tax forms and publications from the IRS Forms Distribution Center listed for your state at the address on this page. Or, if you prefer, you can photocopy tax forms from reproducible copies kept at participating public libraries. In addition, many libraries have reference sets of IRS publications that you can read or copy. Forms may also be downloaded via the Internet.

Detach at this line

If you live in:	Mail to:	Other locations:
Alaska, Arizona, California, Colorado Hawaii, Idaho, Montana, Nevada, New Mexico, Oregon, Utah, Washington, Wyoming, Guam, Northern Marianas, American Samoa	Western Area Distribution Center Rancho Cordova, CA 95743-0001	**Foreign Addresses:** Taxpayers with mail addresses in foreign countries should mail this order blank to either: Eastern Area Distribution Center, P.O. Box 25866, Richmond, VA 23286-6107; or Western Area Distribution Center, Rancho Cordova, CA 95743-0001, whichever is closer. Mail letter requests for other forms and publications to: Eastern Area Distribution Center, P.O. Box 25866, Richmond, VA 23286-8107.
Alabama, Arkansas, Illinois, Indiana, Kansas, Kentucky, Louisiana, Minnesota, Mississippi, Missouri, Nebraska, North Dakota, Ohio Oklahoma, South Dakota, Tennessee, Texas, Wisconsin	Central Area Distribution Center P.O. Box 8903 Bloomington, IL 61072-8903	
Connecticut, Delaware, District of Columbia, Florida, Georgia, Maine, Maryland, Massachusetts, New Hampshire, New Jersey, New York, North Carolina, Pennsylvania, Rhode Island, South Carolina, Vermont, Virginia, West Virginia	Eastern Area Distribution Center P.O. Box 85074 Richmond, VA 23261-5074	**Puerto Rico** — Eastern Area Distribution Center, P.O Box 25866, Richmond, VA 23286-6107 **Virgin Islands** — V.I. Bureau of Internal Revenue, Lockhart Gardens, No. 1-A Charlotte Amalia St. Thomas, VI 00802

----------------------------------- Detach at this line

Order Blank

The IRS will send you two copies of each form and one copy of each publication or set of instructions you circle. Please cut the order blank on the dotted line above and **be sure to print or type your name and address accurately on the bottom portion. Mail to the the IRS address shown above for your state. Be sure to affix proper postage.**

To help reduce waste, please order only the forms, instructions, and publications you think you will need to prepare your return. Use the blank spaces to order items not listed.

You should either receive your order of notification of the status of your order within 7–15 work days after receipt of your request.

1040	Schedule F (1040)	Schedule 3 (1040A) & Instructions	2210 & Instructions	8606 & Instructions	Pub. 502	Pub. 550	Pub. 929
Instructions for 1040 & Schedules	Schedule H (1040)	1040EZ	2441 & Instructions	8822 & Instructions	Pub. 505	Pub. 554	Pub. 936
Schedules A&B (1040)	Schedule R (1040) & Instructions	Instructions for 1040EZ	3903 & Instructions	8829 & Instructions	Pub. 508	Pub. 575	
Schedule C (1040)	Schedule SE (1040)	1040ES (1997) & Instructions	4868 & Instructions	Pub. 1	Pub. 521	Pub. 590	
Schedule C-EZ (1040)	1040A	1040X & Instructions	4562 & Instructions	Pub. 17	Pub. 523	Pub. 596	
Schedule D (1040)	Instructions for 1040A & Schedules	2106 & Instructions	5329 & Instructions	Pub. 334	Pub. 525	Pub. 910	
Schedule E (1040)	Schedule 1 (1040A)	2106EZ & Instructions	8283 & Instructions	Pub. 463	Pub. 527	Pub. 917	
Schedule EIC (1040A or 1040)	Schedule 2 (1040A)	2119 & Instructions	8582 & Instructions	Pub. 501	Pub. 529	Pub. 926	

Name
Street Address
City/State/Zip

For more information: See IRS Publication 334, *Tax Guide for Small Business*

Keeping Your Business Plan Up-to-Date

Your business plan will serve you well if you will revise it often and let it serve as your guide during the lifetime of your business. In order to update it, you, as the owner, will have the final responsibility to analyze what is happening and implement the changes that will make your business more profitable.

☑ **Revising Your Business Plan**

☑ **Implementing Changes in Your Business Plan**

☑ **Anticipating Your Problems**

Revising Your Business Plan

Revision is an on-going process. Changes are constantly taking place in your business. If your business plan is going to be effective either to the business or to a potential lender or investor, it will be necessary for you to update it on a regular basis. Changes necessitating such revisions can be attributed to three primary sources:

Changes within the Company

Any number of changes may occur in your organization. You may be increasing or decreasing the number of employees, upgrading the skill level, or adding new services. You might decide to incorporate or add new partners. Be sure to document these changes in your business plan.

Changes Originating with the Customer

Your product or service may show surges or declines due to your customers' changes in need or taste. This is evident in all the companies who fail because they continue to offer what they like instead of what the customer will buy or use. In the clothing industry, for example, retailers have to pay close attention to current styles, popular materials, and seasonal colors.

Marketing to a new and expanding customer base will also require careful consideration of both demographic and psychographic factors that may differ from those of current customers. If you are planning to sell your products and services internationally, you will need to understand the cultures in order to satisfy the customers.

Technological Changes

You will have to keep your business current with an ever-changing world. As technology advances within your industry, bringing new products and services on the market, you will have to keep up or you will be left behind. The computer industry is a perfect example of fast changes in technology. Developers are challenged daily with the problems of keeping their products current or losing their niche in the marketplace. The toy industry provides another example. Little girls and boys are no longer satisfied with storybook dolls and tinkertoys. They want electronic miracles that are programmed to walk and talk and fly and think and feel.

Technological advances, especially those in the area of communication, are also revolutionizing the *ways* in which we do business. The Internet has enabled small business owners to research information, communicate instantly with venders and customers, process credit cards and transfer funds electronically, and to market and sell products and services to their customers via the Internet. Yesterday's typewriters, telephones, and airmail letters have been replaced with computers, cell phones, and email.

Implementing Changes in Your Business Plan

You, as the owner, must be aware of the changes in your industry, your market, and your community. First, you must determine what revisions are needed in order for you to accomplish the goals you have set for your company. To make this determination, you will have to look at your current plan and decide what you have to do to modify it in order to reflect the changes discussed above.

If this is an overwhelming task for one person, utilize your employees to keep track of the business trends applicable to their expertise. For example, your buyer can analyze the buying patterns of your customers and report to you. Your research and development person might look at changes in technology and materials. Your marketing department can develop a plan that will take advantage of new ways that will help you to reach your potential customers. Each department can be responsible for information that pertains to its particular area and report on a periodic basis.

Be aware, however, that the final judgment as to revisions will rest with you, the owner. You will have to analyze the information and decide on any changes to be implemented. If your decision is wrong, don't dwell on it. Correct your error and cut your losses as soon as possible. With experience, your percentage of correct decisions will increase and your reward will be higher profits.

Anticipating Your Problems

Try to see ahead and determine what possible problems may arise to plague you. For example, you may have to deal with costs that exceed your projections. At the same time, you may experience a sharp decline in sales. These two factors occurring simultaneously can portend disaster if you are not ready for them.

Also, we might add, a good year can give you a false sense of security. Be cautious when things are too good. The increased profits may be temporary. Also, what sells today may not sell tomorrow. As an example, antique clocks were selling extremely well and commanded high prices in the early 1980s. Those prices have decreased by about 40 percent today—and new clocks far outsell the antique ones.

You might think about developing an alternate budget based on possible problems that are likely to be encountered. This may be the time when you will decide that emphasis on a service rather than on a product would be more profitable due to changes in the economy. To again use the clock business as an example, the repair business is currently going strong even though retail trade is down.

Don't Fall into the Trap!

More often than not, a business owner will spend a lot of time and effort writing a business plan when the pressure is on to borrow funds or to get a business started. The intention is there to always keep that plan up-to-date. Before long, things get hectic and the business plan is put in a drawer, never again to be seen.

There is an old saying that *"the business that operates by the seat of its pants will end up with torn pants."*

Do Remember to Revise Your Plan Often

Awareness of changes within your industry and revision of your business plan reflecting those changes will benefit you greatly. Your business plan can be your best friend. If you nurture your relationship with it, you will have a running start on the path to success!

CHAPTER 10

Packaging Your Business Plan

T he packaging of your business plan is an important part of the planning process. Putting your plan together the right way will increase its readability and effectiveness for the business itself and for potential lenders and investors. In this chapter, we will give you some ideas on how to organize and present your business plan for maximum effectiveness.

Because we often get questions regarding business plan software, we will also dedicate some space in this chapter to a discussing what you should look for before making a purchase. Quick fixes may be good when it comes to saving time, but they can be the kiss of death when it comes to something as serious as business planning.

☑ **Business Planning Software**

☑ **Packaging for Success**

☑ **A Final Word**

Business Plan Software

There are several software programs on the market today. What the prospective business plan writer hopes for is a quick solution to a difficult problem—a program with questions that can be answered by filling in the blanks, after which the software will automatically generate a finished business plan.

Do not use a canned program. There are, in fact, some *"fill in the blanks"* software packages. However, it is not advisable for you to use this type of program. There are at least two good reasons:

1. Your business plan serves as the guide for your particular business. Even though you may have the same type of business as someone else, you will have different areas of focus and you will want to fill your own special niche and do things that are unique to your business. These differences should be reflected in your business plan. Therefore, a canned business plan cannot possibly serve you well.

2. If you are going to potential lender or investors, you will find that they will readily recognize the canned statements and generic financial statements that come from a specific piece of software. The resulting *cookie cutter* business plan is an immediate indicator to that person that you have not put much time and effort into the planning process and that you may not know your business well enough to succeed at it. Since the repayment of your loan depends on your business skills, this may indicate that you will be a poor risk.

Effective software programs. Programs should allow for you to do your own research and generate your own organizational and marketing statements. This is the only way that you can create a plan that will make your business unique. Well thought out, individualized organizational and marketing plans will favorably impress your lender or investor by showing them that you have thoroughly researched your business and have the expertise to run it effectively. Thorough planning will also give you the confidence to better run your business.

Automated financial statements (or spreadsheets) can be a great help to you in the financial section of your business plan. If they are pre-formatted and pre-formulated, you will save a great deal of time. You plug in the amounts to the allocated cells and the program should do all of your adding and subtracting. Since the pro forma cash flow statement has approximately 350 figures to work with, your time will be cut considerably. It will also allow you to make changes or create "what if" situations and see the results immediately.

Even here, a note of caution is called for. Many programs have all of the spreadsheets linked into one long integrated spreadsheet. This is a great feature except for its downside. Linked spreadsheets are always generic and not customized for any particular business. If you attempt to customize them and do not have the expertise to make the proper changes throughout the entire spreadsheet (without error), the spreadsheet loses its integrity.

A strong financial plan is your best friend. To preserve that strength, even pre-formatted spreadsheets will need to be altered to reflect the categories of revenues and expenses pertinent to your particular business. Be sure the software program allows you to *completely customize* the spreadsheets to your own Chart of Accounts.

Yes! We Do Have Business Planning Software that Accounts for All of the Above!

In order to help you in the writing of your business plan, we have developed a software program that will guide you neatly through the entire business planning process. **Automate Your Business Plan** *for Windows* is for IBM and compatibles and **does not** require any additional software. The software has its own full-powered word processor and an easy-to-use spreadsheet program with pre-formatted and pre-formulated financial statements that can be completely customized to match your business.

Automate Your Business Plan is *Anatomy of a Business Plan* translated into software. It follows the book step-by-step and will print out a finished business plan.

Packaging for Success

When you have finished writing your business plan, there are a few last considerations that will help in making a favorable impression with a potential lender or investor. Good packaging will also make your plan easier for you to use.

◈ **Binding and cover:** For your working business plan, it is best to use a three-ring binder. That way information can be easily added, updated, or replaced. Your working plan should have a copy of all of your supporting documents. For the plan that you take to a potential lender or investor, you will want to bind it in a nice cover. You can purchase one from an office supply store or take it to your printer and have it done. Use blue, brown, or black covers. Lenders or investors tend to be conservative.

◆ **Length:** Be concise! Generally, you should have no more than 30 to 40 pages in the plan you take to a lender, including Supporting Documents. As you write each section, think of it as being a summary. Include as much information as you can in a brief statement. Potential lenders or investors do not want to search through volumes of material to get to needed information. You can always have an expanded version of your business plan in your own binder, including a complete set of your supporting documents.

◆ **Presentation:** Do your best to make your plan look presentable. However, do not go to the unnecessary expense of paying for professional word processing services unless you cannot do it yourself. The lender or investor is not interested in seeing an expensive looking business plan. What he is looking for is what your business plan says in terms of text and numbers. Paying for frills could even be considered as frivolous by some lenders and investors—a first impression that might indicate that you would not use their loan or investment dollars wisely.

◆ **Table of Contents:** Be sure to include a Table of Contents in your business plan. It will follow the Executive Summary (or Statement of Purpose). Make it detailed enough so you or a lender or investor can locate any of the areas addressed in the plan. It must also list the Supporting Documents and their corresponding page numbers. It might help you to use the Table of Contents in this book as a guide to compiling your own.

◆ **Number of copies:** Make copies for yourself and each lender you wish to approach. Keep track of each copy. Don't try to work with too many potential lenders at one time. If your loan is refused, be sure to retrieve your business plan.

A Final Word

When you are finished, your business plan should look polished and professional, but it should be obvious to the lender or investor that it was done by the people who own and run the business. Your business plan will be the best indication the lender will have to judge your potential for success.

**Be Sure that Your Business Plan Is
Representative of Your Best Efforts!**

It is our hope that you have been able to use this book to help you develop a concise, logical, and appropriate plan for your business. When your work is done and your business plan is complete, don't forget to:

- ◆ **Operate within your business plan.**
- ◆ **Anticipate changes.**
- ◆ **Revise your plan and keep it up-to-date.**

Do these things and we will guarantee that you are well on your way to improving your chances of success and growth as you continue with your business venture. Thank you for including our materials as part of your plan.

Information Resources

The information you need to research and run your business effectively can be found through the resources of public, corporate, or university libraries, in governmental agencies, and in civic organizations. One of our underutilized resources is the public library. The reference librarian in the business section can direct you to the materials you need.

Take some time to write out your questions. Getting the answers will involve reading books, newsletters, and periodicals covering the subject area of your business. You will contact trade and professional associations to get information on trade shows, industry trends, and sources of supply. Attendance and participation at meetings of civic organizations, such as chambers of commerce and at professional organizations unique to your business will provide opportunities for networking. Governmental departments issue publications containing statistical data and projections for their areas of concern. The Internal Revenue Service, Department of Commerce, the Small Business Administration, and many colleges and community service programs offer low-cost classes concerning business development. The following reference section will help you locate the information you need.

☑ **Library Resources**   ☑ **Books**

☑ **Indexes to Periodicals and Magazine Articles**   ☑ **Publications and Periodicals**

☑ **U.S. Government Departments**   ☑ **Internet Resources**

Library Resources

American Business Disc (**American Business Information**): CD-ROM covering 10 million businesses. Can be searched by company name, SIC code, Yellow Page headings, address, and geographically by zip code, city, and state.

American Manufacturers Directory (**American Business Information**): Lists American manufacturers with 25 or more employees.

Bacon's Newspaper/Magazine Directory (**Bacon's Information**): Lists media as source of publicity information.

City and County Data Book (**U.S. Dept. of Commerce**): This book is updated every three years and contains statistical information on population, education, employment, income, housing, and retail sales.

Directory of Directories (**Gale Research Inc.**): Describes over 9,000 buyer's guides and directories.

Discovering Small Business (**Gale Research Inc.**): CD-ROM detailing 300 specific types of ventures with sample business plans, information on financial programs, licensing, and current journal articles.

Dun and Bradstreet Directories (**Dun and Bradstreet**): Lists companies alphabetically, geographically, and by product classification.

Encyclopedia of Associations (**Gale Research Inc.**): Lists trade and professional associations throughout the United States. Many publish newsletters and provide marketing information. These associations can help business owners keep up with the latest industry developments.

Encyclopedia of Associations: National Organizations of the U.S. (**Gale Research Inc.**): CD provides instant access to information on 23,000 national organizations in the U.S.

Encyclopedia of Business Information Sources (**Gale Research Inc.**): Lists handbooks, periodicals, directories, trade associations, and more for over 1200 specific industries and business subjects. Start here to search for information on your particular business.

Federal Yellow Book (**Monitor Leadership Directories, Inc.**): Lists the names, titles, office locations, and telephone numbers of people in hundreds of offices in the Executive Office, Cabinet-level departments, and more than 70 Independent Federal Agencies, such as the EPA and FDA.

Incubators for Small Business (**U.S. Small Business Administration**): Lists over 170 state government offices and incubators that offer financial and technical aid to new small businesses.

Industry Norms and Key Business Ratios (**Dun & Bradstreet**): Provides balance sheet figures for companies in over 800 different lines of business as defined by SIC number.

Lifestyle Market Analyst 2000 (**Standard Rate & Data Service**): Breaks down population geographically and demographically. Includes extensive lifestyle information on the interests, hobbies, and activities popular in each geographic and demographic market.

National Trade and Professional Associations of the U.S. (**Columbia Books, Inc.**): Trade and Professional Associations are indexed by association, geographic region, subject, and budget.

Pratt's Guide to Venture Capital Sources (**Stanley Pratt**): New York, Securities Data Publishing, 1999.

Reference Book for World Traders (**Alfred Croner**): This three-volume set lists banks, chambers of commerce, customs, marketing organizations, invoicing procedures, and more for 185 foreign markets. Sections on export planning, financing, shipping, laws, and tariffs are also included, with a directory of helpful government agencies.

RMA Annual Statement Studies (**Robert Morris Associates**): Industry norms and ratios are compiled from income statements and balance sheets. For each SIC code, three sets of statistics are given with each set representing a specific size range of companies based upon sales.

Research Alert Yearbook (**American Demographics Books**): Information, charts, and graphs covering 53 subject categories and providing information on shopping preferences, expenditure trends.

Small Business Sourcebook (**Gale Research Inc.**): A good starting place for finding consultants, educational institutions, governmental agencies offering assistance, as well as specific information sources for over 140 types of businesses.

Sourcebook for Franchise Opportunities (**Dow-Jones Irwin**): Provides annual directory information for U.S. franchises, and data for investment requirements, royalty and advertising fees, services furnished by the franchiser, projected growth rates, and locations where franchises are licensed to operate.

***Standard Industrial Classification Manual* (U.S. Dept. of Commerce):** This publication list the SIC numbers issued to major areas of business: for example, the SIC number for piano tuning is #7699. This unique number is used in locating statistical data.

***State Business Directories* (American Business Information):** Reference books which include businesses by city, businesses by yellow page category, major employers, and manufacturers by city and product.

***Statistical Abstract of the U.S.* (U.S. Dept. of Commerce):** Updated annually, provides demographic, economic, and social information.

Indexes to Periodicals and Magazine Articles

These references can be found in the library. Periodicals and articles can be researched by subject. Become familiar with periodicals and read articles that contain information specific to your type of business.

***Business Periodicals Index* (H.W. Wilson Company):** An index to articles published in 300 business oriented periodicals.

***Gale Directory of Publications* (Gale Research Company):** Lists periodicals and newsletters.

***Magazines for Libraries* (R.R. Bowker Company):** A directory of publications.

***New York Times Index* (NY Times Company):** A guide to articles published in the *New York Times*.

***Reader's Guide to Periodical Literature* (H.W. Wilson Company):** An index to articles published in 200 popular magazines.

***Ulrich's International Periodicals Directory* (R.R. Bowker Company):** Lists over 100,000 magazines, newsletters, newspapers, journals, and other periodicals in 554 subject areas.

U.S. Government Departments

Federal agencies offer resources that will help you research your industry. Also gather information from governmental agencies on your state and local level. Request to be put on a mailing list to receive appropriate materials and a catalog.

Bureau of Consumer Protection
Division of Special Statutes
6th and Pennsylvania Avenue NW
Washington, DC 20580

Consumer Products Safety Commission
Bureau of Compliance
5401 Westbard Avenue
Bethesda, MD 20207

Department of Agriculture
14th Street and Independence Avenue SW
Washington, DC 20250

Scope of this office includes food safety and inspection, nutrition, veterinary medicine, consumer affairs.

Department of Commerce
Office of Business Liaison
14th Street and Constitution Avenue NW
Washington, DC 20230

The Office of Business Liaison is specifically set up to help guide small businesses through the federal maze and can help locate the federal agency best able to serve your particular needs. The department covers subjects of engineering standards, imports and exports, minority-owned business, patents and trademarks, business outlook analyses, economic and demographic statistics.

Department of Commerce
International Trade Administration
14th Street and Constitution Avenue NW
Washington, DC 20230

Department of Education
400 Maryland Avenue SW
Washington, DC 20202

Scope includes bilingual and adult education, libraries, special education, and educational statistics.

Department of Energy
Forrestal Building
1000 Independence Avenue SW
Washington, DC 20585

Areas covered are conservation, inventions, fusion and nuclear energy, coal, gas, shale, and oil.

Department of Health and Human Services
200 Independence Avenue SW
Washington, DC 20201

Information available on diseases, drug abuse, research, family planning, food safety, occupational safety, and statistical data.

Department of Housing and Urban Development
451 7th Street SW
Washington, DC 20410

Scope involves fair housing, energy conservation, urban studies, and elderly housing.

Department of the Interior
18th and C Streets NW
Washington, DC 20240

Covers the areas of water, natural resources, mapping, geology, fish and wildlife.

Department of Justice
10th Street and Constitution Avenue NW
Washington, DC 20530

Concerned with civil rights, drug enforcement, prisons, antitrust, justice statistics.

Department of Labor
200 Constitution Avenue NW
Washington, DC 20210

Divisions are concerned with labor-management relations, labor statistics, occupational safety and health, women's employment issues, productivity, and technology.

Department of State
2201 C Street NW
Washington, DC 20520

Covers international affairs involving diplomacy, arms, drugs, and human rights.

Department of Transportation
400 7th Street SW
Washington, DC 20590

Scope includes aviation, automobile, boat, rail, and highway standards and safety.

Department of the Treasury
15th Street and Pennsylvania Avenue NW
Washington, DC 20220

Covers the areas of customs, taxpayer assistance, currency research, development, and production.

Environmental Protection Agency
401 M Street SW
Washington, DC 20460

Federal Communications Commission (FCC)
1919 M Street NW
Washington, DC 20554

Federal Trade Commission
Public Reference Branch
Pennsylvania Avenue and 6th Street NW
Washington, DC 20580

Provides information about the FTC Franchise and Business Opportunity Rules.

Food and Drug Administration
FDA Center for Food Safety and Applied Nutrition
200 Charles Street, SW
Washington, DC 20402

Internal Revenue Service

1-800-829-3676 for tax forms and information.

Library of Congress
Copyright Office
101 Independence Ave. SE
Washington, DC 20540

Patent and Trademark Office
U.S. Department of Commerce
P.O. Box 9
Washington, DC 20231

Superintendent of Documents
Government Printing Office
Washington, DC 20402

U.S. Fish and Wildlife Service
Office of Management Authority
4401 N. Fairfax Drive
Arlington VA 22203

U.S. International Trade Commission
500 E Street SW
Washington, DC 20436

U.S. Small Business Administration
1441 L Street NW
Washington, DC 20005

The Small Business Administration offers an extensive selection of information on most business management topics from how to start a business to exporting your products. The SBA has offices throughout the country. Consult the U.S. Government section in your telephone directory for the office nearest you. SBA offers a number of programs and services, including training and educational programs, counseling services, financial programs, and contact assistance. Ask about:

Service Corp of Retired Executives(SCORE): A national organization sponsored by SBA of volunteer business executives who provide free counseling, workshops, and seminars to prospective and existing small business people.

Small Business Development Centers(SBDCs): Sponsored by the SBA in partnership with state and local governments, the educational community, and the private sector. They provide assistance, counseling, and training to prospective and existing business people.

Small Business Institutes (SBIs): Organized through SBA on more than 500 college campuses around the nation. The institutes provide counseling by students and faculty to small business clients.

For more information about SBA business development programs and services, call the SBA Small Business Answer Desk at 1-800-827-5722. SBA has added a home page in the Internet's World Wide Web that provides an interactive guide to SBA programs. (http://www.sba.gov)

Books

Arkebauer, James, and Jack Miller. *Leading-Edge Business Planning for Entrepreneurs*. Chicago: Dearborn, 1999.

Bangs, David. *The Cash Flow Control Guide*. Chicago: Dearborn, 1992.

————. *Financial Troubleshooting*. Boston: Inc. Business Resources, 1999.

————. *Managing by the Numbers*. Chicago: Dearborn, 1992.

Bangs, David, and Linda Pinson. *The Real World Entrepreneur Field Guide*. Chicago: Dearborn, 1999.

Blankenship, A.B., Alan Dutke, and George Breen. *State of the Art Marketing Research*. Chicago: NTC Business Books, 1998.

Clifford, Denis, and Ralph Warner. *The Partnership Book*. Berkeley, CA: Nolo Press, 1997.

Coveney, Patrick. *Business Angels: Securing Start-Up Finances*. New York: John Wiley and Sons, 1998.

Dickey, Terry. *Budgeting for a Small Business*. San Francisco: Crisp Publications, 1994.

Finney, Robert G. *Basics of Budgeting, Purchasing, and Financial Statements with CD-ROM*. New York: Amacom, 1999.

Fletcher, Tana. *Getting Publicity, 2nd edition*. Bellingham, WA: Self-Counsel Press, 1995.

Francese, Peter. *Marketing Know-How*. Ithaca, NY: American Demographics Booms, 1998

Godin, Seth. *The Bootstrapper's Bible*. Chicago: Dearborn, 1998.

Hall, Stephen. *From Kitchen to Market, 2nd edition*. Chicago: Dearborn, 1996.

Levinson, Jay Conrad. *Guerrilla Marketing, 3rd edition*. Boston: Houghton-Mifflin, 1998.

Lipman, Frederick. *Financing Your Business with Venture Capital*. Rocklin, CA: Prima Publishing, 1998.

Pinson, Linda, and Jerry Jinnett. *Keeping the Books, 4th edition*. Chicago: Dearborn, 1998.

————. *Steps to Small Business Start-Up, 4th edition*. Chicago: Dearborn, 2000.

————. *Target Marketing: Researching, Reaching, and Retaining your Target Market, 3rd edition*. Chicago: Dearborn, 1996.

Steingold, Fred. *The Legal Guide for Starting and Running a Small Business, 4th edition*. Berkeley, CA: Nolo Press, 1998.

Steingold, Fred. *The Employer's Legal Handbook, 3rd edition*. Berkeley, CA: Nolo Press, 1999.

Tabet, Joseph, and Jeffrey Slater. *Financial Essentials for Small Business Success*. Chicago: Dearborn, 1994.

Tiernan, Bernadette. *e-tailing*. Chicago: Dearborn, 2000.

Weinstein, Art. *Market Segmentation*. New York: Probus Publishing Company, 1993.

Publications and Periodicals

Business Week, McGraw-Hill, Inc., 1221 Avenue of the Americas, New York, NY 10020.

Entrepreneur, 2392 Morse Avenue, Irvine, CA 92714.

Fast Company, P.O. Box 52760, Boulder, CO 80328.

Home Office Computing, P.O. Box 53538, Boulder, CO 80321.

Inc., 38 Commercial Wharf, Boston, MA 02110.

Nation's Business, 1615 H. Street N.W., Washington, DC 20062-2000.

Small Business Forum: Journal of the Association of Small Business Development Centers, University of Wisconsin SBDC, 432 North Lake Street, Madison, WI 53706.

Small Business Reporter, Bank of America, Department 3120, P.O. Box 37000, San Francisco, CA 94137.

Small Business Success, Pacific Bell Directory, 101 Spear Street, Rm. 429, San Francisco, CA 94105 (800)237-4769 in CA, or (800)848-8000.

Success, 342 Madison Avenue, New York, NY 10173.

Internet Resources

The following Internet addresses provide access to information needed to research your industry, the economy, demographics and other statistics, and to reach government and marketing sites.

A good starting point is BSN (Business Sources on the Net). This site is maintained by librarians and categorizes information sources by topic. You can reach BSN at:

www.hbg.psu.edu/library/bsn.html

There are many search engines available. Perhaps the most thorough in terms of accessing business information is Alta Vista:

www.altavista.digital.com

The SBA (Small Business Administration) site provides access to information and links to sites providing useful information for entrepreneurs and small business owners:

www.sba.gov

Links to services and organizations related to the U.S. Department of Commerce can be found at:

www.doc.gov

Financial Times is one of the best resources for news on international business, politics, and technology:

www.ft.com

Resources to help you make business decisions are available at the Smart Business Supersite: the how-to resource for business:

www.smartbiz.com

The latest news on technological developments from MIT's online journal can be accessed at:

www.techreview.com

Information on government contracts, bids, and procurement can be found through Commerce Business Daily's site:

www.business.gov/

The following companies make a portion of the demographic and industry-related marketing reports available online for free; you may subscribe to their services for a fee:

Forrester Research Inc.	**www.forrester.com**
Quest Information Group	**www.intelliquest.com**
Find/SVP	**www.find.com**
Online Advertising Forum	**www.olaf.net**

Social, demographic, and economic statistics can be obtained from the Website of the U.S. Census Bureau:

www.census.gov

To find specific Internet organization information by geographic location, industry classification, or specific domain name, use the Internet Business Information Services site at:

www.internet.org

Thomas Register of American Manufacturers provides information on products, services, and companies. Over 150,000 U.S. and Canadian companies are in their database:

www.thomasregister.com

Internet/websites that provide sources and information on funding programs and access to venture capital:

www.garage.com or www.sba.gov

Marine Art of California Business Plan

The business plan presented on the following pages is an actual business plan developed by Mr. Robert Garcia for his business, **Marine Art of California**. Mr. Garcia has generously allowed us to use it in *Anatomy of a Business Plan* and **Automate Your Business Plan** to serve as an illustration that will help you with the writing of your own plan.

When Mr. Garcia wrote this plan, he was in the process of organizing his business for start-up and looking for investors in the form of limited partnerships. He has now been in business for three years and updates his plan regularly to reflect what is actually happening in the operation of his venture.

The plan was written prior to start-up. For that reason, it included projections only and the financial section ended with a break-even analysis. After one year in business, Mr. Garcia's business plan would also include historical profit & loss statements, a current balance sheet, and financial statement analysis, all of which would be based on the actual transactions of his business.

We have added to the original plan.

In order to give you a complete example of a business plan, including historical information as well as projections (especially in the financial area), we decided to carry this plan forward one year and create a set of financial statements that would reflect the first year of operation and show how projections are measured against performance.

Because it would be inappropriate to disclose the financial information of a current business, we have created a financial scenario to show what might have happened in the year 1999. The historical financial statements on pages 178 through 181 of this plan are for educational purposes only and <u>do not</u> reflect the actual financial history or industry ratio standards of Marine Art of California. The remainder of the plan is presented as originally written.

This plan can help you.

As you proceed with the writing of your own plan, it may help you to look at Mr. Garcia's business plan to see how he handled each of the corresponding sections. Some of the research material has been condensed and we have not included all of his supporting documents. We have also chosen to omit his personal financial history for privacy reasons.

> ***Warning!*** *The plan is to be examined for Mr. Garcia's handling of content only. It has been used as an example in our book and software because we feel it is a fine example of business plan organization. There is no judgment inferred as to appropriateness or financial potential for lenders or investors. Do not use it as a source of research for your own company.*

We are very pleased that we have the opportunity to include this material in *Anatomy of a Business Plan* and **Automate Your Business Plan**. We hope that it will be of benefit to you. We thank Bob Garcia for being so generous and for allowing us to share his interpretation of business planning with our readers.

MARINE ART OF CALIFORNIA

P.O. Box 10059-251
Newport Beach, CA 92658
(714) 997-9100

BUSINESS PLAN

Robert A. Garcia, President
P.O. Box 10059-251
Newport Beach, CA 92658
(714) 997-9100

Plan prepared*
by
Robert A. Garcia
(Private and Confidential)

* **Financial history updated through December 31, 1999 by the developers of Automate Your Business Plan.** Historical financial statements in this plan show what could have happened in 1999. The 1999 year-end financial statements and financial statement analysis were prepared by *Automate Your Business Plan* developers and are intended to be used for educational purposes only. They were not meant to and <u>do not</u> reflect the actual financial history of Marine Art of California.

Table of Contents

MARINE ART OF CALIFORNIA

Executive Summary

Marine Art of California is a Limited Partnership to be established in 1998. The direct mail order and showroom company will be located in Newport Beach, CA. The company is seeking working capital in the amount of $130,000 for the purpose of start-up operations and to cover estimated operating expenses for a six-month period.

Twenty limited partnerships (2.25% each) are being offered in return investments of $6,500 to be treated as loan funds to be repaid over a 15-year period at the rate of 11%. Limited partnerships will have a duration of four years, at which time the partners' shares will be bought back at the rate of $3,250 for each 2.25% share. At the end of the 15-year loan period, it is projected that the Return on Investment (ROI) for each $6,500 share will amount to $34,084.

The $130,000 in loan funds will enable the company to effectively market its products and services while maintaining proper cash flow. Funding is needed in time for the first catalog issue to be distributed in November 1998 and for a showroom to be operational in the same month for the Christmas buying season. There is a two- to three-week period between order placement and delivery date.

It is projected that the company will reach its break-even point in the latter part of the second year of operation.

Repayment of the loan and interest can begin promptly within 30 days of receipt and can be secured by the percentage of the business to be held as collateral.

I. ORGANIZATIONAL PLAN
Marine Art of California

Description of Business

Marine Art of California is a start-up company in Newport Beach, marketing the works of California artists through a direct mail-order catalog. The product line is a unique combination of art, gift items, and jewelry, all tied together by a marine or nautical theme. This marketing concept is a first! There is no known retailer or catalog company exclusively featuring the works of California artists in either a retail store or by mail-order catalog. I'm targeting a specific genre of the art market that, in terms of marketability, is on the cutting edge.

Having managed Sea Fantasies Art Gallery at Fashion Island Mall in Newport Beach, I was able to discuss my idea personally and collect more than 700 names and addresses of highly interested customers who were marine art lovers. Of these, 90% lived in the surrounding communities and the rest came from across the U.S. and other nations.

Currently, I have begun mailings, taking orders and making sales. I have a large number of artists and vendors throughout California with marketing agreements already in place.

I have assets of about $10,000 of miscellaneous items. These include framed and unframed originals, lithographs, posters, bronzes, acrylic boats, jewelry, videos, cassettes, CDs, T-shirts, glass figurines, greeting cards, shells, and coral.

Sales will be processed by a four-step marketing plan. First is a direct mail-order catalog published bimonthly (six times a year). This allows for complete marketing freedom targeting high-income households, interior designers, and other businesses located in coastal areas. The second is to generate sales through a retail showroom where merchandise can be purchased on-site and large high-end pieces (exhibited on consignment) can be ordered by catalog and drop-shipped from artist/vendor directly to the customer. Third, a comprehensive advertising campaign targeting the surrounding high-income communities shall be conducted, e.g. yellow pages, high-profile magazines, monthly guest artist shows, Grand Opening mailings and fliers with discount coupons. Fourth is to conduct an ongoing telemarketing program aimed at customers on our mail lists in our local area at minimal cost.

Industry trends have stabilized with the bottoming of the current recession. My plan to counter this situation is to obtain exclusive marketing rights on unique designs and the widest selection in the market of quality items priced affordably under $100.00.

My plan is to secure my ranking as the #2 marine art dealer in Southern California, second only to the Wyland Galleries by the end of 2000 and by 2001, through steadily increasing catalog distribution to more than 150,000 copies per mailing, to rank as the #1 dealer in California in gross sales! From 2001 through 2003, projected catalog distribution will increase at a rate of at least 100,000 catalogs per year.

<u>Legal Structure</u>

The structure of the company will consist of one (1) General Partner and up to twenty (20) Limited Partners. The amount of funds needed from the Limited Partners is $130,000, which will equal 45% ownership of the business. Each Limited Partner's investment of $6,500 shall equal 2.25% of the business.

The investment will be treated as a loan and will be paid back over 15 years at 11% interest. The loan repayment amount for each 2.25% share will be $79.03 per month.

No Limited Partner shall have any right to be active in the conduct of the Partnership's business or have the power to bind the Partnership with any contract, agreement, promise, or undertaking.

Exit Strategy from Limited Partnership

The duration of the Partnership is four years. The General Partner will have the option of buying out the Limited Partners at the end of four years for $3,250 for each 2.25% interest. The buyout will not affect the outstanding loan, but the General Partner will provide collateral equal to the loan balance. The value of the business will be used as that collateral.

The distribution of profits shall be made within 75 days of the end of the year. Each Limited Partner will receive 2.25% per share of investment on any profits over and above the following two months' operating expenses (January and February). This amount will be required to maintain operations and generate revenues necessary to keep the company solvent. Following the exit of all limited partners, the company will be restructured as a sole proprietorship.

In the event of a loss, each Limited Partner will assume a 2.25% liability for tax purposes and no profits will be paid. The General Partner will assume 55% of the loss for tax purposes.

A Key Man Insurance Policy in the amount of $250,000 shall be taken out on the General Partner to be paid to the Limited Partners in the event of the General Partner's death. The policy will be divided among the Limited Partners according to their percentage of interest in the company.

* See Copy of Contract in Supporting Documents for remainder of details.

Products and Service

The product line of **Marine Art of California** consists of hand-signed limited editions of bronzes, acrylics, lithographs, and posters with certificates. Included are exclusive designs (covered by signed contracts) of (1) originals and prints, (2) glass figurines, and (3) fine jewelry. Rounding out the line are ceramic figures, videos, cassettes, CDs, marine life books, nautical clocks, marine jewelry (14k gold, sterling silver, genuine gemstones), and many more gift items, as well as a specific line for children. The marketing areas covered are both Northern California and Southern California.

The suppliers are artists and vendors from throughout California. They number over 260! I chose them because they best express, artistically, the growing interest in the marine environment. However, due to catalog space, only 30 to 50 artists/vendors can be represented. The retail showroom will be able to accommodate more.

My framing source for art images is a wholesale operation in Fullerton that services many large accounts including Disney Studios.

With an extremely large artist/vendor pool to draw from, I virtually eliminate any supply shortage that cannot be replaced quickly. Also, my shipping policy specifies a maximum of 3 weeks delivery time for custom-made pieces such as limited edition bronzes that need to be poured at foundries. Almost all of my suppliers have been in business for years and understand the yearly marketing trends.

Management

At present, I, Robert A. Garcia, am sole proprietor. I possess a wealth of business environment experience as indicated on my resume. My first long-term job was in the grocery industry with Stater Bros. Markets. I worked from high school through college, rising to the position of second assistant manager. The most valuable experience I came away with was the ability to work cohesively with a variety of personalities in demanding customer situations. It was at this point that I learned the importance and value of the customer in American business. The customers' needs are placed first! They are the most important link in the chain.

With the opportunity for better pay and regular weekday hours, I left Stater Bros. for employment with General Dynamics Pomona Division. For the next eleven years I was employed in Production Control and earned the title of Manufacturing Coordinator, supervising a small number of key individuals. I was responsible for all printed circuit board assemblies fabricated in off-site facilities located in Arizona and Arkansas. My duties included traveling between these facilities as needed. On a daily basis, I interfaced with supporting departments of Engineering, Quality Assurance, Procurement, Shipping and Receiving, Inspection, Stockroom and Inventory Control, Data Control Center, Electronic Fabrication, Machine Shop, and Final Assembly areas.

The programs involved were the Standard Missile (Surface to Air Weapon System), Phalanx Close I Weapons System, Stinger System, and Sparrow Missile. My group was responsible for all analysis reports for upper management, Naval personnel, and corporate headquarters in St. Louis, Missouri.

Management (cont.)

Duties included: solving material shortages, scheduling work to be released to maintain starts and completions, and to drive all support departments to meet Final Assembly needs for contract delivery. Problem solving was the name of the game. The importance of follow-up was critical. Three key concepts that we used as business guidelines were (1) production of a **QUALITY PRODUCT** (2) at a **COMPETITIVE PRICE** (3) delivered **ON SCHEDULE**.

I'm currently in contact on a regular basis with 8 advisors varying in backgrounds of marketing, advertising, corporate law, small business start-up, finance, direct mail-order business, and catalog production. Two individuals are college professors with active businesses, one a publisher of my business plan reference book, and two are retired executives with backgrounds in marketing and corporate law involved in the SCORE program through the Small Business Administration (SBA). I meet with these two executives every week.

Pertinent Courses and Seminars Completed

College Course	Supervisory Training	Mt. San Antonio College
College Course	Successful Business Writing	Mt. San Antonio College
Seminar	Producing a Direct Mail Catalog	Coastline Community College
Seminar	Business Taxes & Recordkeeping	SCORE Workshop
Seminar	Business Plan Road Map	SCORE Workshop

Note: See resume in Supporting Documents

Manager Salary Plan: Upon the signing of limited partnership agreements, I will maintain the status as managing partner and decision maker. For the duration of the partnership (planned for four years), as the manager, I will draw a monthly salary of $2,000, as per the agreement. In addition, I will retain 55% ownership of the company.

Personnel

The total number of employees to be hired initially will be four. Interviews have been conducted for each position, and all are tentatively filled. I will be on the premises during all business hours for both retail and catalog ordering operations during the first month of business. It will be the owner's duty to hire the following employees:

1. **Store Manager** - part time - $11.00 per hour

2. **1st Asst. Manager** - part time - $9.00 per hour

3. **2nd Asst. Manager** - part time - $8.00 per hour

4. **Sales Consultant** - part time - $5.50 per hour

5. **Administrative Asst.** - part time - $10.00 per hour

Personnel (cont.)

<u>TRAINING:</u>

1. All employees will be cross-trained in the following areas:

    a. Knowledge of product line

    b. Daily Sales Reconciliation Report (DSR)

    c. Catalog order processing

    d. Familiarity with key suppliers

    e. Company policy regarding customer relations

    f. Charges: VISA / MasterCard

<u>PERSONNEL DUTIES:</u>

1. Manager: Reports directly to Owner

    a. Open store (Key)—dust and vacuum

    b. Write work schedule

    c. Verify previous day's sales figures

    d. Follow up on any problems of previous day

    e. Head biweekly wall-to-wall inventory

    f. Reconcile any business discrepancies

    g. Responsible for store and catalog operations

    h. Order inventory

    i. Have access to safe

    j. Process catalog orders

    k. Conduct telemarketing in spare time

    l. Authorize employee purchase program (EPP)

2. Administrative Assistant: Reports to Manager

    a. Open store (Key)

    b. Write work schedule

    c. Perform office functions

        (1) Daily Sales Reconciliation Report   (DSR)

        (2) Accounts Receivable   (A/R)

        (3) Accounts Payable   (A/P)

        (4) Payroll   (P/R)

        (5) General Ledger   (G/L)

        (6) Typing—60 wpm

        (7) Computer—WP/Lotus/D-Base

        (8) 10-Key Adding Machine

    d. Have access to safe

    e. Process catalog orders

    f. Authorize employee purchase program (EPP)

Personnel (cont.)

3. 1st Assistant Manager: Reports to Manager

    a. Close store (Key)

    b. Order inventory

    c. Complete Daily Sales Reconciliation Report (DSR)

    d. Follow up on day's problems not yet solved

    e. Have access to safe

    f. Process catalog orders

    g. Conduct telemarketing in spare time

4. 2nd Assistant Manager: Reports to 1st Assistant Manager

    a. Is familiar with all 1st Assistant Manager tasks

    b. Process catalog orders

    c. Assist in Customer Relations follow-up

    d. Dust and vacuum showroom

    e. Conduct telemarketing in spare time

5. Sales Consultant: Reports to 2nd Assistant Manager

    a. Cover showroom floor

    b. Process catalog orders

    c. Assist in Customer Relations follow-up

    d. Dust and vacuum showroom

    e. Conduct telemarketing in spare time

EMPLOYEE PROFILE

1. Personable, outgoing, reliable, in good health

2. College background

3. High integrity and dedication

4. Neat in appearance

5. Able to take on responsibilities

6. Able to follow directives

7. Demonstrates leadership qualities

8. Previous retail experience

9. Basic office skills

10. Sincere interest in marine art and environment

11. Likes water sports

12. Team worker

Accounting and Recordkeeping

All bookkeeping activities shall be done by the Administrative Assistant. Financial Reports will be filed by John Horist, CPA. John brings more than 40 years experience in his field. His hourly fee is very reasonable.

I would like to point out the key areas of recordkeeping required in the business and explain the software to be used and why. The areas are as follows:

Mail Lists: List & Mail Plus Software from Avery. It stores, sorts and prints up to 64,000 addresses with no programming required. It contains pre-defined label formats, or I can create my own. Searching and extracting subsets of the mailing list is possible. It also checks for duplicate entries.

Labels: MacLabel Pro Software from Avery. The features include preset layouts for Avery laser labels and dot matrix labels, drawing tools and graphic sizing, built-in clip art and easy mail merge.

Accounting: Sybiz Windows Accounting Software. This program automatically updates all accounts, customers, payroll, suppliers, inventory, and ledgers in one step. Windows graphics, fonts, and integration make it easy to use.

The simplicity and power of these reasonably-priced programs makes them very attractive.

Insurance

Prospective Carrier:	State Farm Insurance	
	2610 Avon, Suite C	
	Newport Beach, CA 92660	
	(714) 645-6000	
Agent:	Kim Hiller	
Type of Insurance:	Business/Personal:	$ 150,000.00
	Deductible:	$ 1,000.00
	Liability:	$1,000,000.00
Premium:	Annual Premium:	$ 3,100.00
	Monthly Premium:	$ 258.00
	Workers' Comp: 1.43 per/1K of Gross Payroll	

<u>Security</u>

PROBLEM SITUATIONS TO BE CONSIDERED AND PROTECTIVE MEASURES TO BE USED:

1. Internal Theft: Employee Dishonesty

a. Shoplifting of store merchandise: two closed circuit monitoring cameras recording showroom activity each business day.

b. Cash theft: $400 limit of cash on hand. Timely safe drops and daily maintenance of Daily Sales Reconciliation Report will balance cash with receipts.

c. Falsifying receipts: DSR will detect discrepancies.

d. Employee Purchase Plan: will reduce inclination to steal. Employee discount is 35% off retail price. Can purchase layaway (20% down—balance over 60 days) or by payroll deduction (deducted from each check over four pay periods). Processed by authorized personnel other than oneself (two signatures required).

e. Employee Orientation Program: will stress security procedures and employee integrity.

f. Biweekly wall-to-wall inventory: will reveal any losses.

2. External Theft: Customer shoplifting or Robbery

a. Walk-in theft: two closed circuit monitoring cameras recording showroom activity each business day.

b. Break-in theft: robbery—alarm system plus closed circuit monitoring cameras. All fine jewelry is displayed in locked cases, removed and stored in safe each night.

c. Wall-to-wall biweekly inventory will reveal any merchandise loss.

II. MARKETING PLAN
Marine Art of California

<u>Target Market</u>

Who are my customers?

1. Profile:

Economic level: middle to upper class.

Psychological makeup: art lover, jewelry lover, fashion conscious, ocean lover, eclectic taste, college educated, discriminating buyer, upwardly mobile life-style.

Age: 35 to 55.

Sex: Male/Female.

Income level: $75,000 and above.

Habits: high-expense entertainment, travel, marine-oriented hobbies (shell/dolphin collectors, scuba diver, boat/yacht owner, etc.), patrons of performing arts, concerts, and museums.

Work: professional, business owners, business executives, middle management, interior designers.

Shop: middle to high-profile retail establishments.

2. Location:

Orange County: coastal areas—home value of $500,000 and above.

San Francisco County, San Diego County, San Bernardino County

3. Market size:

Mail list purchased through wholesale mail list companies. The consumer base will range from 20,000 to 100,000 in the first year of operations.

4. Competition:

Minimal due to unique two-pronged marketing concept of marketing exclusively California marine art, custom-designed jewelry, and giftware by way of (1) direct mail-order catalog and (2) retail showroom. No known operation in either category.

5. Other factors:

As acting distributor for several artists I am able to retain exclusive marketing rights and, in most cases, have contracted to purchase at **10–15% below published wholesale price lists.**

Competition

The two areas of competition to consider will be (1) competitors to the retail showroom and (2) competitors to the direct mail-order operation.

(1) Competition to Retail Showroom

Following this page are attached Competition Evaluation Worksheets for each competitor within a radius of three miles of proposed store site.[1] Retail Stores to be evaluated will have at least 1 of the four categories of my product line:

A. MARINE ART: Framed (custom) and framed

B. MARINE SCULPTING: Cast in bronze and acrylic

C. MARINE AND NAUTICAL GIFT ITEMS

D. MARINE AND CONTEMPORARY JEWELRY DESIGNS: Fine and fashion

(2) Competition to Direct Mail-Order Catalog

After investigating scores of catalog companies across the nation for the past year and speaking to artists and vendors across the state of California, we are aware of only one mail-order company with a similar theme but with a very different line and profile than **Marine Art of California**.

Methods of Distribution

Two-Way Distribution Program

A. Direct Mail-Order Catalog

1. Catalog mailings are distributed through target marketing.

2. Orders are processed via telephone (1-800 #) or by return mail-order forms, accepting checks, VISA/MC, or American Express.

3. Shipping in most cases is done by the artist or vendor directly to the customer per my instructions. All other shipping is done by **Marine Art of California**.

4. Shipping costs are indicated in the catalog for each item. The customer is charged for shipping costs to reimburse the vendor.

5. UPS shipping is available throughout the United States.

---

[1] Supporting documents are not included in this sample.

Methods of Distribution (cont.)

B. Retail Showroom

1. All items shown in the catalog will be available for purchase in the retail store.

2. High-ticket items will be carried on consignment with previous agreements already made with individual artists.

3. General Catalogs will be displayed on an order counter for all products not stocked in the store and that can be shipped on request.

4. All large items will be delivered anywhere in Orange County **at no charge**.

Since I am dealing with more than 260 artists and vendors across the state there should be no problem with the availability of merchandise. I am only able to carry about 55 artists and vendors in the catalog. Most items can be ordered for the store and be in stock within a 2 to 3 day turnaround.

For more detailed information on shipping arrangements, please see copy of Terms and Conditions for Participants in Supporting Documents section.[2]

Advertising

Pacific Bell:	Yellow/white pages: 1 line	No charge
	Bold: $5.00 extra each	
Pac Bell/Sammy	Sales order # N74717625 (8/21)	
740-5211	Business line installation	$70.45
	Monthly rate	$11.85
	DEADLINE: August 19. Cannot change without $18.00 per month rate increase	
	Display: ¼ column listing (per month)	$49.00
	(Yearly cost $588.00)	
	Disconnect w/message (new #) 1 year	No charge
Donnelly:	White pages: one line	No charge
1-800-834-8425	Yellow pages: two lines	No charge
	three or more	$10.00
	½ add (per month)	$27.00
	DEADLINE - August 21 (30 days to cancel)	
	Change deadline: September 10	
	Deposit due September 11	$183.00
	Monthly rate	$91.50
	(Yearly cost $1,098.00)	

---

[2] Supporting documents are not included in this sample.

Advertising (cont.)

Metropolitan Magazine: 757-1404	Circulation 40,000 Monthly rate	129.00

Kim Moore
4940 Campus Drive
Newport Beach,CA 92660

California Riveria:	⅙ page (per month)	$300.00
494-2659	Art charge: one time	$50.00
Leslie	40% discount—new subscriber	
Box 536	Can hold rate for six months (Reg. $575.00)	
Laguna Beach,	Color (per month)	$600.00
CA 92652	Articles	No charge
	Print month end	
	Circulation: 50,000:29K High Traffic	
	21K Direct Mail (92660 - 92625)	

Grand Opening:	4 x 6 Postcard—color	$400.00
	Catering	$200.00
	Artist show	
	Discount coupons	
	Fliers	
	Newspaper ads (OC Register: one time cost—$100)	

Orange County News: 714-565-3881	Will get advertising estimates after six months in business

Orange County Register:	Monthly rate	$100.00

Advertising (cont.)

DONNELLY LISTINGS:

Five Categories:

    1. Art Dealer, Galleries

    2. Interior Designers and Decorators

    3. Framers

    4. Jewelers

    5. Gift Shops

    1. ART DEALERS:

    Original Art, Lithos, Posters, Custom Framing, Bronze & Acrylic Sculptings, Int. Designer Prices, Ask for Catalog.

    2. INTERIOR DECORATORS AND DESIGNERS:

    Original Art, Lithos, Posters, Custom Framing, Bronze & Acrylic Sculptings, Dealer Prices, Ask for Catalog.

    3. FRAMERS:

    Large Selection of California Marine Art, Coastal Scenes, Custom Framing, Matting, Ask for Mail-Order Catalog

    4. JEWELERS:

    Specialty, Marine/Nautical Custom Designs by California Artists, 14K Gold, Sterling, Gemstones, Ask for Catalog

    5. GIFT SHOPS:

    Unique Line of Marine/Nautical Gifts, Glass Figurines, Acrylic Boats, Clocks, Art, Jewelry, Bronzes, Ask for Catalog

Pricing

A. Purchasing: As stipulated in my Terms and Conditions, I request a 10 - 15% discount off published wholesale prices from artists and vendors in lieu of a participation fee. In about 95% of all agreements made, I am receiving this important discount!

B. Catalog Pricing

> 1. Non-Jewelry Items: To recover publication costs, I have "keystoned" (100% markup) all items plus an additional 10-50%. Keystoning is typical in the retail industry. The added margin will cover any additional shipping charges that may not be covered by the indicated shipping fee paid by the customer.

> 2. Jewelry Items: Typical pricing in the industry is "Key" plus 50% (150% markup) to triple "Key" (200% markup). My markup is "Key" plus 10-30% to stay competitive.

C. Store Pricing: All items will be "Keystone" plus 10 - 20% to allow a good margin for sales on selected items.

D. Wholesale: Mailings and advertising will target Interior Decorators and Designers. To purchase wholesale, one must present a copy of their ASID or ISID license number and order a minimum purchase of $500.00 or more. The discount will be 20% off retail price.

Below is a sample of the computer data base with 17 fields of information on each item in inventory and how the retail price is computed.

File: Price List
Record 1 of 49

Item:	Fisherman's Wharf
Make:	Poster
Vendor	A Chrasta
Exclusive:	So California
Size:	21.5 26 Sq.
Vendor #:	NAC102WM
Image Pr:	$5.00
Type:	Poster
Frame:	PT4XW
Frame Price:	$31.50
Whsl. Price:	$36.50
Disc:	50% IM
Adj. Whsl:	$36.50
Key+:	10%
Retail Price:	$79.50
Group:	1

Gallery Design

After managing Sea Fantasies Gallery at Fashion Island Mall in Newport Beach, I have decided to recreate its basic layout. My goal is to create the most stunning and unique showroom design in Orange County with a product line that appeals to the high-profile customer's taste.

The design theme is to give the customer a feeling of being underwater when they enter. This would be accomplished by the use of glass display stands, live potted tropical plants to simulate lush, green underwater vegetation. Overhead curtains 18 inches wide would cleverly hide the track lighting while reflecting the light on the curtain sides, creating the illusion of an underwater scene with sunlight reflecting on the ocean surface.

A large-screen TV would continuously play videos of colorful underwater scenes with mood music playing on the store's sound system. A loveseat for shoppers to relax in would face the screen. Along with creating a soothing and relaxing atmosphere, the videos, CDs and cassettes would be available for sale. All fine art pieces (bronzes and framed art) would be accented with overhead track lighting, creating a strong visual effect.

Large coral pieces would be used for display purposes, such as for jewelry. Others would be strewn around the showroom floor area for a natural ocean floor effect.

Certain end displays would be constructed of glass with ocean floor scenes set inside consisting of an arrangement of coral, shells, and brightly painted wooden tropical fish on a two-inch bed of sand! All display stands would be available for sale.

This design concept was generally considered to be the most outstanding original store plan in Fashion Island as expressed by Mall customers and the Management Office. By incorporating these tried and proven concepts with my own creative designs, this gallery will have the most outstanding and unique appearance of any gallery from Long Beach to San Clemente.

The showroom area will be approximately 800 square feet. The rear and stock area is about 200 sq./ft.

<u>Timing of Market Entry</u>

Considering the fact that most of my product line could be viewed as gift items, the upcoming Holiday Season is of **CRITICAL IMPORTANCE**! This is typically the peak sales period in the retail industry. Catalogs from large retailers and mail-order houses are already appearing in the mail for the holidays. These are the dates to consider:

1. **OCTOBER 8**:   Camera-ready artwork goes to film separator.

    Turnaround time: three days!

2. **OCTOBER 11**:   All slides and artwork must be ready to be delivered to the printer, Bertco graphics, in Los Angeles.

    Turnaround time: 11 working days!

3. **OCTOBER 22**:   Printed catalogs must be delivered to Towne House Marketing in Santa Ana.

    Turnaround time: three days!

4. **OCTOBER 29**:   Catalogs shipped to Santa Ana Main Post Office.

    Turnaround time: two working days!

5. **NOVEMBER 1**:   **CUSTOMER RECEIVES CATALOG**—Ordering begins.

6. **DECEMBER 4**:   Last ordering date to ensure Christmas delivery! Can send via Federal Express all stocked items and all stocked items at vendors.

    Problem Items:
       a) High-end cast bronzes
       b) Hand-made glass figurines
       c) Original paintings

    Turnaround time: three weeks!

Location

The prime business location targeted for **Marine Art of California** retail showroom is 1,000 square feet at 106 Bayview Circle, Newport Beach, CA 92660. This site was chosen because of large front display windows, excellent visibility and access for the showroom, as well as adequate floor space to house inventory for catalog shipping. Both operations require certain square footage to operate successfully. Demographics and surrounding stores are extremely favorable.

Proposed site: Newport Beach, California

Features:
- Retail Shop space of 1,000 sq. ft.
- Located in the primary retail and business sector of Newport Beach, Orange County's most affluent and growing community
- Excellent visibility and access
- Median household income in 1 mile radius is $90,000.00

Demographics[3]	1 Mile	3 Miles	5 Miles
Population:	1,043	111,983	308,906
Income:	$90,000	$61,990	$59,600

Private Sector Employment (Daytime pop.)

1 Mile	3 Miles	5 Miles
43,921	113,061	306,313

Socio-Economic Status Indicator (SESI)

1 Mile	3 Miles	5 Miles
73	79	79

Population by Age

	1 Mile	3 Miles	5 Miles
25–29		9.2%	8.4%
30–34		9.4%	9.9%
35–44		16.1%	18.6%
45–54		12.3%	12.1%
25–54 TOTAL		**47.0%**	**49.0%**

Leasing Agent: Chuck Sullivan
CB Commercial
4040 MacArthur Blvd.
Newport Beach CA 92660
(714) 955-6431

---

[3] Donnelly Marketing Information Service

Industry Trends

Information extracted from: ABI/INFORM DATABASE at UCI Library for Business Research.

Title: **Sharper Image Revamps Product Line. Sells Items Consumers Can Actually Buy.**

Journal: **Marketing News** Vol. 26, Issue 10, Pg. 2

Summary: Although shoppers will still find upscale items at Sharper Image, the company has doubled the amount of goods that are more affordable. The addition of low-priced items is part of a continuing shift that will last, even if the economy improves.

Title: **What's Selling, and Why**

Journal: **Catalog Age** Vol. 9, Issue 5, Pg. 5

Summary: Market researcher Judith Langer believes today's mailers must create a value package that combines quality and price. Merchandise is reflecting consumer sentiment about the economy and the desire to buy U.S. goods and services.

Title: **Tripping the Gift Market Fantastic**

Journal: **Catalog Age** Vol. 9, Issue 6, Pg. 30

Summary: Christmas Fantastic and Celebration Fantastic catalogs feature gifts and decorative accessories and target upscale females age 25 and over. Response has been strong. Average orders of $95.00 for Christmas Fantastic and $85.00 for Celebration Fantastic have surpassed company expectations.

Title: **Spring Sales Blossom**

Journal: **Catalog Age** Vol. 9, Issue 6, Pg. 36

Summary: Spring sales appear to be much stronger than in the previous year. Many mailers believe the latest upturn in sales will be long-lasting.

Title: **Your Catalog's List Is Its Greatest Asset**

Journal: **Target Marketing** Vol. 15, Issue 2, Pp.44-45

Summary: There are a number of reasons why greater attention should be paid to the customer mail list rather than prospecting for new customers: (1) It is the primary source of profit for the company. (2) It is the cataloger's most valuable asset. (3) It will outperform a rented list by as much as 10 times in response rate and average order.

Note: The above articles have been condensed for brevity.

Publications and Services Utilized

Art Business News (Monthly)

> Monthly trade magazine for art dealers and framers. Foremost business journal in the art industry. It provided readers with a wide range of art industry news, features, sales and marketing trends, and new product information. Reports on trade shows nationally and internationally.

National Jeweler (Monthly)

> Dealer magazine. Provides jewelry industry news, features, sales and marketing trends, fashions, and styles. Lists major manufacturers and wholesalers.

Catalog Age (Monthly)

> Monthly journal featuring articles on mail-order companies. Provides inside information on statistics for mail-order business. Highly informative.

Target Marketing (Monthly) Trade journal.

Orange County Business Journal (Weekly)

Small Business Administration

> Free Publications: **Selling by Mail Order**
> **Tax & Regulatory Requirements in Orange County**
> **Partnership Agreements—Planning Checklist**
> **Understanding Cash Flow**
> **Developing A Strategic Business Plan**
> **Insurance Checklist for Small Business**

Anatomy of a Business Plan: Pinson & Jinnett (Dearborn Financial Publishing)

Automate Your Business Plan 6.0: Pinson (Out of Your Mind… and Into the Marketplace)

Direct Marketing Handbook: Edward L. Nash (McGraw-Hill)

The Catalog Handbook: James Holland

Direct Marketing Association: Membership organization for catalogers.

Orange County Demographic Overview: Demographic reports, charts and maps provided by the market research department of the Orange County Register.

ABI/INFORM Data Base: University of California, Irvine (see Industry Trends section)

> On-line database located in the library. Contained in this database are abstracts and indexes to business articles published in more than 800 different journals. ABI/INFORM is an excellent source of information on:

Companies	Trends	Marketing & Advertising
Products	Corporate Strategies	
Business Conditions	Management Strategies	

Orange County Demographic Overview—Demographic reports, charts, and maps provided by the market research department of the *Orange County Register*.

III. FINANCIAL DOCUMENTS
Marine Art of California

<u>Summary of Financial Needs</u>

I. **Marine Art of California**, a limited partnership, is seeking equity capital for start-up purposes.

   A. Direct Mail-Order Catalog

   B. Retail/Wholesale Showroom

II. **Funds needed to accomplish above goal** will be $130,000. See "Loan Fund Dispersal Statement" for distribution of funds and backup statement.

<u>Loan Fund Dispersal Statement</u>

I. DISPERSAL OF LOAN FUNDS

Marine Art of California will utilize funds in the amount of $130,000 for start-up of two retail functions: (1) A direct mail-order catalog and (2) a retail showroom to conduct related functions.

II. BACKUP STATEMENT

Direct mail-order catalog:	a) 24 pages		
	b) 2 editions		
	c) Quantities:	20K:	$ 20,000.00
		30K:	23,200.00
Start-up expense of warehouse—One Time Cost:			25,275.00
3 Months Operating Expense:			58,364.00
3 Month Total Loan Repayment Cost:			3,161.00
(@ $1,560.00 per month)			
		TOTAL:	$130,000.00

Catalog revenues will result in a net profit sufficient to pay all expenses and loan payments beginning in 30 days and continuing.

21

Pro Forma Cash Flow Statement

Page 1 (Pre-Start-Up and January thru May)

Marine Art of California

For the Year 1999	Start-Up Nov-Dec	Jan	Feb	Mar	Apr	May	Jun
BEGINNING CASH BALANCE	0	75,575	65,312	50,837	49,397	37,807	43,559
CASH RECEIPTS							
A. Sales/revenues	41,620	22,065	16,040	42,350	30,300	67,744	47,696
B. Receivables (credit accts.)	0	0	0	0	0	0	0
C. Interest income	0	0	0	0	0	0	0
D. Sale of long-term assets	0	0	0	0	0	0	0
TOTAL CASH AVAILABLE	41,620	97,640	81,352	93,187	79,697	105,551	91,255
CASH PAYMENTS							
A. Cost of goods to be sold							
Inventory purchases	29,900	12,213	9,200	22,375	16,375	35,122	25,123
B. Variable expenses							
1. Advertising/marketing	1,042	221	221	221	521	521	521
2. Car delivery/travel	200	100	100	100	100	100	100
3. Catalog expense	27,600	9,600	10,800	10,800	14,600	14,600	16,400
4. Gross wages	5,120	2,560	2,560	2,560	2,560	3,520	3,520
5. Payroll expense	384	192	192	192	192	269	269
6. Shipping	800	400	400	400	400	400	400
7. Misc. var. exp.	3,000	500	500	500	500	500	500
Total variable expenses	38,146	13,573	14,773	14,773	18,873	19,910	21,710
C. Fixed expenses							
1. Accounting and legal	820	160	160	160	160	160	160
2. Insurance + workers' comp	904	302	302	302	302	320	320
3. Rent	3,900	1,300	1,300	1,300	1,300	1,300	1,300
4. Repairs and maintenance	60	30	30	30	30	30	30
5. Guaranteed pay't (mgr. partner)	4,000	2,000	2,000	2,000	2,000	2,000	2,000
6. Supplies	600	300	300	300	300	300	300
7. Telephone	1,050	600	600	700	700	1,000	1,000
8. Utilities	630	290	290	290	290	290	290
9. Misc. (inc. licenses/permits)	175	0	0	0	0	0	0
Total fixed expenses	12,139	4,982	4,982	5,082	5,082	5,400	5,400
D. Interest expense	1,192	1,192	1,192	1,192	1,192	1,192	1,192
E. Federal/state income tax	0	0	0	0	0	0	0
F. Capital purchases (office)	9,000	0	0	0	0	0	0
G. Capital purchases (showroom)	5,300	0	0	0	0	0	0
H. Loan payments	368	368	368	368	368	368	368
I. Equity withdrawals	0	0	0	0	0	0	0
TOTAL CASH PAID OUT	96,045	32,328	30,515	43,790	41,890	61,992	53,793
CASH BALANCE/DEFICIENCY	(54,425)	65,312	50,837	49,397	37,807	43,559	37,462
LOANS TO BE RECEIVED	130,000	0	0	0	0	0	0
EQUITY DEPOSITS	0	0	0	0	0	0	0
ENDING CASH BALANCE	75,575	65,312	50,837	49,397	37,807	43,559	37,462

1. $130,000 15-year loan. 20 limited partners @ $6,500 in exchange for 2.5% equity (each) in company (see proposal in Supporting Documents)
2. Cash business: Prepaid orders and paid on-site purchases only; no open accounts or receivables.

Pro Forma Cash Flow Statement

Page 2 (May thru December + 6 and 12-month Totals)

Marine Art of California

6-MONTH TOTALS	Jul	Aug	Sep	Oct	Nov	Dec	12-MONTH TOTALS
75,575	37,462	48,996	46,287	47,992	37,772	80,527	75,575
226,195	83,508	58,672	67,950	47,700	154,200	105,700	743,925
0	0	0	0	0	0	0	0
0	0	0	0	0	0	0	0
0	0	0	0	0	0	0	0
301,770	120,970	107,668	114,237	95,692	191,972	186,227	819,500
120,408	43,054	30,661	35,275	25,150	78,375	54,125	387,048
2,226	521	521	521	521	521	521	5,352
600	100	100	100	100	100	100	1,200
76,800	16,400	18,200	18,200	20,000	20,000	20,000	189,600
17,280	3,520	3,520	3,520	3,520	3,520	3,520	38,400
1,306	269	269	269	269	269	269	2,920
2,400	400	400	400	400	400	400	4,800
3,000	500	500	500	500	500	500	6,000
103,612	21,710	23,510	23,510	25,310	25,310	25,310	248,272
960	160	160	160	160	160	160	1,920
1,848	320	320	320	320	320	320	3,768
7,800	1,300	1,300	1,300	1,300	1,300	1,300	15,600
180	30	30	30	30	30	30	360
12,000	2,000	2,000	2,000	2,000	2,000	2,000	24,000
1,800	300	300	300	300	300	300	3,600
4,600	1,250	1,250	1,500	1,500	1,800	1,800	13,700
1,740	290	290	290	290	290	290	3,480
0	0	0	0	0	0	0	0
30,928	5,650	5,650	5,900	5,900	6,200	6,200	66,428
7,152	1,192	1,192	1,192	1,192	1,190	1,190	14,300
0	0	0	0	0	0	0	0
0	0	0	0	0	0	0	0
0	0	0	0	0	0	0	0
2,208	368	368	368	368	370	370	4,420
0	0	0	0	0	0	0	0
264,308	71,974	61,381	66,245	57,920	111,445	87,195	720,468
37,462	48,996	46,287	47,992	37,772	80,527	99,032	99,032
0	0	0	0	0	0	0	0
0	0	0	0	0	0	0	0
37,462	48,996	46,287	47,992	37,772	80,527	99,032	99,032

Quarterly Budget Analysis
Marine Art of California

For the Quarter Ending: December 31, 1999

BUDGET ITEM	THIS QUARTER			YEAR-TO-DATE		
	Budget	Actual	Var.	Budget	Actual	Var.
Sales/revenues	**307,600**	**300,196**	**(7,404)**	**743,925**	**730,379**	**(13,546)**
a. Catalog sales	285,500	275,238	(10,262)	672,920	647,380	(25,540)
b. Showroom sales	15,300	16,382	1,082	46,325	53,805	7,480
c. Wholesale sales	6,800	8,576	1,776	24,680	29,194	4,514
Less cost of goods	**159,650**	**146,315**	**13,335**	**375,048**	**369,502**	**5,546**
a. Purchases	167,650	154,172	13,478	387,048	380,914	6,134
Catalog products	152,750	137,619	15,131	336,460	323,690	12,770
Showroom products	10,650	11,191	(541)	35,163	38,903	(3,740)
Wholesale products	4,250	5,362	(1,112)	15,425	18,321	(2,896)
b. Less change in ending inventory	8,000	7,857	143	12,000	11,412	588
Gross profits	**147,950**	**153,881**	**5,931**	**368,877**	**360,877**	**(8,000)**
Variable expenses						
1. Advertising/marketing	1,563	4,641	(3,078)	5,352	16,431	(11,079)
2. Car delivery/travel	300	268	32	1,200	1,193	7
3. Catalog expense	60,000	54,852	5,148	189,600	172,263	17,337
4. Gross wages	10,560	10,560	0	38,400	38,400	0
5. Payroll expense	807	807	0	2,920	2,920	0
6. Shipping	1,200	1,732	(532)	4,800	5,591	(791)
7. Miscellaneious selling expense	1,500	1,328	172	6,000	4,460	1,540
8. Depreciation (showroom assets)	265	265	0	1,060	1,060	0
Fixed expenses						
1. Accounting and legal	480	450	30	1,920	2,035	(115)
2. Insurance + workers' comp	960	960	0	3,768	3,768	0
3. Rent	3,900	3,900	0	15,600	15,600	0
4. Repairs and maintenance	90	46	44	360	299	61
5. Guaranteed pay't (mgr. partner)	6,000	6,000	0	24,000	24,000	0
6. Supplies	900	500	400	3,600	2,770	830
7. Telephone	5,100	5,134	(34)	13,700	13,024	676
8. Utilities	870	673	197	3,480	2,447	1,033
9. Miscellaneous admin. expense	0	197	(197)	0	372	(372)
10. Depreciation (office equip)	450	450	0	1,800	1,800	0
Net income from operations	**53,005**	**61,118**	**8,113**	**51,317**	**52,444**	**1,127**
Interest income	0	0	0	0	0	0
Interest expense	3,858	3,858	0	14,300	14,300	0
Net profit (loss) before taxes	**49,147**	**57,260**	**8,113**	**37,017**	**38,144**	**1,127**
Taxes (partnership*)	0	0	0	0	0	0
(Partners taxed individually according to distributive shares of profit/loss)						
PARTNERSHIP: NET PROFIT (LOSS)	**49,147**	**57,260**	**8,113**	**37,017**	**38,144**	**1,127**

NON-INCOME STATEMENT ITEMS

1. Long-term asset repayments	0	0	0	0	0	0
2. Loan repayments	1,104	1,104	0	4,420	4,420	0
3. Equity withdrawals	0	0	0	0	0	0
4. Inventory assets	8,000	7,857	143	12,000	11,412	588

BUDGET DEVIATIONS

	This Quarter	Year-to-Date
1. Income statement Items:	$ 8,113	$ 1,127
2. Non-income statement items:	$ 143	$ 588
3. Total deviation	$ 8,256	$ 1,715
Cash Position Year-To-Date:	**Projected = $99,032**	**Actual = $100,747**

Three-Year Income Projection
Marine Art of California

Updated: September 26, 1998

	Nov-Dec 1998 Pre-Start-Up	YEAR 1 1999	YEAR 2 2000	YEAR 3 2001	TOTAL 3 YEARS
INCOME					
1. Sales/revenues	41,620	743,930	2,651,856	4,515,406	7,952,812
Catalog sales	33,820	672,925	2,570,200	4,421,500	7,698,445
Showroom sales	4,600	46,325	53,274	61,266	165,465
Wholesale sales	3,200	24,680	28,382	32,640	88,902
2. Cost of goods sold (c – d)	23,900	375,048	1,329,476	2,261,783	3,990,207
a. Beginning inventory	6,000	6,000	18,000	25,000	6,000
b. Purchases	23,900	387,048	1,336,476	2,268,783	4,016,207
Catalog	19,600	336,460	1,285,100	2,210,750	3,851,910
Showroom (walk-in)	2,300	35,163	33,637	37,633	108,733
Wholesale	2,000	15,425	17,739	20,400	55,564
c. C.O.G. avail. sale (a + b)	29,900	393,048	1,354,476	2,293,783	4,022,207
d. Less ending inventory (12/31)	6,000	18,000	25,000	32,000	32,000
3. Gross profit on sales (1 – 2)	17,720	368,882	1,322,380	2,253,623	3,962,605
EXPENSES					
1. Variable (selling) (a thru h)	38,146	249,332	734,263	1,316,291	2,338,032
a. Advertising/marketing	1,042	5,352	5,727	6,127	18,248
b. Car delivery/travel	200	1,200	1,284	1,374	4,058
c. Catalog expense	27,600	189,600	670,400	1,248,000	2,135,600
d. Gross wages	5,120	38,400	41,088	43,964	128,572
e. Payroll expenses	384	2,920	3,124	3,343	9,771
f. Shipping	800	4,800	5,280	5,808	16,688
g. Miscellaneous selling expenses	3,000	6,000	6,300	6,615	21,915
h. Depreciation (showroom assets)	0	1,060	1,060	1,060	3,180
2. Fixed (administrative) (a thru h)	12,139	68,228	71,609	75,268	227,244
a. Accounting and legal	820	1,920	2,054	2,198	6,992
b. Insurance + workers' comp	904	3,768	4,032	4,314	13,018
c. Rent	3,900	15,600	16,692	17,860	54,052
d. Repairs and maintenance	60	360	385	412	1,217
e. Guaranteed pay't (mgr. partner)	4,000	24,000	24,000	24,000	76,000
f. Supplies	600	3,600	3,852	4,123	12,175
g. Telephone	1,050	13,700	15,070	16,577	46,397
h. Utilities	630	3,480	3,724	3,984	11,818
i. Miscellaneous fixed expense	175	0	0	0	175
j. Depreciation (Office Assets)	0	1,800	1,800	1,800	5,400
Total operating expenses (1 + 2)	50,285	317,560	805,872	1,391,559	2,565,276
Net income operations (GPr – Exp)	(32,565)	51,322	516,508	862,064	1,397,329
Other income (interest income)	0	0	0	0	0
Other expense (interest expense)	1,192	14,300	13,814	13,274	42,580
Net profit (loss) for partnership	(33,757)	37,022	502,694	848,790	1,354,749
Taxes: (partnership)*	0	0	0	0	0
* (partners taxed individually according to	0	0	0	0	0
distributive shares of profit or loss)	0	0	0	0	0
PARTNERSHIP: NET PROFIT (LOSS)	(33,757)	37,022	502,694	848,790	1,354,749

Projected Balance Sheet

Business Name:

Marine Art of California

Date of Projection: September 30, 1998
Date Projected for: December 31, 1999

ASSETS			% of Assets
Current assets			
Cash	$	98,032	73.96%
Petty cash	$	1,000	0.75%
Sales tax holding account	$	4,067	3.07%
Accounts receivable	$	0	0.00%
Inventory	$	18,000	13.58%
Short-term investments	$	0	0.00%
Long-term investments	$	0	0.00%
Fixed assets			
Land (valued at cost)	$	0	0.00%
Buildings	$	0	0.00%
1. Cost 0			
2. Less acc. depr. 0			
Showroom improvements	$	4,240	3.20%
1. Cost 5,300			
2. Less acc. depr. 1,060			
Office improvements	$	4,160	3.14%
1. Cost 5,200			
2. Less acc. depr. 1,040			
Office equipment	$	3,040	2.29%
1. Cost 3,800			
2. Less acc. depr. 760			
Autos/vehicles	$	0	0.00%
1. Cost 0			
2. Less acc. depr. 0			
Other assets			
1.	$	0	0.00%
2.	$	0	0.00%
TOTAL ASSETS	$	132,539	100.00%

LIABILITIES			% of Liabilities
Current liabilities			
Accounts payable	$	0	0.00%
Notes payable	$	4,906	3.79%
Interest payable	$	0	0.00%
Taxes payable (partnership)			
Federal income tax	$	0	0.00%
Self-employment tax	$	0	0.00%
State income tax	$	0	0.00%
Sales tax accrual	$	4,067	3.15%
Property tax	$	0	0.00%
Payroll Accrual	$	0	0.00%
Long-term liabilities			
Notes payable to investors	$	120,306	93.06%
Notes payable others	$	0	0.00%
TOTAL LIABILITIES	$	129,279	100.00%

NET WORTH (EQUITY)			% of Net Worth
Proprietorship	$	0	0.00%
or			
Partnership			
1. Bob Garcia, 55% equity	$	1,793	55.00%
2. Ltd. Prtnrs., 45% equity	$	1,467	45.00%
or			
Corporation			
Capital stock	$	0	0.00%
Surplus paid in	$	0	0.00%
Retained earnings	$	0	0.00%
TOTAL NET WORTH	$	3,260	100.00%

Assets – Liabilities = Net Worth
and
Liabilities + Equity = Total Assets

1. See Financial Statement Analysis for ratios and notations.

Break-Even Analysis
Marine Art of California

Date of Analysis: September 29, 1998

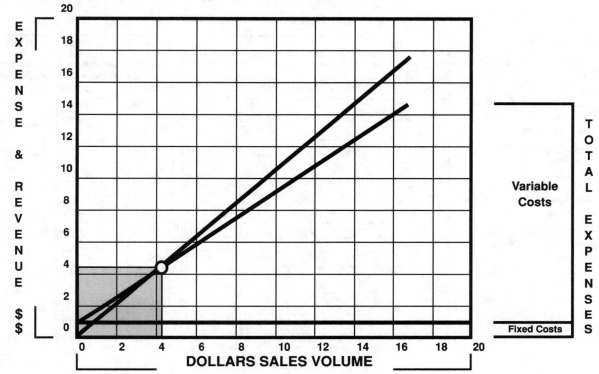

NOTE: Figures shown in 2 hundreds of thousands of dollars (Ex: 2 = $ 400,000)

Marine Art of California
Break-Even Point Calculation

B-E POINT (SALES) = Fixed costs + [(Variable costs/Est. revenues) X Sales]

B-E Point (Sales) = $ 181,282.00 + [($ 2,750,165.00 / $ 3,437,406.00) X Sales]

B-E Point (Sales) = $ 181,282.00 + [.8001 X Sales]

S - .8001S = $181,282.00   S - .8001S = $181,282.00   .19992S = $181,282.00

S = $181,282.00/.1999

Break-Even Point
S = $906,700*

*rounded figure

FC (Fixed costs)	= (Administrative expenses + Interest)	$	181,282
VC (Variable costs)	= (Cost of goods + Selling expenses)	$	2,750,165
R (Est. revenues)	= (Income from sale of products and services)	$	3,437,406
BREAK-EVEN POINT =		$	906,727

The financial figures below in no way represent an actual Profit & Loss Statement for Mr. Garcia's business. This statement is for illustrative purposes only and is an example of what "might have happened" during Marine Art of California's first year of business.

Profit and Loss (Income) Statement
Marine Art of California
Page 1 (January thru June + 6-Month Totals)

For the Year: 1999	Jan	Feb	Mar	Apr	May	Jun	6-MONTH TOTALS AMOUNT	% of Total Revenues PERCENT
INCOME								
1. Sales/revenues	21,073	17,916	40,640	31,408	66,858	50,034	227,929	100.00%
a. Catalog sales (60%-40%)	16,700	13,700	34,786	24,600	61,540	42,846	194,172	85.19%
b. Showroom sales (walk-in)	1,825	2,356	3,900	4,670	3,170	4,648	20,569	9.02%
c. Wholesale sales	2,548	1,860	1,954	2,138	2,148	2,540	13,188	5.79%
2. Cost of goods sold	10,622	9,960	22,799	16,417	35,137	25,580	120,515	52.87%
a. Beginning inventory	6,000	7,234	7,465	6,230	6,784	6,345	6,000	2.63%
b. Purchases	11,856	10,191	21,564	16,971	34,698	26,335	121,615	53.36%
(1) Catalog goods (50%)	8,350	6,850	17,393	12,300	30,770	21,423	97,086	42.59%
(2) Showroom (50%+$1Kp/m)	1,913	2,178	2,950	3,335	2,585	3,324	16,285	7.14%
(3) Wholesales (x.625)	1,593	1,163	1,221	1,336	1,343	1,588	8,244	3.62%
c. C.O.G. available for sale	17,856	17,425	29,029	23,201	41,482	32,680	127,615	55.99%
d. Less ending inventory	7,234	7,465	6,230	6,784	6,345	7,100	7,100	3.12%
3. Gross profit	10,451	7,956	17,841	14,991	31,721	24,454	107,414	47.13%
EXPENSES								
1. Variable (selling) expenses								
a. Advertising/marketing	836	836	836	1,547	1,547	1,547	7,149	3.14%
b. Car delivery/travel	94	126	78	83	112	97	590	0.26%
c. Catalog expense	9,600	10,770	10,770	11,960	11,960	11,960	67,020	29.40%
d. Gross wages	2,560	2,560	2,560	2,560	3,520	3,520	17,280	7.58%
e. Payroll expense	192	192	192	192	269	269	1,306	0.57%
f. Shipping	385	432	391	406	389	391	2,394	1.05%
g. Miscell. variable expenses	538	147	268	621	382	211	2,167	0.95%
h. Deprec. (showroom)	88	88	89	88	88	89	530	0.23%
Total variable expenses	14,293	15,151	15,184	17,457	18,267	18,084	98,436	43.19%
1. Fixed (admin) expenses								
a. Accounting and legal	150	150	150	385	150	150	1,135	0.50%
b. Insurance + workers' comp	302	302	302	302	320	320	1,848	0.81%
c. Rent	1,300	1,300	1,300	1,300	1,300	1,300	7,800	3.42%
d. Repairs and maintenance	0	12	56	0	0	72	140	0.06%
e. Guar. pay't (mgr. partner)	2,000	2,000	2,000	2,000	2,000	2,000	12,000	5.26%
f. Supplies	287	246	301	223	259	172	1,488	0.65%
g. Telephone	542	634	556	621	836	872	4,061	1.78%
h. Utilities	287	263	246	164	168	172	1,300	0.57%
i. Misc. fixed expenses	23	17	0	46	39	0	125	0.05%
j. Deprec. (office equip)	150	150	150	150	150	150	900	0.39%
Total fixed expenses	5,041	5,074	5,061	5,191	5,222	5,208	30,797	13.51%
Total operating expense	19,334	20,225	20,245	22,648	23,489	23,292	129,233	56.70%
Net income from operations	(8,883)	(12,269)	(2,404)	(7,657)	8,232	1,162	(21,819)	-9.57%
Other income (interest)	0	0	0	0	0	0	0	0.00%
Other expense (interest)	1,192	1,192	1,192	1,192	1,192	1,192	7,152	3.14%
Net profit (loss) before taxes	(10,075)	(13,461)	(3,596)	(8,849)	7,040	(30)	(28,971)	-12.71%
Taxes: partnership*	0	0	0	0	0	0	0	0.00%
*(partners taxed individually on	0	0	0	0	0	0	0	0.00%
distributive shares of profits)	0	0	0	0	0	0	0	0.00%
PARTNERSHIP: NET PROFIT (LOSS)	(10,075)	(13,461)	(3,596)	(8,849)	7,040	(30)	(28,971)	-12.71%

The financial figures below in no way represent an actual Profit & Loss Statement for Mr. Garcia's business. This statement is for illustrative purposes only and is an example of what "might have happened" during Marine Art of California's first year of business.

Profit and Loss (Income) Statement
Marine Art of California
Page 2 (July thru December + 12-Month Totals)

For the Year: 1999

	Jul	Aug	Sep	Oct	Nov	Dec	12-MONTH TOTALS AMOUNT	of Total Revenues PERCENT
INCOME								
1. Sales/revenues	81,092	57,014	64,148	67,684	127,390	105,122	730,379	100.00%
a. Catalog sales (60%-40%)	72,740	47,890	57,340	57,468	120,550	97,220	647,380	88.64%
b. Showroom sales (walk-in)	5,490	6,734	4,630	6,340	4,280	5,762	53,805	7.37%
c. Wholesale sales	2,862	2,390	2,178	3,876	2,560	2,140	29,194	4.00%
2. Cost of goods sold	41,819	28,641	32,212	33,942	63,689	48,684	369,502	50.59%
a. Beginning inventory	7,100	7,256	8,421	9,555	10,940	12,267	6,000	0.82%
b. Purchases	41,975	29,806	33,346	35,327	65,016	53,829	380,914	52.15%
(1) Catalog goods (50%)	36,370	23,945	28,670	28,734	60,275	48,610	323,690	44.32%
(2) Showroom (50%+$1Kp/m)	3,745	4,367	3,315	4,170	3,140	3,881	38,903	5.33%
(3) Wholesales (x.625)	1,860	1,494	1,361	2,423	1,601	1,338	18,321	2.51%
c. C.O.G. available for sale	49,075	37,062	41,767	44,882	75,956	66,096	386,914	52.97%
d. Less ending inventory	7,256	8,421	9,555	10,940	12,267	17,412	17,412	2.38%
3. Gross profit	39,273	28,373	31,936	33,742	63,701	56,438	360,877	49.41%
EXPENSES								
1. Variable (selling) expenses								
a. Advertising/marketing	1,547	1,547	1,547	1,547	1,547	1,547	16,431	2.25%
b. Car delivery/travel	136	107	92	96	84	88	1,193	0.16%
c. Catalog expense	15,125	17,633	17,633	18,284	18,284	18,284	172,263	23.59%
d. Gross wages	3,520	3,520	3,520	3,520	3,520	3,520	38,400	5.26%
e. Payroll expense	269	269	269	269	269	269	2,920	0.40%
f. Shipping	516	467	482	534	617	581	5,591	0.77%
g. Miscell. variable expenses	459	184	322	721	265	342	4,460	0.61%
h. Deprec. (showroom)	88	88	89	88	88	89	1,060	0.15%
Total variable expenses	21,660	23,815	23,954	25,059	24,674	24,720	242,318	33.18%
1. Fixed (admin) expenses								
a. Accounting and legal	150	150	150	150	150	150	2,035	0.28%
b. Insurance + workers' comp	320	320	320	320	320	320	3,768	0.52%
c. Rent	1,300	1,300	1,300	1,300	1,300	1,300	15,600	2.14%
d. Repairs and maintenance	0	0	113	46	0	0	299	0.04%
e. Guar. pay't (mgr. partner)	2,000	2,000	2,000	2,000	2,000	2,000	24,000	3.29%
f. Supplies	164	231	387	143	164	193	2,770	0.38%
g. Telephone	1,164	1,287	1,378	1,422	1,943	1,769	13,024	1.78%
h. Utilities	159	148	167	193	217	263	2,447	0.34%
i. Misc. fixed expenses	41	9	0	22	0	175	372	0.05%
j. Deprec. (office equip)	150	150	150	150	150	150	1,800	0.25%
Total fixed expenses	5,448	5,595	5,965	5,746	6,244	6,320	66,115	9.05%
Total operating expense	27,108	29,410	29,919	30,805	30,918	31,040	308,433	42.23%
Net income from operations	12,165	(1,037)	2,017	2,937	32,783	25,398	52,444	7.18%
Other income (interest)	0	0	0	0	0	0	0	0.00%
Other expense (interest)	1,192	1,192	1,192	1,192	1,190	1,190	14,300	1.96%
Net profit (loss) before taxes	10,973	(2,229)	825	1,745	31,593	24,208	38,144	5.22%
Taxes: partnership*	0	0	0	0	0	0	0	0.00%
*(partners taxed individually on	0	0	0	0	0	0	0	0.00%
distributive shares of profits)	0	0	0	0	0	0	0	0.00%
PARTNERSHIP: NET PROFIT (LOSS)	10,973	(2,229)	825	1,745	31,593	24,208	38,144	5.22%

The financial figures below in no way represent an actual Profit & Loss Statement for Mr. Garcia's business.

This statement is for illustrative purposes only and is an example of what "might have happened" during Marine Art of California's first year of business.

Profit & Loss (Income) Statement
Marine Art of California

Beginning: January 1, 1999   **Ending: December 31, 1999**

			% Total Revenues
INCOME			
1. Sales revenues		$ 730,379	100.00%
a. Catalog sales (60%-40%)	647,380		88.64%
b. Showroom sales (walk-in)	53,805		7.37%
c. Wholesale sales	29,194		4.00%
2. Cost of goods sold (c-d)		369,502	50.59%
a. Beginning inventory	6,000		0.82%
b. Purchases	380,914		52.15%
(1) Catalog goods (50%)	323,690		44.32%
(2) Showroom (50%+$1K p/m)	38,903		5.33%
(3) Wholesale (x .625)	18,321		2.51%
c. C.O.G. avail. sale (a+b)	386,914		52.97%
d. Less ending inventory (12/31)	17,412		2.38%
3. Gross profit on sales (1 – 2)		$ 360,877	49.41%
EXPENSES			
1. Variable (selling) (a thru I)		242,318	33.18%
a. Advertising/marketing	16,431		2.25%
b. Car delivery/travel	1,193		0.16%
c. Catalog expense	172,263		23.59%
d. Gross wages	38,400		5.26%
e. Payroll expense	2,920		0.40%
f. Shipping	5,591		0.77%
g. Misc. variable selling expense	4,460		0.61%
h. Depreciation (showroom)	1,060		0.15%
2. Fixed (administrative) (a thru I)		66,115	9.05%
a. Accounting and legal	2,035		0.28%
b. Insurance and workers' comp	3,768		0.52%
c. Rent	15,600		2.14%
d. Repairs and maintenance	299		0.04%
e. Guaranteed payment (mgr. partner)	24,000		3.29%
f. Supplies	2,770		0.38%
g. Telephone	13,024		1.78%
h. Utilities	2,447		0.34%
i. Misc. fixed (admin) expenses	372		0.05%
j. Depreciation (administrative assets)	1,800		0.25%
Total operating expenses (1 + 2)		308,433	42.23%
Net income from operations (GP – Exp)		$ 52,444	7.18%
Other income (interest income)	0		0.00%
Other expense (interest expense)	14,300		1.96%
Net profit (loss) before taxes		$ 38,144	5.22%
Taxes: partnership*	0		0.00%
* (partners taxed individually on distributive	0	0	0.00%
shares of profits or losses)	0		0.00%
PARTNERSHIP: NET PROFIT (LOSS)		$ 38,144	5.22%

Balance Sheet

Business Name:

Marine Art of California   Date: December 31, 1999

ASSETS			% of Assets
Current assets			
Cash	$	100,102	75.43%
Petty cash	$	645	0.49%
Sales tax holding account	$	3,107	2.34%
Accounts receivable	$	0	0.00%
Inventory	$	17,412	13.12%
Short-term investments	$	0	0.00%
Long-term investments	$	0	0.00%
Fixed assets			
Land (valued at cost)	$	0	0.00%
Buildings	$	0	0.00%
1. Cost	0		
2. Less acc. depr.	0		
Showroom improvements	$	4,240	3.20%
1. Cost	5,300		
2. Less acc. depr.	1,060		
Office improvements	$	4,160	3.13%
1. Cost	5,200		
2. Less acc. depr.	1,040		
Office equipment	$	3,040	2.29%
1. Cost	3,800		
2. Less acc. depr.	760		
Autos/vehicles	$	0	0.00%
1. Cost	0		
2. Less acc. depr.	0		
Other assets			
1.	$	0	0.00%
2.	$	0	0.00%
TOTAL ASSETS	$	132,706	100.00%

LIABILITIES			% of Liabilities
Current liabilities			
Accounts payable	$	0	0.00%
Notes payable	$	4,906	3.82%
Interest payable	$	0	0.00%
Taxes payable			
Federal income tax	$	0	0.00%
Self-employment tax	$	0	0.00%
State income tax	$	0	0.00%
Sales tax accrual	$	3,107	2.42%
Property tax	$	0	0.00%
Payroll accrual	$	0	0.00%
Long-term liabilities			
Notes payable to investors	$	120,306	93.76%
Notes payable others	$	0	0.00%
TOTAL LIABILITIES	$	128,319	100.00%

NET WORTH (EQUITY)			% of Net Worth
Proprietorship	$	0	0.00%
or			
Partnership			
1. Bob Garcia, 55% equity	$	2,413	55.00%
2. Ltd. Prtnrs., 45% equity	$	1,974	45.00%
or			
Corporation			
Capital stock	$	0	0.00%
Surplus paid in	$	0	0.00%
Retained earnings	$	0	0.00%
TOTAL NET WORTH	$	4,387	100.00%

Assets - Liabilities = Net Worth
and
Liabilities + Equity = Total Assets

Financial Statement Analysis Summary

The following is a summary of the1999 financial statement analysis information developed on the next five pages of spreadsheets (pages 33-37):

*Writer must research industry forstandards.

1999	PROJECTED	ACTUAL	INDUSTRY* STANDARD
1. Net working capital	$112,126	$113,253	$100,000 +
2. Current ratio	13.5	15.1	2.0 +
3. Quick ratio	11.5	13.0	1.0 +
4. Gross profit margin	49.60%	49.4%	45.0%
5. Operating profit margin	6.9%	7.2%	6.8%
6. Net profit margin	5.0%	5.2%	12.4%
7. Debt to assets	97.5%	96.7%	33.0%
8. Debt to equity	39.7:1	29.3:1	1.0:1 +
9. ROI (return on investment)	28.0%	28.7%	11% +
10. Vertical income statement analysis **			
Sales/revenues	100.0%	100.0%	
Cost of goods	50.4%	50.6%	50.0% -
Gross profit	49.6%	49.4%	40.0% +
Operating expense	42.7%	42.2%	35.0% +
Net income operations	6.9%	7.2%	15.0% +
Interest income	0/0%	0.0%	N/A
Interest expense	1.9%	2.0%	Variable
Net profit (pre-tax)	5.0%	5.2%	10.0% +
** All items stated as % of total revenues			
11. Vertical balance sheet analysis ***			
Current assets	91.2%	91.4%	85.0%
Inventory	13.6%	13.1%	28.0%
Total assets	3.7%	96.7%	
Current liabilities	3.7%	3.7%	20.0% -
Total liabilities	97.5%	96.7%	
Net worth	2.5%	3.3%	50.0% +
Total liabilities + Net worth	100.0%	100.0%	

*** All Asset items stated as % of Total Assets;
    Liability & Net Worth items stated as % of Total Liabilities + Net Worth

Notes:

Marine Art of California has an excessively high debt ratio (96.7%). However, the company has survived the first year of business, maintained its cash flow ($100,000+), and returned a higher amount than originally promised to its investors. Sales for the first year were less than projected (-2%), but the net profit was still in excess of projections by 0.2%. Good management of the company by Mr. Garcia + a timely product with a solid niche would seem to be a good indicator that this company's profits will continue to increase rapidly and that the company will be more than able to fulfill its obligations to its limited partners/investors.

Financial Statement Analysis
Marine Art of California

For the Year: 1999

Type of Analysis	Formula	Projected: Year 1		Historical: Year 1	
1. Liquidity Analysis	**Balance Sheet**	Current Assets	121,099	Current Assets	121,266
	Current Assets	Current Liabilities	8,973	Current Liabilities	8,013
a. Net Working Capital	— Current Liabilities	**Net Working Capital**	**$112,126**	**Net Working Capital**	**$113,253**
	Balance Sheet	Current Assets	121,099	Current Assets	121,266
b. Current Ratio	Current Assets	Current Liabilities	8,973	Current Liabilities	8,013
	Current Liabilities	**Current Ratio**	**13.50**	**Current Ratio**	**15.13**
	Balance Sheet	Current Assets	121,099	Current Assets	121,266
c. Quick Ratio	Current Assets minus Inventory	Inventory	18,000	Inventory	17,412
	Current Liabilities	Current Liabilities	8,973	Current Liabilities	8,013
		Quick Ratio	**11.49**	**Quick Ratio**	**12.96**
2. Profitability Analysis	**Income Statement**	Gross Profits	368,882	Gross Profits	360,877
a. Gross Profit Margin	Gross Profits	Sales	743,930	Sales	730,379
	Sales	**Gross Profit Margin**	**49.59%**	**Gross Profit Margin**	**49.41%**
b. Operating Profit Margin	Income from Operations	Income From Ops.	51,322	Income From Ops.	52,444
	Sales	Sales	743,930	Sales	730,379
		Op. Profit Margin	**6.90%**	**Op. Profit argin**	**7.18%**
c. Net Profit Margin	Net Profits	Net Profits	37,022	Net Profits	38,144
	Sales	Sales	743,930	Sales	730,379
		Net Profit Margin	**4.98%**	**Net Profit Margin**	**5.22%**
4. Debt Ratios	**Balance Sheet**	Total Liabilities	129,279	Total Liabilities	128,319
	Total Liabilities	Total Assets	132,539	Total Assets	132,706
a. Debt to Assets	Total Assets	**Debt to Assets Ratio**	**97.54%**	**Debt to Assets Ratio**	**96.69%**
	Total Liabilities	Total Liabilities	129,279	Total Liabilities	128,319
b. Debt to Equity	Total Owners' Equity	Total Owners' Equity	3,260	Total Owners' Equity	4,387
		Debt to Equity Ratio	**3965.61%**	**Debt to Equity Ratio**	**2924.98%**
4. Measures of Investment	**Balance Sheet**	Net Profits	37,022	Net Profits	38,144
a. ROI	Net Profits	Total Assets	132,539	Total Assets	132,706
(Return on Investment)	Total Assets	**ROI (Ret. on Invest.)**	**27.93%**	**ROI (Ret. on Invest.)**	**28.74%**
5. Vertical Financial Statement Analysis	**Balance Sheet** 1. Each asset % of Total Assets 2. Liability & Equity % of Total L&E **Income Statement** 3. All items % of Total Revenues	**NOTE:** *See Attached* **Balance Sheet and** **Income Statement**		**NOTE:** *See Attached* **Balance Sheet and** **Income Statement**	
6. Horizontal Financial Statement Analysis	**Balance Sheet** 1. Assets, Liab & Equity measured against 2nd year. Increases and decreases stated as amount & % **Income Statement** 2. Revenues & Expenses measured against 2nd year. Increases and decreases stated as amount & %	**NOTE:** **Horizontal Analysis** **Not Applicable** **Only one year in business**		**NOTE:** **Horizontal Analysis** **Not Applicable** **Only one year in business**	

33

The financial figures below in no way represent an actual Profit & Loss (Income) Statement for Mr. Garcia's business.
This statement is for illustrative purposes only and is an example of what "might have happened" during Marine Art of California's first year of business.

Vertical Income Statement Analysis
Marine Art of California

Historical For the Year: 1999		Begin: January 1, 1999 End: December 31, 1999	

	AMOUNT		% Total Revenues
INCOME			
1. Sales/revenues		$ 730,379	100.00%
a. Catalog sales	647,380		88.64%
b. Showroom sales	53,805		7.37%
c. Wholesale sales	29,194		4.00%
2. Cost of goods sold (c – d)		369,502	50.59%
a. Beginning inventory	6,000		0.82%
b. Purchases	380,914		52.15%
(1) Catalog products	323,690		44.32%
(2) Showroom (walk-in) products	38,903		5.33%
(3) Wholesale products	18,321		2.51%
c. C.O.G. avail. sale (a+b)	386,914		52.97%
d. Less ending inventory (12/31)	17,412		2.38%
3. Gross profit on sales (1 – 2)		$ 360,877	49.41%
EXPENSES			
1. Variable (selling) (a thru l)		242,318	33.18%
a. Advertising/marketing	16,431		2.25%
b. Car delivery/travel	1,193		0.16%
c. Catalog expense	172,263		23.59%
d. Gross wages	38,400		5.26%
e. Payroll expense	2,920		0.40%
f. Shipping	5,591		0.77%
g. Miscellaneous variable selling expense	4,460		0.61%
h. Depreciation (prod/serv assets)	1,060		0.15%
2. Fixed (administrative) (a thru l)		66,115	9.05%
a. Accounting and legal	2,035		0.28%
b. Insurance and workers' comp	3,768		0.52%
c. Rent	15,600		2.14%
d. Repairs and maintenance	299		0.04%
e. Guaranteed payment (mgr. partner)	24,000		3.29%
f. Supplies	2,770		0.38%
g. Telephone	13,024		1.78%
h. Utilities	2,447		0.34%
i. Miscellaneous fixed (admin) expenses	372		0.05%
j. Depreciation (administrative assets)	1,800		0.25%
Total operating expenses (1 + 2)		308,433	42.23%
Net income from operations (GP – Exp)		$ 52,444	7.18%
Other income (interest income)	0		0.00%
Other expense (interest expense)	14,300		1.96%
Net profit (loss) before taxes		$ 38,144	5.22%
Taxes: (partnership)			
	0		0.00%
* (partners taxed individually according to	0	0	0.00%
distributive shares of profit or loss)	0		0.00%
PARTNERSHIP: NET PROFIT (LOSS)		$ 38,144	5.22%

This financial statement is for illustrative purposes only and the figures in no way represent an actual Balance Sheet for Mr. Garcia's business. The example below represents a "possible scenario" for the asset, liability, and net worth positions of Marine Art of California after one year of business.

Vertical Balance Sheet Analysis

(All Asset %'s represent % of Total Assets; All Liability or Equity %'s represent % of Total Liabilities + Total Equity)

Analysis of Historical Balance Sheet	Date of Balance Sheet: December 31, 1999

Marine Art of California

ASSETS			% of Total Assets	LIABILITIES			% of Total L + NW
Current assets				**Current liabilities**			
Cash	$	100,102	75.43%	Accounts payable	$	0	0.00%
Petty cash	$	645	0.49%	Notes payable	$	4,906	3.70%
Sales tax holding account	$	3,107	2.34%	Interest payable	$	0	0.00%
Accounts receivable	$	0	0.00%				
Inventory	$	17,412	13.12%	Taxes payable			
Short-term investments	$	0	0.00%	Federal income tax	$	0	0.00%
				Self-employment tax	$	0	0.00%
Long-term investments	$	0	0.00%	State income tax	$	0	0.00%
				Sales tax accrual	$	3,107	2.34%
Fixed assets				Property tax	$	0	0.00%
Land (valued at cost)	$	0	0.00%				
				Payroll accrual	$	0	0.00%
Buildings	$	0	0.00%				
1. Cost	0			**Long-term liabilities**			
2. Less acc. depr.	0			Notes payable to investors	$	120,306	90.66%
				Notes payable others	$	0	0.00%
Showroom improvements	$	4,240	3.20%				
1. Cost	5,300			**TOTAL LIABILITIES**	$	128,319	96.69%
2. Less acc. depr.	1,060						
Office improvements	$	4,160	3.13%				
1. Cost	5,200						
2. Less acc. depr.	1,040			**NET WORTH (EQUITY)**			
Office equipment	$	3,040	2.29%				
1. Cost	3,800			**Proprietorship**	$	0	0.00%
2. Less acc. depr.	760			or			
				Partnership			
Autos/vehicles	$	0	0.00%	1. Bob Garcia, 55% equity	$	2,413	1.82%
1. Cost	0			2. Ltd. Prtnrs., 45% equity	$	1,974	1.49%
2. Less acc. depr.	0			or			
				Corporation			
				Capital stock	$	0	0.00%
Other assets				Surplus paid in	$	0	0.00%
1.	$	0	0.00%	Retained earnings	$	0	0.00%
2.	$	0	0.00%				
				TOTAL NET WORTH	$	4,387	3.31%
TOTAL ASSETS	$	132,706	100.00%	**LIABILITIES + NET WORTH**	$	132,706	100.00%

Assets – Liabilities = Net Worth -or- Liabilities + Equity = Assets

Projected Vertical Income Statement Analysis

(Percentages for all categories are in terms of % of Total Sales/Revenues)

Marine Art of California

Projections For Years Ended: 12/31/98 12/31/99 12/31/00 + 1992-2000 Combined Analysis

	Pre-Start-Up: 1998		Year 1: 1999		Year 2: 2000		Total: 2 Yrs. + Pre-Start-Up	
	AMOUNT	%	AMOUNT	%	AMOUNT	%	AMOUNT	%
INCOME								
1. Sales/revenues	41,620	100.00%	743,930	100.00%	2,651,856	100.00%	3,437,406	100.00%
a. Catalog sales	33,820	81.26%	672,925	90.46%	2,570,200	96.92%	3,276,945	95.33%
b. Showroom sales	4,600	11.05%	46,325	6.23%	53,274	2.01%	104,199	3.03%
c. Wholesale sales	3,200	7.69%	24,680	3.32%	28,382	1.07%	56,262	1.64%
2. Cost of goods sold (c – d)	23,900	57.42%	375,048	50.41%	1,329,476	50.13%	1,728,424	50.28%
a. Beginning inventory	6,000	14.42%	6,000	0.81%	18,000	0.68%	6,000	0.17%
b. Purchases	23,900	57.42%	387,048	52.03%	1,336,476	50.40%	1,747,424	50.84%
(1) Catalog products	19,600	47.09%	336,460	45.23%	1,285,100	48.46%	1,641,160	47.74%
(2) Showroom (walk-In)	2,300	5.53%	35,163	4.73%	33,637	1.27%	71,100	2.07%
(3) Wholesale products	2,000	4.81%	15,425	2.07%	17,739	0.67%	35,164	1.02%
c. C.O.G. avail. sale (a+b)	29,900	71.84%	393,048	52.83%	1,354,476	51.08%	1,753,424	51.01%
d. Less ending inventory (12/31)	6,000	14.42%	18,000	2.42%	25,000	0.94%	25,000	0.73%
3. Gross profit on sales (1 – 2)	17,720	42.58%	368,882	49.59%	1,322,380	49.87%	1,708,982	49.72%
EXPENSES								
1. Variable (selling) (a thru h)	38,146	91.65%	249,332	33.52%	734,263	27.69%	1,021,741	29.72%
a. Advertising/marketing	1,042	2.50%	5,352	0.72%	5,727	0.22%	12,121	0.35%
b. Car delivery/travel	200	0.48%	1,200	0.16%	1,284	0.05%	2,684	0.08%
c. Catalog expense	27,600	66.31%	189,600	25.49%	670,400	25.28%	887,600	25.82%
d. Gross wages	5,120	12.30%	38,400	5.16%	41,088	1.55%	84,608	2.46%
e. Payroll expense	384	0.92%	2,920	0.39%	3,124	0.12%	6,428	0.19%
f. Shipping	800	1.92%	4,800	0.65%	5,280	0.20%	10,880	0.32%
g. Miscellaneous selling expense	3,000	7.21%	6,000	0.81%	6,300	0.24%	15,300	0.45%
h. Depreciation (showroom assets)	0	0.00%	1,060	0.14%	1,060	0.04%	2,120	0.06%
2. Fixed (administrative) (a thru h)	12,139	29.17%	68,228	9.17%	71,609	2.70%	151,976	4.42%
a. Accounting and legal	820	1.97%	1,920	0.26%	2,054	0.08%	4,794	0.14%
b. Insurance + workers' comp	904	2.17%	3,768	0.51%	4,032	0.15%	8,704	0.25%
c. Rent	3,900	9.37%	15,600	2.10%	16,692	0.63%	36,192	1.05%
d. Repairs and maintenance	60	0.14%	360	0.05%	385	0.01%	805	0.02%
e. Guar. payment (mgr. partner)	4,000	9.61%	24,000	3.23%	24,000	0.91%	52,000	1.51%
f. Supplies	600	1.44%	3,600	0.48%	3,852	0.15%	8,052	0.23%
g. Telephone	1,050	2.52%	13,700	1.84%	15,070	0.57%	29,820	0.87%
h. Utilities	630	1.51%	3,480	0.47%	3,724	0.14%	7,834	0.23%
i. Misc. fixed expenses	175	0.42%	0	0.00%	0	0.00%	175	0.01%
j. Depreciation (office assets)	0	0.00%	1,800	0.24%	1,800	0.07%	3,600	0.10%
Total operating expenses (1 + 2)	50,285	120.82%	317,560	42.69%	805,872	30.39%	1,173,717	34.15%
Net income operations (GPr – Exp)	(32,565)	-78.24%	51,322	6.90%	516,508	19.48%	535,265	15.57%
Other income (interest income)	0	0.00%	0	0.00%	0	0.00%	0	0.00%
Other expense (interest expense)	1,192	2.86%	14,300	1.92%	13,814	0.52%	29,306	0.85%
Net profit (loss) before taxes	(33,757)	-81.11%	37,022	4.98%	502,694	18.96%	505,959	14.72%
Taxes: (partnership)	0	0.00%	0	0.00%	0	0.00%	0	0.00%
* (partners taxed individually according	0	0.00%	0	0.00%	0	0.00%	0	0.00%
to distributive shares of profit or loss)	0	0.00%	0	0.00%	0	0.00%	0	0.00%
PARTNERSHIP: NET PROFIT (LOSS)	(33,757)	-81.11%	37,022	4.98%	502,694	18.96%	505,959	14.72%

Projected Vertical Balance Sheet Analysis

(All Asset %'s represent % of Total Assets; All Liability or Equity %'s represent % of Total Liabilities + Total Equity)

Date Projected for : December 31, 1999	Date of Projection : September 30, 1998

Marine Art of California

ASSETS			% of Total Assets	LIABILITIES			% of Total L + NW
Current assets				**Current liabilities**			
Cash	$	98,032	73.96%	Accounts payable	$	0	0.00%
Petty cash	$	1,000	0.75%	Notes payable	$	4,906	3.70%
Sales tax holding account	$	4,067	3.07%	Interest payable	$	0	0.00%
Accounts receivable	$	0	0.00%				
Inventory	$	18,000	13.58%	Taxes payable			
Short-term investments	$	0	0.00%	Federal income tax	$	0	0.00%
				Self-employment tax	$	0	0.00%
Long-term investments	$	0	0.00%	State income tax	$	0	0.00%
				Sales tax accrual	$	4,067	3.07%
Fixed assets				Property tax	$	0	0.00%
Land (valued at cost)	$	0	0.00%				
				Payroll accrual	$	0	0.00%
Buildings	$	0	0.00%				
1. Cost	0			**Long-term liabilities**			
2. Less acc. depr.	0			Notes payable to investors	$	120,306	90.77%
				Notes payable others	$	0	0.00%
Showroom improvements	$	4,240	3.20%				
1. Cost	5,300			**TOTAL LIABILITIES**	$	129,279	97.54%
2. Less acc. depr.	1,060						
Office improvements	$	4,160	3.14%				
1. Cost	5,200						
2. Less acc. depr.	1,040			**NET WORTH (EQUITY)**			
Office equipment	$	3,040	2.29%	**Proprietorship**	$	0	0.00%
1. Cost	3,800			or			
2. Less acc. depr.	760			**Partnership**			
				1. Bob Garcia, 55% equity	$	1,793	1.35%
Autos/vehicles	$	0	0.00%	2. Ltd. Prtnrs., 45% equity	$	1,467	1.11%
1. Cost	0			or			
2. Less acc. depr.	0			**Corporation**			
				Capital Stock	$	0	0.00%
				Surplus Paid In	$	0	0.00%
Other assets				Retained Earnings	$	0	0.00%
1.	$	0	0.00%				
2.	$	0	0.00%	**TOTAL NET WORTH**	$	3,260	2.46%

TOTAL ASSETS	$	132,539	100.00%	**LIABILITIES + NET WORTH**	$	132,539	100.00%

Assets - Liabilities = Net Worth -or- Liabilities + Equity = Assets

IV. SUPPORTING DOCUMENTS
Marine Art of California

Personal Resume

Letter of Reference

Proposal for Limited Partnership

Catalog Cost Analysis

Competition Comparison Analysis

Terms & Conditions for Participants

Robert A. Garcia

P.O. Box 10059-251   (714) 722-6478
Newport Beach CA 92658

Manufacturing Management

Record of accomplishments in 12+ years in manufacturing and distribution. Experience in start-up and turn-around operations. In-depth understanding of multi-facility high-tech production systems/methods. Strengths in project management, problem solving, and coordinating/managing critical manufacturing functions: purchasing, engineering, inventory control, tracking, scheduling, and quality assurance developed with General Dynamics.

PROFILE

Hands-on management style: coordinated five support groups in Arizona, Arkansas, and California facilities in production of 57 complex assemblies, each having up to 100 components per circuit board.

Experience in product development for target markets; multi-product experience.

Set priorities, provided clear direction, energized others, got positive results.

Enthusiastic rapport builder, analytical self-starter, persistent, persuasive.

ACHIEVEMENT OVERVIEW

Turnaround Operations

Production of systems seven months behind schedule, inventory control unreliable, purchasing not aggressively seeking critical components from vendors.

- Procured materials for electronic circuit card assemblies in support of off-site and final assembly of missile systems.
- Created, along with other members of special task team, procedures and internal tracking system to show how specific part shortages would impact production schedules up to six months ahead.
- Chaired weekly inventory status meetings with Purchasing and Quality Assurance representatives.
- Supervised five analysts.
- Coordinated sub-assembly activities between offsite facilities in Arizona and Arkansas and final assembly in California in order to deliver product to customers against tight time constraints.
- Trained new hires.
- Provided data analysis to upper management for review.

Results Achieved: Corrected inventory accuracy from 70% to 97% within nine months.

cont. next page

Robert A. Garcia Page 2

Start-up Production/Distribution—Part Time Operation (secondary income)

- Researched market, found great potential for product, Bonsai trees.
- Studied plant propagation methods, built large greenhouse, implemented methods learned, marketed product.
- Participated in various home and garden shows, county fairs, three major shows/year.
- Employed staff of 8, wholesaled products to nurseries in LA and Orange Counties.

Results Achieved: Grew and operated business successfully for eight years, increased net profit from $4,500 to $12,000 within four years.

CAREER HISTORY

Freelance Photography/Marine Art of California *Owner/President*	1992–Current
Sea Fantasies Gallery *Store Manager*	1991–1992
General Dynamics Corporation *Manufacturing Coordinator*	1980–1989
Casa Vallarta Restaurant *Controller (part-time)*	1986–1987
B & D Nursery (secondary income) *Operations Manager*	1973–1981
Stater Bros. Markets *Journeyman Clerk*	1969–1980

EDUCATION

Completed course work in History, California State Polytechnic University. Independent studies in Psychology of Supervision, Written Communication

AFFILIATIONS/INTERESTS

Coordinator on Service Board for Orange County
Alanon and Alateen Family Groups, 1988–1990

Regularly cast in musical productions.
Have appeared at Orange County Performing Arts Center and Fullerton Civic Light Opera.

Powell and Associates
Marketing Consultants

1215 West Imperial Highway - Suite 103 - Brea, CA 92621 Keith Powell - President Tel: (714) 680-8306

Dear Prospective Investor:

It is indeed a pleasure to write a reference letter for Bob A. Garcia.

I have known Bob over the past five years and have found him to be an extremely creative and enthusiastic individual. I have been associated with Bob through several community and civic organizations for which he is an active participant. He has also held office in several of these organizations and has always fulfilled his duties with aplomb.

Bob approached me well over a year ago to meet with him on a regular basis to become a "mentor" of a then dream, now a reality, his company MARINE ART OF CALIFORNIA. Along with several other mentors that he has been seeking advice from, I have had the privilege of reviewing, commenting and assisting in the development of his plan. He has evidenced great discipline, follow through, creativity and a willingness to do his homework on this business venture.

I would most highly recommend he be given the consideration he seeks. Bob has evidenced the qualities needed to succeed in any business venture, that of commitment, dedication, optimism and follow through.

If you have any further questions, please do not hesitate to contact me. My direct line is 714-680-8306.

Cordially,

Keith P. Powell
President

PROPOSAL FOR LIMITED PARTNERSHIP

Borrow $130,000.00 from private investors as limited partners as outlined:

$130,000.00 = 45% of Marine Art of California

$130,000.00 = 20 shares @ $6,500.00 each

1 share = 2.25% of Marine Art of California

Limited Partners will own 2.25% of the business for each $6,500.00 invested. The investment will be treated as a loan and paid back at 11% interest over 15 years at $78.00 per month per shareholder.

1 share = $78.00 per month for 15 years

20 shares = $1560.00 per month

The General Partner, Robert A. Garcia, will own 55% of the business. The Limited Partners will own 45% of the business for the duration of the partnership.

The duration of the partnership is four years. The General Partner will have the option of buying out the Limited Partners at the end of four years for $3,250.00 for each 2.25% interest. The buyout will not affect the outstanding loan, but the General Partner will provide collateral equal to the loan balance. The value of inventory will be used as that collateral.

Return On Investment (ROI) for each $6,500.00 share:

A.
Principal (15 years)		Interest (15 years)		Buy-out (4 years)		Total (15 years)
$6,500.00	+	$7,540.00	+	$3,250.00	=	$17,290.00

B. PROJECTED Annual Profits (Loss) for 1 share (2.25%):

1998	1999	2000	2001		4 Year Total
($759.53)	$833.00	$11,310.62	$19,097.78	=	$30,481.87

- Principal and Interest (15 years) $14,040.00
- Buy-Out (4 years) $ 3,250.00
- Projected Profits/loss (4 years) $30,481.87

Total Projected Return on Investment   **$47,771.87**

or

$$\frac{\textbf{Net Profits}}{\textbf{Assets}} = \frac{\$41,271}{\$6,500} = 635\%$$

Contract Highlights:

1. **1st Right of Refusal:** Limited Partners agree to extend the 1st Right of Refusal to the General Partner, Robert A. Garcia in the event the Limited Partner desires to sell, grant, or trade his share of the business.

2. **Key Man Insurance:** A Life Insurance Policy valued at $250,000.00 shall be taken out on General Partner, Robert A. Garcia, which is approximately double the amount of the $130,000.00 loan needed. In the event of the death of Robert A Garcia, the payments of the full policy amount will be divided among the Limited Partners equal to the amount invested (e.g. 2.25% investment would equal a 1/20th layout of $12,500.00)

3. **Limited Partner Purchase Program**: General Partner, Robert A. Garcia, agrees to grant **at cost buying privileges** on all product line items for the purchase of 3 or more shares. For 1–2 shares, a 45% discount shall be extended. These shall be in effect for the life of the Limited Partnership Contract (minimum four years before exercising buyout option). For remainder of the loan contract, (two years) a discount of 35% off retail price will be extended. At the completion of the loan repayment, a **Lifetime Discount of 20%** off retail will be extended to Limited Partners. These privileges are non-transferable.

43

Catalog Cost Analysis

PRINTING QUANTITY	20,000	30,000	40,000	50,000	60,000
CATALOG ITEMS					
24-page: Price per 1000	521.37	413.92	360.07	336.11	306.49
Weight - 2.208 OZ.					
Extended cost	10,427.40	12,417.60	14,402.80	16,305.50	18,389.40
Prep and delivery	756.00	970.00	1,235.00	1,500.00	1,765.00
Mail list costs - $50.00 per/1000	1,000.00	1,500.00	2,000.00	2,500.00	3,000.00
Postage - $170 per/1000	3,200.00	4,800.00	6,400.00	8,000.00	9,600.00
Film separations - $64 per/page	3,600.00	2,500.00	2,500.00	2,500.00	2,500.00
Art work	1,000.00	1,000.00	1,000.00	1,000.00	1,000.00
TOTAL COSTS	**19,983.40**	**23,187.60**	**27,537.80**	**31,805.50**	**36,254.40**
Rounded numbers	20,000.00	23,200.00	27,600.00	32,000.00	36,500.00
Unit costs	1.00	0.77	0.69	0.64	0.61
Costs per page	0.04	0.03	0.03	0.03	0.03
Costs per/1000	999.17	772.92	688.44	636.11	604.24

PRINTING QUANTITY	70,000	80,000	90,000	100,000	
CATALOG ITEMS					
24-page: Price per 1000	291.72	280.29	268.85	261.00	
Weight - 2.208 OZ.					
Extended cost	20,420.40	22,423.20	24,196.50	26,100.00	
Prep and delivery	2,030.00	2,295.00	2,560.00	2,825.00	
Mail list costs - $50.00 per/1000	3,500.00	4,000.00	4,500.00	5,000.00	
Postage - $170 per/1000	11,900.00	13,600.00	15,300.00	17,000.00	
Film separations - $64 per/page	2,500.00	2,500.00	2,500.00	2,500.00	
Art work	1,000.00	1,000.00	1,000.00	1,000.00	
TOTAL COSTS	**41,350.40**	**45,818.20**	**50,056.50**	**54,425.00**	
Rounded numbers	41,500.00	46,000.00	50,500.00	55,000.00	
Unit costs	0.59	0.57	0.56	0.54	
Costs per page	0.02	0.02	0.02	0.02	
Costs per/1000	590.72	572.73	556.18	544.25	

FOREIGN PRINTING QUANTITY	40,000.00	50,000.00	60,000.00	70,000.00	
NOTE: 20% will be deducted for foreign printing. Prices are reflected in Profit Analysis	27,600.00	32,000.00	36,500.00	41,500.00	
	0.80	0.80	0.80	0.80	
FOREIGN PRINTING COSTS	**22,080.00**	**25,600.00**	**29,200.00**	**33,200.00**	

FOREIGN PRINTING QUANTITY	80,000.00	90,000.00	100,000.00		
	46,000.00	50,500.00	55,000.00		
	0.80	0.80	0.80		
FOREIGN PRINTING COSTS	**36,800.00**	**40,400.00**	**44,000.00**		

Competition Comparison Analysis

	Price Range	Total Retail Prices	% of Total Prices	# of Items	Item RNG %		
COMPANY NAME							
Wild Wings	-50.00	2,092.35	3%	68	19%		
Spring	-100.00	5,269.50	7%	68	19%	-100.00	38%
32 Pages	-200.00	11,302.00	15%	78	22%		
	-500.00	39,905.00	54%	124	35%		
	-999.00	11,045.00	15%	19	5%		
	$1,000.00	4,745.00	6%	2	1%		
		$74,358.85	100%	359	100%		
						Avg item price	$207.13
			(Based on keystone pricing)			Avg item profit	$103.56
Sharper Image	-50.00	1,580.65	9%	47	39%		
Jul/Aug	-100.00	2,418.45	14%	31	26%	-100.00	64%
24 of 60 Pages	-200.00	3,898.75	23%	25	21%		
	-500.00	4,879.45	29%	13	11%		
	-999.00	2,797.85	17%	4	3%		
	$1,000.00	1,195.00	7%	1	1%		
		$16,770.15	100%	121	100%		
						Avg item price	$138.60
			(Based on keystone pricing)			Avg Item Profit	$69.30
Sharper Image	-50.00	2,223.60	10%	73	42%		
Jul/Aug	-100.00	3,227.95	15%	41	24%	-100.00	66%
32 of 60 Pages	-200.00	5,088.35	23%	33	19%		
	-500.00	7,129.10	33%	20	12%		
	-999.00	4,047.75	19%	6	3%		
	$1,000.00	0.00	0%	0	0%		
		$21,716.75	100%	173	100%		
						Avg Item Price	$125.53
			(Based on keystone pricing)			Avg item profit	$62.77
Marine Art of California	-50.00	2,826.95	13%	108	54%		
Nov/Dec	-100.00	3,587.65	17%	46	23%	-100.00	77%
40 Pages	-200.00	3,461.85	16%	23	12%		
	-500.00	4,528.25	21%	15	8%		
	-999.00	4,281.00	20%	6	3%		
	$1,000.00	2,600.00	12%	1	1%		
		$21,285.70	100%	199	100%		
						Avg item price	$106.96
			(Based on keystone pricing)			Avg item profit	$53.48

MARINE ART OF CALIFORNIA
Robert A. Garcia
P.O. Box 10059-251
Newport Beach, CA 92658
(714) 722-6478

TERMS AND CONDITIONS FOR PARTICIPANTS

1. **Artist/Vendor** agrees to drop ship stocked items within 48 hours of notification to indicated customer with Instructions for Shipping provided by **Marine Art of California**. A time schedule is needed for custom made pieces such as bronzes acrylics, or original art works requiring longer delivery. Customer will pay shipping.

2. **Artist/Vendor** agrees to provide 48 hour Federal Express Delivery with added shipping charges for all stocked items.

3. **Artist/Vendor** agrees to use only shipping labels provided by **Marine Art of California**.

4. **Artist/Vendor** guarantees that all items shipped will be free of any business names, logos, addresses, phone numbers or any other printed material referencing said **Artist/Vendor** (engravings or signatures of **Artist** on pieces not included).

5. Each **Artist** shall include a pre-approved autobiographical sheet with each shipment.

6. **Artist/Vendor** shall include required Certificates of Authenticity on all Limited Edition pieces shipped.

7. Exclusive marketing rights for a selected art item made for **Marine Art of California** shall be covered in a separate contract.

8. **Artist/Vendor** agrees to fax a copy of the shipping manifest or phone in shipping information and date of pickup on same day of transaction.

9. **Artist/Vendor** guarantees insurance coverage for the full retail value.

10. **Artist/Vendor** shall agree to 10 day full refund period beginning from the date customer receives shipped merchandise.

11. **Artist/Vendor** agrees to extend 30 days net payment plan to **Marine Art of California**.

12. **Artist/Vendor** shall not record names nor addresses of buyers for purposes of any sales or marketing contact within 24 months of shipment of the order.

Terms and Conditions, page 2

13. In lieu of any participation fee, **Artist/Vendor** agrees to extend a 15% discount on published wholesale prices to **Marine Art of California**. This is justifiable due to advertising, printing, mailing and target marketing costs and project volume sales.

14. Each **Artist/Vendor** shall be notified 2 weeks prior to the mailing of the first catalog issue.

15. Artist/Vendor agrees to provide goods and services as stated above for a minimum duration of 60 days after publication date.

I hereby acknowledge and accept these terms and conditions set forth by **Marine Art of California.**

_____

(Company)

_____

(Print Name and Title)

_____

(Signature and Title of Authorized Representative)

Date:_____

Dayne Landscaping, Inc. Business Plan

The business plan presented on the following pages is based on current research for a landscaping and snow removal business in New Hampshire. It was developed by international marketing specialist, Robin Dayne, President of rtd Marketing International, Inc. in Nashua, New Hampshire. Robin wrote this plan specifically for you (readers of *Anatomy of a Business Plan* and the users of **Automate Your Business Plan** software. It will show you how you can follow our format and write a winning business plan for your own company.

Dayne Landscaping, Inc. Scenario

Dayne Landscaping, Inc. is a fictitious one-year-old business that provides landscaping and snow removal services in Nashua, New Hampshire. The business had a successful first year (1999) and is planning to expand its customer base and purchase its present site (currently leased) for $375,000. In order to purchase the location, Dayne Landscaping, Inc. will use $100,000 of its own funds and seek a loan for the remaining $275,000.

How is this business plan organized?

The Organizational and Marketing Plans for Dayne Landscaping, Inc. reflect the company's current status and its plans for its future expansion. It is extremely important that the marketing plan be strong enough to ensure that it can repay the loan and interest and still maintain its profitability.

Financial Documents need to reflect the company's history and project its future. This company has been in business for one year (1999) and is seeking a loan. Therefore, the financial documents need to begin with a summary of financial needs and dispersal of loan funds statement. The next section includes projections for 2000 and historical financial statements for the 1999 business year. They will show how well the company met its original projections and what its current financial status is. The third area to be covered in financial documents will address the company's projections for the future—projected cash flow, three-year income projections, and projected balance sheet. The closing pages of the financial section contain a financial statement analysis of the company's history and future projections. Utilizing the financial information developed previously, ratios are computed and matched against industry standards.

This plan can help you.

As you proceed with the writing of your own plan, it may help you to look at Dayne Landscaping, Inc.'s business plan to see how Robin handled each of the corresponding sections. Some of the research material has been condensed and we have not included all of the necessary supporting documents. We have also chosen to omit any business or personal financial history that the writer or lender may wish to include in copies of the business plan.

> ***Warning!*** *This plan is to be examined for Ms. Dayne's handling of content only. It has been used as an example in our book and software because we feel it is a fine example of business plan organization. There is no judgment inferred as to appropriateness or financial potential for lenders or investors. Do not use it as a source of research for your own company.*

We are very pleased that Robin Dayne has provided us with this excellent example of a business plan for inclusion in *Anatomy of a Business Plan* and **Automate Your Business Plan**. We hope that Dayne Landscaping, Inc.'s plan will be of benefit to you. We thank Robin for being so generous and for allowing us to share her interpretation of business planning with our readers.

Robin Dayne is an international marketing consultant who specializes in creating increased revenues through Customer Base Management™. Through her firm, rtd Marketing International, Inc., any company can have its customer base analyzed and have a marketing plan and strategy designed to fit the needs of the business. If you would like to contact Robin for information on her services, you can write to her at: rtd Marketing International, Inc., 81 Walden Pond Drive, Nashua, NH 03060 Tel: (603) 880-0136.

Dayne Landscaping, Inc.

22 San Carlos Dr.
Nashua, New Hampshire 03060
603-335-8200

Robin T. Dayne, President

22 San Carlos Dr.
Nashua, New Hampshire 03060
(603)-335-8200

Joe Sanborn, Vice-President

56 Gingham St.
Nashua, NH 03990
(603) 446-9870

Fred Ryan, Treasurer

98 Canon St.
Nashua, NH 06223
(603) 883-0938

Trudy St. George, Secretary

31 Mill St.
Nashua, NH 08876
(603) 595-3982

**Plan Prepared November 1999
by the Corporate Officers**
(Private and Confidential)

Copy 1 of 5

TABLE OF CONTENTS

* *Note: We have included only part of the supporting documents in this sample business plan.*

Dayne Landscaping Inc.

Executive Summary

Dayne Landscaping, Inc. is a one-year-old landscaping and snow removal company established in January of 1999. The company is located at 22 San Carlos Ave., Nashua, New Hampshire. The currently leased location is available for sale at $375,000. Dayne Landscaping, Inc. has $100,000 to invest and is seeking a $275,000 loan to complete the purchase. By owning the facility, the company can increase its equity for an amount equivalent to the current rental expense.

Dayne Landscaping has established its niche in the landscaping and snow removal business during 1999. Projections for 2000 show that it is reasonable to expect expansion of customer base to new markets and territories. Cash Flow projections support the assumption that the company will have sufficient funds to purchase equipment and hire additional employees to support implementation of the marketing programs.

Today the business services 100 residential accounts, 15 small business accounts, and currently no large corporate accounts. The services include: landscaping and design, lawn care and maintenance, snow plowing and removal, and tree maintenance and removal. The success of the company has been a direct result of our ability to provide personal service at a competitive rate, thus creating a dedicated customer base. Currently, the average cost for lawn maintenance of a residential home is $25 to 30 per hour, small business accounts $50 to 100 per hour, and large corporate accounts are negotiated on a per contract basis. Due to the seasonal changes in New Hampshire, snow removal becomes an important part of the business to maintain the company's revenues during the slower winter months of December, January, February, and March.

The projected growth rate for the landscaping industry, based the previous years is 28 percent. We will be expanding our business with new equipment, marketing, and additional employees to meet and exceed that demand. We are expecting to grow our customer base by 50 percent based on our first year's track record, our unique offering, and planned marketing activities.

The $275,000 in loan funds will be required for April 2000 closing. Repayment of the 15-year loan, plus interest, can begin promptly in May. Early retirement of the loan is anticipated as early as 2003. In addition to the property and facility, itself, the loan can further be secured by the owner's home equity which is currently $167,000.

Dayne Landscaping Inc.

I. The Organizational Plan

<u>Description of the Business</u>

Dayne Landscaping, Inc., established in January 1999 as a corporation, handles landscaping, lawn maintenance, and snow removal, of residential homes, and small businesses in New Hampshire. It began with 20 residential accounts and two small business accounts. As of November 1999, it has grown to 100 residential accounts and 15 small business accounts, totaling $750,000 in revenue, a growth of 520 percent.

The company has been very successful due to the high standard of service and care provided to the customer and because of its reputation for quick response times during snowstorms. The company also offers a unique service of oriental garden design landscaping, the only one in the tri-state area. Today that service is offered in New Hampshire only. Twenty-five of the 115 accounts have contracted for these unique gardens. Our plan is to open markets in Connecticut and Massachusetts over the next three years. It is important to note that these gardens are a not only a unique service; they are also our premium high ticket service and provide a larger profit margin, directly impacting the company's bottom line.

The company's growth strategy is to buy out smaller landscaping companies as we expand the business into Massachusetts and Connecticut and increase our Large Corporate accounts for snow removal. Currently, with local corporations "downsizing," "out-sourcing" these services to local businesses has become prevalent.

The company currently leases a 20,000 square feet area, which includes a 4,000 square feet building for the main office, a large attached garage for trucks, maintenance equipment, and supplies, two large lots, one fenced-in for parking equipment, plows, flatbeds, and storage of trees, shrubs, and plants.

Legal Structure

Dayne Landscaping, Inc. is a corporation filed under the same name.

The legal and financial advisers recommended a corporation as the most efficient structure based on our current plans for expansion. There have been 300 shares of stock applied for, and 100 issued to the sole shareholder (President) at the time of incorporation. This will leave the flexibility of having additional shares on hand should we need to use them in negotiations of larger landscaping company buy-outs.

The officers of the company, a President, Vice President, Treasurer, and Secretary, determine the direction of the corporation through its board meetings.

Additionally, there is an incentive plan for board members to acquire company stock based on set profit goals.

It should be noted that the President is the only officer working in the day-to-day business. All other officers interact at the monthly board meetings. This allows the company to have access to expertise and advice at large cost savings, which has a direct impact on the bottom line and growth of the company.

Products and Services

Dayne Landscaping offers three categories of landscaping services to three varieties of customers. The customers consist of residential homes, small businesses, and large corporations. Each group has the option of purchasing the same types of services. Lawn care, which includes mowing, weeding, planting, re-sod, pest control, and tree and shrub maintenance. Customized landscape design can be purchased on a contract basis, including specialties in oriental gardens, tree sculpture, and complete landscape design. The third service offered is snow plowing and removal.

All the plantings are high quality and are purchased from a local nursery that has been in the business for over 35 years. We also have an arrangement to use the nursery as a consultant when there is a need for it.

3

Products and Services (cont.)

<u>Customer Profiles</u>

The following are descriptions of the three types of customers and the services that are typically purchased by each.

1. **Residential homes** in mid- to high-income areas, typically purchase lawn care that consists of mowing, weeding, pest control, and tree/scrub maintenance. There are two people assigned per job: two part-time college students, overseen by a supervisor. This job can take an average of two hours to complete. Each home receives a contract for two visits per month unless there is a special need, which is an additional cost to the basic contract. These lawn contacts run from March to November. Additionally, 50 percent of the residential customers also purchase winter snow removal for their driveways, and these customers are charged a minimal flat fee and a per-call fee, with an up-front deposit to ensure they get priority service.

2. **Small business account or office park** is the second type of customer. They typically consist of banks, or small office buildings, and require shrub and landscaping care, weed and pest control, and minimal lawn mowing. The average time required to service this type of account is three to four hours with one supervisor and two or three part-time employees. All the small business accounts have a contract for snow removal. A pre-determined amount for the contract is negotiated in October for the four months November to February, with a per-call fee for the month of March, which can have unpredictable snow storms. These customers require quick response times and are charged for that level of service, as they need to accommodate their own customers during business hours.

3. **Large corporate account or condo complex** are the third type of customer. They require the same services as the small corporate account, but require many more hours, employees, and equipment. Additionally, included in their lawn maintenance is routine watering. The accounts that are being targeted will require an average of one week of maintenance per month. This is the area to be expanded over the next three years. To support the watering needed every other day during the summer months, one part-time worker is hired and dedicated to watering for every two companies. Corporate account contracts are negotiated individually, and range from 60K to 350K per year, depending on the amount of square footage and specific landscaping requirements. These customers also require immediate response times, especially in winter during the snow season.

4

Management and Personnel

Management

At present, Robin Dayne is the President and sole shareholder in Dayne Landscaping, Inc. Robin has five prior years of experience in the landscaping business, working for a local competitor. Previously she worked in a variety of service industries selling and marketing products and services.

Dayne Landscaping, Inc. has been incorporated for almost one year, realizing a 520 percent growth rate between January to November. The growth rate is attributed to high standards set for customer service. Many customers shifted from the prior company because of their loyalty to Robin Dayne. She has set up an incentive plan for her employees that rewards them for outstanding customer service, based on year-end survey results, or when contracts are renewed or new business is closed.

Under Ms. Dayne's management, a strong team of very dedicated people who love to work with nature has been formed. As manager, her role is to identify new business, develop and implement marketing activities, and to negotiate and close new contracts.

The four (4) supervisors manage the accounts and part-time workers. They also determine staffing and equipment needed to maintain the account. There is also a design specialist who is specifically trained in oriental garden design and tree topiaries.

Corporate Officers

The corporate officers are:

    Robin Dayne, President
    Joe Sanborn, Vice President and Accountant
    Fred Ryan, Treasurer
    Trudy St. George, Secretary and Legal Counsel

The VP/Accountant, Secretary/Legal Counsel, and Treasurer do not interact in the day-to-day business of the company. Their services are used as needed.

Personnel

There are three full-time office employees—one office manager and two administrative assistants. Four supervisors and two design specialists work in the field. The remainder are part-time workers, numbering from four to twenty-five or more, depending on the time of the year and work load.

1. Owner-President: 1999 Guaranteed Salary $65,000 with yearly increases justified by profitability.
2. Design Specialists: Two in 2000; Salaries @ $25,000 + 5 percent commission on new business contracts.
3. Four Supervisors: Salaries @ $15,000 + 3 percent bonus per contract for any excellent customer surveys at year end.
4. Office Manager: Salary @ $22,000 per year.
5. Administrative Assistants: (one in 1999, two in 2000): Salaries @ $15,000 per year.
6. Part-time workers: 5-25 @ $7 per hour; (more added as volume increases).

Management and Personnel (cont.)

Training:

1. All employees receive training from the President and the Supervisor in the following areas:

Given by the President
   a. Company policies and procedures regarding the customers and company standards
   b. Landscaping orientation at the time they are hired
   c. Liability and safety procedures
   d. Equipment care and theft policies

Given by the Supervisors
   a. Overview of each account assignment
   b. Equipment assignment and training—operation of mowers, tools, and supplies
   c. Chemicals precautions

Personnel Duties:

1. **President/Owner**
   a. Sets company policies and trains all new employees
   b. Solicits, interviews, and hires new employees
   c. Assigns accounts to Supervisors
   d. Negotiates new and large contracts
   e. Approves the purchases of equipment and supplies
   f. Handles customer service issues that cannot be satisfied by Supervisor
   g. Reviews and signs all checks
   h. Follows up on Supervisor sales leads

2. **Four Supervisors—reports to President**
   a. Manages, on average, 25 residential accounts and 4 small business accounts
   b. Will be managing one to two Large Corporate accounts
   c. Responsible for training part-time help on account profiles and equipment
   d. Forecasts supplies needed for each account
   e. Forecasts and manages work schedules
   f. Conducts second round of interviews of part-timers and approves
   g. Handles account problems related to service and quality issues
   h. Solicits new business leads to President.
   i. Responsibility for inventory and equipment assigned to his/her team

Personnel Duties (cont.)

3. **Office Manager—reports to President**
   a. Manages account scheduling
   b. Supports Supervisors—back-up supplies misc.
   c. Takes account calls and passes to Supervisors
   d. Performs yearly customer survey
   e. Answers phone
   f. Dispatches and is in "beeper" contact with Supervisors
   g. Assigns and maintains equipment for Supervisors

4. **Administrative Assistant—reports to President**
   a. Responsible for Bookkeeping functions of:
      1. Daily sales reconciliation
      2. Accounts receivable
      3. Accounts Payable
      4. Payroll
      5. General Ledger
   b. Computer Typing—60 WPM, with software knowledge: WP/Excel/D-Base
   c. 10-key adding machine
   d. Access to safe
   e. Tracks orders placed for equipment and supplies

5. **Part-Time Employees—reports to Supervisor**
   a. Assigned to work specific accounts
   b. Mows, weeds, does manual labor
   c. Identifies any problems
   d. Follows instructions from supervisor
   f. Manages inventory of supplies

Employee Profile

All employees must be:
   a. Hard working
   b. Like working outdoors
   c. Good communicators
   d. Team workers
   e. Educated for full-time work with a minimum HS degree, or in College
   f. Neat in appearance
   g. Able to follow directives and be a quick learner
   h. Dedicated to doing an outstanding job
   i. Responsible, regarding safety

Accounting and Recordkeeping

All bookkeeping is kept on computer on a regular basis by the Administrative Assistant on the software "Quickbooks" from Intuit. At the end of the year, the files are printed and passed to the accountant, Bob Sanborn, CPA who has been a personal friend for many years and has 35 years experience as a CPA. His fees are reasonable and there is a high level of trust in his input to the business, as he is the Vice President for the corporation as well.

The customer base and prospect database is kept on the software "ACT" from Contact Software International, which allows us to keep precise time lines of our scheduling and manage our accounts accurately. "Office" from Microsoft allows us to perform WP, develop customized Spreadsheets, and develop proposals and presentations to larger accounts. All the above programs are "off-the-shelf" and are easy to get support for at very reasonable prices.

Insurance

Carrier: Primercia
111 Shoe St.
Manchester, New Hampshire

Agent: Sam Bickford

Type of Insurance:

	Business/personal	600,000
	Deductible	4,000
	Liability	1,000,000
Equipment		40,000
	Deductible	500
	Liability	2,000,000
Vehicles		150,000
	Deductible	1,000
	Liability	1,000,000
	Annual Premium	8,000
	Monthly Premium	670
	Workers Comp. 1.43 per/1k gross Payroll	

Security

Problem situations to be considered and protective measures to be taken:

1. **Internal theft—Employee Dishonesty**

   a. Shoplifting of supplies: four (4) closed-circuit cameras in garage recording 24 hours.

   b. Cash theft: petty cash limit of $600. Daily receipt drop-off to bank of all receivable.

   c. Falsifying signatures: all checks signed by President at the end of the day.

   d. Employee orientation: to reduce theft and stress security procedures.

   e. Monthly inventory: responsibility of the Supervisors.

2. **External**

   a. Walk-in theft cameras at each doorway exit (2).

   b. Cameras in garage and on parking area, and fenced-in plant lot.

   c. Break-in theft/robbery: Alarms set nightly and connected directly to local police station.

Dayne Landscaping, Inc.

II. Marketing Plan

Target Market

Target #1

Large Corporate Facilities and Condominiums

Who: Corporations that are "out-sourcing" the landscaping maintenance of their facilities to outside vendors, and condominium complexes. There are approximately 75 accounts that are potential customers within a 50-mile radius. Our goal is to secure 5 in 2000.

What: Telemarket for background information, and send a direct mail with telemarketing follow-up. Describe landscaping, lawn maintenance, pest control, and all other landscaping services, such as tree removal and replacement, landscaping design and care, and snow plowing and removal from their parking lots and driveways. Provide a guarantee for the services and show competitive comparison pricing from local companies.

When: Begin January to determine the bidding process and RFP schedule to determine the timing of proposals. Call each account to determine the timing and arrange for an on-site inspection, to determine the amount of work needed and special needs to develop an estimate. If possible, inquire what the previous years costs were and if the customer was satisfied with the work of the current landscaper.

Where: Position joint services with local garden stores for promotions and advertising.

Target Market (cont.)

Target #2

Small Businesses or Office Parks

Who: All small businesses and office parks that have outdoor grounds that want to save money, or are unhappy with their present landscaping company. In the 50-mile radius, there are approximately 125 accounts that are potential customers. Our goal is to add 15 new contracts in this category in 2000.

What: Telemarket for background information and send a direct mail with telemarketing follow-up. Describe all the same landscaping services and snow plowing, referencing exciting satisfied customers. Provide a guarantee for services rendered, show the cost savings using Dayne Landscaping, Inc., and develop a plan for continued snow and landscape maintenance. Offer the company's quality guarantee and comparison chart of competitive pricing.

When: Begin January to determine when existing contracts expire and provide information on the company and services. Request an on-site evaluation to determine costs and uncover any problem areas needing work.

Where: Position joint services with local garden stores for promotions and advertising. Advertise in the local papers, Yellow Pages, and Business to Business Directory.

Target #3

Residential Homes

Who: Target all residential homes in the 50-mile radius that are in mid to high income areas and over three+ acres. Contact all existing customers with satisfaction survey, and solicit at the same time for:

    a. Additional business—renew contracts for next year

    b. New customers—referrals

What: Develop and send company brochure that targets the residential homes supplying them with information on all services offered by Dayne Landscaping, Inc. with price comparisons.

When: Develop brochure in January and mail in February prior to Spring and Summer contracts. Follow-up with existing customers and potential customers in September for the snow plowing contracts.

Where: Position joint services with local garden stores for promotions and advertising.

Competition

Dayne Landscaping currently has two competitors in the local area: The Garden Shop and Landscaping Plus. While they have been in the New Hampshire area for several years, they are family-owned businesses that have a limited number of clientele and the same number of accounts year after year. They also have no type of landscaping specialty. Only the Garden Shop offers snow removal. Landscaping Plus has only three snow plows that are active during the winter months.

Methods of Distribution

Dayne Landscaping sells directly to the customer, and is primarily a service business, with the exception of selling the landscaping plants and shrubs, which come from a local nursery wholesaler.

Promotional Activities

Paid Advertising: We currently participate in several forms of advertising:

1. Newspaper ads: All ad copy is identical, and includes information required by the newspaper:

A. Ad information: 1. Ad size: The ad is two column x three inches

2. Timing: Monthly

3. Section: Garden section

B. Ad location, contact and fees:

Nashua Telegraph
P.O. Box 1008
Nashua, NH 03061-1008

Contact: Mark Potts
Circulation: 50,000
Fee: $126.00

Manchester Union Leader
100 William Loeb Drive
Manchester, NH 03109

Contact: Ken Coose
Circulation: 125,000
Fee: $171.99

Lowell Sun
15 Kearney Square
Lowell, MA 01852-1996

Contact: Carol McCabe
Circulation; 75,000
Fee: $153.00

Hartford Daily News
100 Main St.
Hartford, CT 10002

Contact: Sue Betz
Circulation: 150,000
Fee: $190.00

Paid Advertising (cont.)

2. Phone books: Yellow Pages and directories

A. NYNEX Phone Book—Yellow Pages

Ad Information:

Coverage:	So. NH area
Yearly Fee:	$650.00
Ad Size:	1/4 page
Renewal date:	February 1st
Contact:	Sam Moore

B. Business to Business Directory (NH only)

Ad Information

Coverage:	All NH
Yearly Fee:	$250.00
Ad Size:	1/4 page
Renewal Date:	January 1st
Contact:	Karl Hess

3. Local Cable Channels

A. Channel 13—Local Nashua station reaching all of Southern NH

Ad Information:

Length of ad "spot":	60 seconds
Development costs:	$250.00 (one time fee)
Length of campaign:	3 mos.
Runs per month:	Three times per day, everyday
Cost for three months:	$300.00
Total campaign cost:	$550.00

B. Weather Channel "tag line"—reaching 400,000 homes

Ad Information:

Length of ad "spot":	15 seconds
Development costs:	$100. (one time fee)
Length of campaign:	3 mos.
Runs per month:	20 times per day, everyday
Cost for three months:	$900.00
Total campaign cost:	$1,000.00

Direct Mail

Note: There was no direct mail done in the first year of business. With the development of the Marketing plan, two direct mail pieces will need to be developed to target our three potential customer bases for 2000 (see detailed plan of this activity).

Direct mail #1

Designed for:	Target market #1: large corporations and condominiums
	Target market #2: small business and office parks
Creative Strategy:	Design needs to be glossy, appropriate for corporate, professional environment.
Highlight:	

Customer service: testimonials

Quick response time

All services

Guarantee

Free evaluation

Direct mail #2

Designed for:	Target market #3: residential homes
Creative Strategy:	Design should be a tri-fold brochure "self-mailer" (no envelope required)
	Direct highlights for the homeowner.
Highlight:	

Customer service: testimonials

Quick response time

All services

Guarantee

Free evaluation

Community Involvement

Member of the Chamber of Commerce in Nashua. Board Member of the local Garden Club, involved with teaching kids about plants and nature, as well as involved with the "Beautification of Nashua" program.

Note: In this sample plan, we have included the promotion for target market #1 only. All target markets should have their own separate plan using the same format.

14

Worksheet for
Individual Marketing Promotion

Market: Large Corporate or Condo Landscaping   **Date:** 2/00

Program Name: Corporate Promo   **Media:** Direct Mail and Telemarketing

Program Objectives:

- Generate a minimum of 500k in additional revenue in the year 2000
- Increase corporate account base by five new accounts
- Establish Dayne Landscaping as a landscaping provider to large corporations and condominiums

Audience:

Direct Mail

Who: the 70 identified accounts consisting of condominiums and large corporations.

What: Send direct mail (company brochure) to Corporate and Condo contacts listing services and benefits of Dayne Landscaping. Position money back guarantee as an added promotion.

Where: in the New Hampshire and Massachusetts areas (50 mile radius).

When: Drop mail in mid-January.

Telemarketing (Prior to mailing):

Who: Call all accounts to identify landscaping contact in the large corporation, or property management company of the condominium.

What: Find out the contract renewal dates and bid submission dates for each prospect.

When: Make phone calls first two weeks of January.

Where: NA

15

Marketing Worksheet (cont.)

Telemarketing (Post Direct Mail):

Who: Call all contacts and confirm bid dates

What: ask if they received the direct mail and offer a free landscaping consultation

When: Calling begins five to eight working days after the direct mail is received

Where: NA

List Source:

The list was taken from the library in the *New Hampshire Corporate Directory*, and *Massachusetts Corporate Directory* as well as the Realty listing of Condominiums.

Creative Strategy for Direct Mail:

- Position Dayne Landscaping, Inc. as a leader in quality service
- Position Guarantee
- Leverage existing customer base with success stories
- Position against the competition
- Position "free" consulting offer
- The telemarketing call back in a week

Creative Strategy for Telemarketing:

- Develop script with the same messages as the direct mail will have
- If possible position—Company and Promotional offer

Components of Mailing:

Tri-fold brochure: components

- Self-mailer, with reply card
- Address handwritten on the backside

Marketing Worksheet (cont.)

Timing:

Pre-Mailing Telemarketing

% Called	Location	Call dates
50%	New Hampshire	1/2–1/9
50%	Massachusetts	1/9–1/18

Direct Mail

% Mailed	Location	Mail date
50%	New Hampshire	1/12
50%	Massachusetts	1/19

Post- Mailing Telemarketing

% Called	Location	Call dates
50%	New Hampshire	1/22
50%	Massachusetts	1/29

Call to Action:

Reply card to be sent to office or/and 800 number can be called

Lead Criteria:

"Hot" leads are classified as anyone getting a proposal, evaluation, or call back from the mailing or telemarketing. They have the potential of closing in 2000.

"Warm" leads are any accounts that are interested and cannot do anything until 2001 due to their current contracts.

"Cold" leads are those accounts who are not interested at all and have no revenue potential in the future.

Marketing Worksheet (cont.)

Training:

Employees in the field: will be given an overview of the entire promotion to prepare them for customers asking questions, while on the job.

Office staff: will receive training and instructions on how to answer the phone and track the responses from the 800 and mailer. They will also be assisting on the pre- and post-telemarketing activities.

Expenses: Will not exceed $3,000 for the entire promotion.

Measurement:

Revenue Goal	500k
Expenses	3K
Total # (list)	70
# or responses	TBD
# of leads	TBD
Cost/ per Response	TBD
Cost/ per Lead	TBD
Revenue/Expense ratio	TBD

TBD = To be determined at the end of the program.

Assumptions:

- Average value per contract = 100K

- Response rate = 2.0 % on the Direct mail and 15-20% on the telemarketing or 1.5 responses on the direct mail, and 10 to 14 on the telemarketing.

- "Hot" lead rate = 0.5% on the direct mail and 5% to 7% on the telemarketing or 3.5 leads on the direct mail and 3.5-5 leads on the telemarketing

Lead Tracking Process:

- All Direct mail responses will be tracked

- All Phone calls will be logged when responding on the 800.

- All regular calls will be screened, "Are you calling regarding our direct mail promotion?"

Program Review: 30 days after last telemarketing follow-up call.

Dayne Landscaping, Inc.

Part III. Financial Documents

Sources and Uses of Loan Funds

1999 Financial Statements

2000 Financial Projections

Financial Statement Analysis

Summary of Financial Needs

I. Dayne Landscaping. Inc. is seeking a loan to increase its equity capital through real estate investment:

    A. By purchasing the buildings currently being leased by the company.

    B. By purchasing the parcel of land on which the buildings now stand.

II. Dayne Landscaping, Inc. has $100,000 in cash to invest. An additional amount of $275,000 in loan funds is needed to complete the purchase.

Loan Fund Dispersal Statement

1. Dispersal of Loan Funds

Dayne Landscaping, Inc. will utilize the anticipated loan in the amount of $275,000 to purchase the facility (land and buildings) that it currently leases. The full purchase price is $375,000. The present owner of the premises is John S. Strykker. The parcel and accompanying buildings located at 22 San Carlos Drive in Nashua, New Hampshire are currently owned by John S. Strykker.

2. Back-Up Statement

a. The land is currently appraised at $200,000. Attached buildings appraise at $175,000. The owner, Mr. John S. Strykker is agreeable to close of escrow on or about April 15, 2000.

b. Dayne Landscaping, Inc. has appropriated $100,000 in retained earnings to be used as for a capital investment in the facility. The additional $275,000 in loan funds will make up the full purchase amount of $375,000.

c. The buildings sit on a 20,000-square-foot parcel of land, centrally located in Nashua, New Hampshire. The land is currently appraised at $200,000 and the buildings at $175,000. There are two large lots. One is fenced-in for parking equipment and also serves as a storage area for trees, shrubs, and plants. There is a 4,000-square-foot building that serves as the main office and a large attached garage to house trucks, maintenance equipment, and supplies.

d. The $275,000 in loan funds are needed by April 1 in order to proceed with escrow. Loan repayment can begin promptly on May 1st for a 15-year period. The company has a strong cash flow and a rapidly-growing market. Early payoff is anticipated.

e. Dayne Landscaping is currently paying $2,850 in monthly rental expense. Payments on the anticipated $275,000, 15-year loan @9% would amount to $2,789. Purchase of the land and the buildings will enable Dayne Landscaping, with no additional expense, to repay the loan + interest and to divert the current rental expense into equity growth.

1999 Cash to Be Paid Out Projections
Dayne Landscaping, Inc.

Time Period Covered: January 1, 1999 to December 31, 1999

1. START-UP COSTS		12,550
a. Business license	150	
b. Corporation filing	250	
c. Legal fees	650	
Other start-up costs:	0	
(1) Lawn equipment	6,500	
(2) Office equipment	5,000	
(3) Security deposit—office rental	5,700	
2. INVENTORY PURCHASES		98,000
Cash out for goods intended for resale		
a. Fertilizer	20,000	
b. Pesticide	10,000	
c. Plants/shrubs	18,000	
d. Salt/sand	5,000	
e. Seed	45,000	
3. VARIABLE EXPENSES (SELLING)		
a. Design specialist salary/payroll taxes	20,000	
b. Machinery, tools, equipment	5,000	
c. Marketing	5,411	
d. Part-time worker salaries/payroll taxes	150,000	
e. Sales bonuses	1,500	
f. Sales commission	8,000	
g. Supervisor salaries/payroll taxes	60,000	
h. Travel expense	9,500	
i. Miscellaneous selling expense	1,000	
Total selling expense		260,411
4. FIXED EXPENSES (ADMIN)		
a. Administration fees — legal/acct.	2,000	
b. Insurance — liability, casualty, fire, theft	11,600	
c. Licenses and permits	4,200	
d. Office equipment	1,200	
e. Office salaries/payroll taxes	42,000	
f. Owner guaranteed payments	65,000	
g. Rent expense	34,200	
h. Utilities	4,320	
i. Miscellaneous administrative expense	200	
Total administrative expense		164,720
5. ASSETS (LONG-TERM PURCHASES)		18,719
a. Machinery, equipment, trucks, large mowers	17,333	
b. Interest expense on assets	1,386	
6. LIABILITIES		0
Cash outlay for retiring debts, loans,		
and/or accounts payable		
7. OWNER EQUITY		0
Dividends to be paid to stockholders		
TOTAL CASH TO BE PAID OUT		$ 554,400

1999 Sources of Cash Projections
Dayne Landscaping, Inc.

Time Period Covered: From January 1, 1999 thru December 31, 1999

1. CASH ON HAND		$ 0
2. SALES (REVENUES)		
Product sales income		4,000
Miscellaneous accessories	4,000	
Services income		564,000
Landscaping — residential	185,000	
Lanscaping — small business	65,000	
Landscaping — customized	174,000	
Snow removal — residential	15,000	
Snow removal — small business	125,000	
Deposits on sales or services		5,000
5% up-front for snow removal contracts		
Collections on accounts receivable		0
3. MISCELLANEOUS INCOME		
Interest income		1,250
5% of $25k savings		
Payments to be received on loans		0
4. SALE OF LONG-TERM ASSETS		0
5. LIABILITIES		0
Loan Funds (to be received during current period; from banks,		
through the SBA, or from other lending institutions)		
6. EQUITY		
Owner investments (sole prop/partners)		0
Paid-in (corporation)		25,000
Sale of stock (corporation)		0
Venture capital		0

	A. Without product sales =	$ 595,250
TOTAL CASH AVAILABLE		
	B. With product sales =	$ 599,250

1999 Cash Flow Statement
One-Year Cash Flow Projection and Cash Flow History
Dayne Landscaping, Inc.

For the Year 1999	Projected for: 1999	Historical for: 1999
BEGINNING CASH BALANCE (January 1, 1995)	0	0
CASH RECEIPTS		
A. Sales/revenues	**$573,000**	**$777,864**
1. Landscaping — residential	185,000	216,000
2. Landscaping — small business	65,000	160,700
3. Landscaping — customized	174,000	199,374
4. Snow removal — residential	15,000	18,250
5. Snow removal — small business	125,000	167,100
6. 5% Snow removal contracts	5,000	8,500
7. Sale of miscellaneous accessories	4,000	7,940
B. Receivables	0	0
C. Interest income	1,250	1,250
D. Sale of long-term assets	0	0
TOTAL CASH AVAILABLE	**$574,250**	**$779,114**
CASH PAYMENTS		
A. Cost of goods to be sold		
1. Fertilizer	20,000	19,000
2. Pesticide	10,000	11,000
3. Plants/shrubs	18,000	23,000
4. Salt/sand	5,000	8,030
5. Seed	45,000	45,000
Total cost of goods	**$98,000**	**$106,030**
B. Variable expenses (selling)		
1. Design specialist salary/payroll taxes	20,000	20,000
2. Machinery, tools, equipment	11,500	11,000
3. Marketing	5,411	5,400
4. Part-time worker salaries/payroll taxes	150,000	182,000
5. Sales bonuses	1,500	2,000
6. Sales commissions	8,000	10,800
7. Supervisor salaries/payroll taxes	60,000	60,000
8. Travel expense	9,500	10,400
9. Miscellaneous selling expense	1,000	1,200
Total variable expenses	**$266,911**	**$302,800**
C. Fixed expenses (administrative)		
1. Administrative fees (legal/accounting)	3,050	3,050
2. Insurance (liability, casualty, fire, theft)	11,600	11,600
3. Licenses and permits	4,200	4,200
4. Office equipment	5,700	7,700
5. Office salaries/payroll taxes	42,000	42,000
6. Owner's guaranteed payment	57,000	65,000
7. Rent expense + security deposit	39,900	39,900
8. Utilities	4,320	4,320
9. Miscellaneous administrative expense	200	500
Total fixed expenses	**$167,970**	**$178,270**
D. Interest expense	1,386	5,535
E. Federal and state income tax	7,196	65,220
F. Other uses	0	0
G. Long-term asset payments	17,334	15,081
H. Loan payments	0	0
I. Capital distributions	0	0
TOTAL CASH PAID OUT	**$558,797**	**$672,936**
CASH BALANCE/DEFICIENCY	15,453	106,178
LOANS TO BE RECEIVED	0	0
CAPITAL CONTRIBUTION	25,000	25,000
ENDING CASH BALANCE (December 31, 1999)	**$40,453**	**$131,178**

1999 Quarterly Budget Analysis
Dayne Landscaping, Inc.

For the Quarter Ending: December 31, 1999

BUDGET ITEM	THIS QUARTER			YEAR-TO-DATE		
	Budget	Actual	Variation	Budget	Actual	Variation
SALES/REVENUES	**95,900**	**121,050**	**25,150**	**573,000**	**777,864**	**204,864**
Landscaping — residential	17,800	24,000	6,200	185,000	216,000	31,000
Landscaping — small business	9,600	14,000	4,400	65,000	160,700	95,700
Landscaping — customized	0	0	0	174,000	199,374	25,374
Snow removal — residential	4,200	3,950	(250)	15,000	18,250	3,250
Snow removal — small business	58,300	70,300	12,000	125,000	167,100	42,100
5% Snow removal contracts	6,000	8,500	2,500	5,000	8,500	3,500
Miscellaneous accessories	0	300	300	4,000	7,940	3,940
Less cost of goods	**3,520**	**(1,000)**	**4,520**	**98,000**	**101,030**	**(3,030)**
a. Fertilizer	0	0	0	20,000	19,000	1,000
b. Pesticide	0	0	0	10,000	11,000	(1,000)
c. Plants/shrubs	0	0	0	18,000	23,000	(5,000)
d. Salt/sand	3,520	4,000	(480)	5,000	8,030	(3,030)
e. Seed	0	0	0	45,000	45,000	0
Less ending inventory (12/31)	0	5,000	0	0	5,000	(5,000)
GROSS PROFITS	**92,380**	**122,050**	**29,670**	**475,000**	**676,834**	**201,834**
VARIABLE EXPENSES						
a. Design specialist salary/taxes	5,000	2,500	2,500	20,000	20,000	0
b. Machinery, tools, equipment	0	0	0	11,500	11,000	500
c. Marketing	1,350	1,000	350	5,411	5,400	11
d. Part-time worker salaries/taxes	18,700	33,000	(14,300)	150,000	182,000	(32,000)
e. Sales bonuses	0	0	0	1,500	2,000	(500)
f. Sales commission	1,450	1,750	(300)	8,000	10,800	(2,800)
g. Supervisor salaries/payroll taxes	15,000	15,000	0	60,000	60,000	0
h. Travel expense	2,000	1,600	400	9,500	10,400	(900)
i. Miscellaneous variable expense	0	0	0	1,000	1,200	(200)
j. Depreciation expense	3,801	3,801	0	15,200	15,200	0
FIXED EXPENSES						
a. Administration fees—legal/acct.	500	501	(1)	3,050	3,050	0
b. Insurance (liability, casualty, fire, theft)	2,900	2,898	2	11,600	11,600	0
c. Licenses and permits	1,050	0	1,050	4,200	4,200	0
d. Office equipment	300	400	(100)	5,700	7,700	(2,000)
e. Office salaries/taxes	10,500	10,500	0	42,000	42,000	0
f. Owner's guaranteed payment	16,250	16,248	2	65,000	65,000	0
g. Rent expense + security deposit	8,550	8,550	0	39,900	39,900	0
h. Utilities	1,080	1,080	0	4,320	4,320	0
i. Miscellaneous fixed expense	0	0	0	200	500	(300)
NET INCOME FROM OPERATIONS	**3,949**	**23,222**	**16,773**	**16,919**	**180,564**	**163,645**
INTEREST INCOME	347	312	(35)	1,250	1,250	0
INTEREST EXPENSE	2,400	348	(2,052)	1,386	5,535	4,149
NET PROFIT (Pretax)	**1,896**	**23,186**	**21,290**	**16,783**	**176,279**	**159,496**
TAXES (federal and state)	1,282	12,549	(11,267)	7,196	65,220	(58,024)
NET PROFIT (After Tax)	**614**	**10,637**	**10,023**	**9,587**	**111,059**	**101,472**

NON-INCOME STATEMENT ITEMS

	Budget	Actual	Variation	Budget	Actual	Variation
1. Long-term asset repayments	4,335	3,883	452	17,333	15,081	2,252
2. Loan repayments	0	0	0	0	0	0
3. Dividend payments	0	0	0	0	0	0
4. Capital contribution	0	0	0	25,000	25,000	0
5. Inventory assets	0	5,000	(5,000)	0	5,000	(5,000)

BUDGET DEVIATIONS	This Quarter	Year-to-Date
1. Income statement items:	$ 10,023	$ 101,472
2. Non-income statement items:	$ (4,548)	$ (2,748)
3. Total deviation	**$ 5,475**	**$ 98,724**

24

1999 Profit & Loss (Income) Statement
Dayne Landscaping, Inc.

Beginning: January 1, 1999   **Ending: December 31, 1999**

			% Total Revenues
INCOME			
1. Sales/revenues		$ 777,864	100.00%
Landscaping — residential	216,000		27.77%
Landscaping — small business	160,700		20.66%
Customized landscaping	199,374		25.63%
Snow removal — residential	18,250		2.35%
Snow removal — small business	167,100		21.48%
5% Snow removal contracts	8,500		1.09%
Miscellaneous accessories	7,940		1.02%
2. Cost of goods sold (c – d)		101,030	12.99%
a. Beginning inventory	0		0.00%
b. Purchases	106,030		13.63%
(1) Fertilizer	19,000		2.44%
(2) Pesticide	11,000		1.41%
(3) Plants/shrubs	23,000		2.96%
(4) Salt/sand	8,030		1.03%
(5) Seed	45,000		5.79%
c. C.O.G. avail. sale (a + b)	106,030		13.63%
d. Less ending inventory (12/31)	5,000		0.64%
3. Gross profit on sales (1 – 2)		$ 676,834	87.01%
EXPENSES			
1. Variable (selling) (a thru l)		318,000	40.88%
a. Design specialist salary/payroll taxes	20,000		2.57%
b. Machinery, hand tools, equipment	11,000		1.41%
c. Marketing	5,400		0.69%
d. Part-time worker salaries/payroll taxes	182,000		23.40%
e. Sales bonuses	2,000		0.26%
f. Sales commission	10,800		1.39%
g. Supervisor salaries/payroll taxes	60,000		7.71%
h. Travel expense	10,400		1.34%
i. Miscellaneous variable expense	1,200		0.15%
j. Depreciation (selling assets)	15,200		1.95%
2. Fixed (administrative) (a thru l)		178,270	22.92%
a. Administration fees — legal/acct.	3,050		0.39%
b. Insurance — liability, casualty, fire/theft	11,600		1.49%
c. Licenses and permits	4,200		0.54%
d. Office equipment	7,700		0.99%
e. Office salaries/payroll taxes	42,000		5.40%
f. Owner's guaranteed payment	65,000		8.36%
g. Rent expense	39,900		5.13%
h. Utilities	4,320		0.56%
i. Miscellaneous fixed expense	500		0.06%
j. Depreciation (administrative assets)	0		0.00%
Total operating expenses (1 + 2)		496,270	63.80%
Net Income from Operations (GP – Exp)		$ 180,564	23.21%
Other Income (Interest Income)	1,250		0.16%
Other Expense (Interest Expense)	5,535		0.71%
Net Profit (Loss) Before Taxes		$ 176,279	22.66%
Provision for Income Taxes			
a. Federal	51,999		6.68%
b. State	13,221	65,220	1.70%
c. Local	0		0.00%
NET PROFIT (LOSS) AFTER TAXES		$ 111,059	14.28%

1999 Profit & Loss (Income) Statement
Dayne Landscaping, Inc.
Page 1 (January thru June + 6-Month Totals)

For the Year: 1999

INCOME	Jan	Feb	Mar	Apr	May	Jun	6-MONTH TOTALS AMOUNT	% of Total Revenues PERCENT
1. Sales/revenues	71,200	39,700	139,150	90,230	77,080	71,250	488,610	100.00%
Landscaping — residential	0	0	55,000	33,000	28,000	22,000	138,000	28.24%
Landscaping — small business	0	0	37,000	23,000	22,000	22,000	104,000	21.28%
Landscaping — customized	0	0	46,000	32,000	26,000	26,250	130,250	26.66%
Snow removal — residential	8,250	5,550	500	0	0	0	14,300	2.93%
Snow removal — small business	62,850	33,950	0	0	0	0	96,800	19.81%
Miscellaneous accessories	100	200	650	2,230	1,080	1,000	5,260	1.08%
5% Snow removal contracts	0	0	0	0	0	0	0	0.00%
2. Cost of goods to be sold	2,530	500	30,800	17,700	21,000	18,500	91,030	18.63%
a. Beginning inventory	0	0	0	0	0	0	0	0.00%
b. Purchases	2,530	500	30,800	17,700	21,000	18,500	91,030	18.63%
(1) Fertilizer	0	0	7,000	0	6,000	0	13,000	2.66%
(2) Pesticide	0	0	0	3,500	0	4,500	8,000	1.64%
(3) Plants/Shrubs	0	0	8,800	6,200	5,000	2,000	22,000	4.50%
(4) Salt/Sand	2,530	500	0	0	0	0	3,030	0.62%
(5) Seed	0	0	15,000	8,000	10,000	12,000	45,000	9.21%
c. C.O.G. Available for sale	2,530	500	30,800	17,700	21,000	18,500	91,030	18.63%
d. Less ending inventory	0	0	0	0	0	0	0	0.00%
3. GROSS PROFIT	68,670	39,200	108,350	72,530	56,080	52,750	397,580	81.37%
EXPENSES								
1. Variable (selling) expenses								
a. Design specialist salary	0	0	2,500	2,500	2,500	2,500	10,000	2.05%
b. Machinery, hand tools, equip.	5,000	0	0	2,000	0	2,000	9,000	1.84%
c. Marketing	315	650	925	650	350	315	3,205	0.66%
d. Part-time worker salaries	12,000	9,000	12,000	12,500	13,000	13,750	72,250	14.79%
e. Sales bonuses	0	0	500	500	500	500	2,000	0.41%
f. Sales commission	600	300	800	2,100	1,000	1,500	6,300	1.29%
g. Supervisor salaries	5,000	5,000	5,000	5,000	5,000	5,000	30,000	6.14%
h. Travel expense	800	700	1,100	1,900	1,150	1,050	6,700	1.37%
i. Miscellaneous selling expense	200	100	250	350	0	0	900	0.18%
j. Depreciation (variable assets)	1,266	1,266	1,266	1,266	1,267	1,267	7,598	1.56%
Total Variable Expenses	25,181	17,016	24,341	28,766	24,767	27,882	147,953	28.23%
1. Fixed (Administrative) Expenses								
a. Admin. fees — legal/acct.	1,216	166	167	166	167	166	2,048	0.42%
b. Insurance (liab, cas, fire, theft)	967	967	967	967	967	967	5,802	1.19%
c. Licenses and permits	100	200	1,250	2,500	150	0	4,200	0.86%
d. Machinery, tools, equipment	1,500	2,250	750	950	650	600	6,700	1.37%
e. Office salaries	3,500	3,500	3,500	3,500	3,500	3,500	21,000	4.30%
f. Owner's guaranteed payment	5,417	5,417	5,417	5,417	5,417	5,417	32,502	6.65%
g. Rent expense + security dep.	8,550	2,850	2,850	2,850	2,850	2,850	22,800	4.67%
h. Utilities	360	360	360	360	360	360	2,160	0.44%
i. Miscellaneous fixed expense	0	0	100	100	100	100	400	0.08%
j. Depreciation (fixed assets)	0	0	0	0	0	0	0	0.00%
Total Fixed Expenses	21,610	15,710	15,361	16,810	14,161	13,960	97,612	19.98%
Total Operating Expense	46,791	32,726	39,702	45,576	38,928	41,842	245,565	48.21%
Net Income From Operations	21,879	6,474	68,648	26,954	17,152	10,908	152,015	33.16%
Other income (interest)	105	104	104	104	104	104	625	0.13%
Other expense (interest)	507	499	490	482	474	466	2,918	0.60%
Net Profit (Loss) Before Taxes	21,477	6,079	68,262	26,576	16,782	10,546	149,722	32.69%
Provision for income taxes								
a. Federal	3,222	912	16,694	10,156	6,545	4,113	41,642	8.52%
b. State	1,611	456	5,120	1,993	1,259	791	11,230	2.30%
NET PROFIT (LOSS) AFTER TAXES	16,644	4,711	46,448	14,427	8,978	5,642	96,850	21.87%

1999 Profit & Loss (Income) Statement
Dayne Landscaping, Inc.
Page 2 (July thru December + 12-Month Totals)

For the Year: 1999	Jul	Aug	Sep	Oct	Nov	Dec	12-MONTH TOTALS AMOUNT	% of Total Revenues PERCENT
INCOME								
1. Sales/revenues	**60,330**	**51,012**	**56,862**	**38,200**	**32,800**	**50,050**	**777,864**	**100.00%**
Landscaping — residential	18,000	14,000	22,000	24,000	0	0	216,000	27.77%
Landscaping — small business	16,500	10,900	15,300	14,000	0	0	160,700	20.66%
Landscaping — customized	25,150	24,912	19,062	0	0	0	199,374	25.63%
Snow removal — residential	0	0	0	0	950	3,000	18,250	2.35%
Snow removal — small business	0	0	0	0	23,250	47,050	167,100	21.48%
Miscellaneous accessories	0	0	0	0	8,500	0	8,500	1.09%
5% Snow removal contracts	680	1,200	500	200	100	0	7,940	1.02%
2. Cost of goods to be sold	**4,000**	**6,000**	**1,000**	**0**	**1,000**	**(2,000)**	**101,030**	**12.99%**
a. Beginning inventory	0	0	0	0	0	0	0	0.00%
b. Purchases	**4,000**	**6,000**	**1,000**	**0**	**1,000**	**3,000**	**106,030**	**5.79%**
(1) Fertilizer	0	6,000	0	0	0	0	19,000	2.44%
(2) Pesticide	3,000	0	0	0	0	0	11,000	1.41%
(3) Plants/shrubs	1,000	0	0	0	0	0	23,000	2.96%
(4) Salt/sand	0	0	1,000	0	1,000	3,000	8,030	1.03%
(5) Seed	0	0	0	0	0	0	45,000	5.79%
c. C.O.G. Available for sale	4,000	6,000	1,000	0	1,000	3,000	106,030	5.79%
d. Less ending inventory	0	0	0	0	0	5,000	5,000	0.64%
3. GROSS PROFIT	**56,330**	**45,012**	**55,862**	**38,200**	**31,800**	**52,050**	**676,834**	**87.01%**
EXPENSES								
1. Variable (selling) expenses								
a. Design specialist salary/p.tax	2,500	2,500	2,500	2,500	0	0	20,000	2.57%
b. Machinery, hand tools, equip.	1,000	0	1,000	0	0	0	11,000	1.41%
c. Marketing	206	650	339	400	300	300	5,400	0.69%
d. Part-time worker salaries	25,250	25,250	26,250	10,000	12,500	10,500	182,000	23.40%
e. Sales bonuses	0	0	0	0	0	0	2,000	0.26%
f. Sales commission	400	1,100	1,250	250	1,000	500	10,800	1.39%
g. Supervisor salaries/payroll tax	5,000	5,000	5,000	5,000	5,000	5,000	60,000	7.71%
h. Travel expense	850	650	600	620	480	500	10,400	1.34%
i. Misc. variable expense	100	200	0	0	0	0	1,200	0.15%
j. Depreciation (variable assets)	1,267	1,267	1,267	1,267	1,267	1,267	15,200	1.95%
Total Variable Expenses	**36,573**	**36,617**	**38,206**	**20,037**	**20,547**	**18,067**	**318,000**	**40.88%**
1. Fixed (Administrative) Expenses								
a. Admin. fees — legal/acct.	167	167	167	167	167	167	3,050	0.39%
b. Insurance (liab, cas, fire, theft)	967	967	966	966	966	966	11,600	1.49%
c. Licenses and permits	0	0	0	0	0	0	4,200	0.54%
d. Machinery, tools, equipment	100	200	300	200	100	100	7,700	0.99%
e. Office salaries	3,500	3,500	3,500	3,500	3,500	3,500	42,000	5.40%
f. Owner's guaranteed payment	5,417	5,417	5,416	5,416	5,416	5,416	65,000	8.36%
g. Rent expense	2,850	2,850	2,850	2,850	2,850	2,850	39,900	5.13%
h. Utilities	360	360	360	360	360	360	4,320	0.56%
i. Miscellaneous fixed expense	100	0	0	0	0	0	500	0.06%
i. Depreciation (fixed assets)	0	0	0	0	0	0	0	0.00%
Total Fixed Expenses	**13,461**	**13,461**	**13,559**	**13,459**	**13,359**	**13,359**	**178,270**	**22.92%**
Total Operating Expense	**50,034**	**50,078**	**51,765**	**33,496**	**33,906**	**31,426**	**496,270**	**63.80%**
Net Income From Operations	**6,296**	**(5,066)**	**4,097**	**4,704**	**(2,106)**	**20,624**	**180,564**	**23.21%**
Other Income (Interest)	105	104	104	104	104	104	1,250	0.16%
Other Expense (Interest)	457	449	441	432	423	415	5,535	0.71%
Net Profit (Loss) Before Taxes	**5,944**	**(5,411)**	**3,760**	**4,376**	**(2,425)**	**20,313**	**176,279**	**22.66%**
Provision for Income Taxes								
a. Federal	2,318	($2,110)	1,466	1,707	($946)	7,922	51,999	6.68%
b. State	446	($406)	282	328	($182)	1,523	13,221	1.70%
NET PROFIT (LOSS) AFTER TAXES	**3,180**	**(2,895)**	**2,012**	**2,341**	**(1,297)**	**10,868**	**111,059**	**14.28%**

27

Balance Sheet

Business Name:
Dayne Landscaping, Inc.

Date: December 31, 1999

ASSETS

		% of Assets
Current Assets		
Cash	$ 31,178	15.83%
Savings (land and building)	$ 100,000	50.77%
Petty cash	$ 0	0.00%
Accounts receivable	$ 0	0.00%
Inventory	$ 5,000	2.54%
Long-Term Investments	$ 0	0.00%
Fixed Assets		
Land (valued at cost)	$ 0	0.00%
Buildings	$ 0	0.00%
1. Cost — 0		
2. Less acc. depr. — 0		
Improvements	$ 0	0.00%
1. Cost — 0		
2. Less acc. depr. — 0		
Equipment	$ 12,800	6.50%
1. Cost — 16,000		
2. Less acc. depr. — 3,200		
Furniture	$ 0	0.00%
1. Cost — 0		
2. Less acc. depr. — 0		
Autos/Vehicles	$ 48,000	24.37%
1. Cost — 60,000		
2. Less acc. depr. — 12,000		
Other Assets		
1.	$ 0	0.00%
2.	$ 0	0.00%
TOTAL ASSETS	$ 196,978	100.00%

LIABILITIES

		% of Liabilities
Current Liabilities		
Accounts payable	$ 0	0.00%
Notes payable	$ 16,332	26.81%
Interest payable	$ 0	0.00%
Pre-paid deposits	$ 0	0.00%
Taxes payable		
Accrued federal income tax	$ 0	0.00%
Accrued state income tax	$ 0	0.00%
Accrued payroll tax	$ 0	0.00%
Accrued sales tax	$ 0	0.00%
Payroll accrual	$ 0	0.00%
Long-Term Liabilities		
Notes payable to investors	$ 0	0.00%
Notes payable others	$ 44,587	73.19%
TOTAL LIABILITIES	$ 60,919	100.00%

NET WORTH (EQUITY)

		% of Net Worth
Proprietorship	$ 0	0.00%
or		
Partnership		
1. (Name 1), ___% equity	$ 0	0.00%
2. (Name 2), ___% equity	$ 0	0.00%
or		
Corporation		
Capital stock	$ 20,000	14.70%
Surplus paid in	$ 5,000	3.67%
Retained earnings, appropriated	$ 100,000	73.50%
Retained earnings, unappropriated	$ 11,059	8.13%
TOTAL NET WORTH	$ 136,059	100.00%

Assets – Liabilities = Net Worth
and
Liabilities + Equity = Total Assets

1. See Financial Statement Analysis for ratios and notations

Break-Even Analysis

Based on 1999 Financial Statements - Not a Projection

Dayne Landscaping, Inc.

Date of Analysis: December 31, 1999

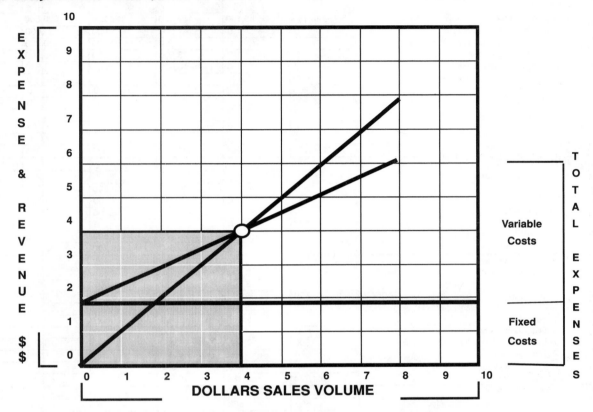

NOTE: Figures shown in hundreds of thousands of dollars (Ex: 1 = $ 100,000)

B-E POINT (SALES) = Fixed costs + [(Variable Costs / Revenues) x Sales]

B-E Point (Sales) = $ 183,805 + [($ 419,030 / $ 777,864)   x   Sales]

Dayne Landscaping, Inc.

BREAK-EVEN POINT CALCULATION

FC (Fixed Costs) =	(Administrative Expenses + Interest)	$ 183,805
VC (Variable Costs) =	(Cost of Goods + Selling Expenses)	$ 419,030
R (Revenues)	= (Income from sale of products and services)	$ 777,864
BREAK-EVEN POINT =		$ 398,444

2000 Pro Forma Cash Flow Statement
Dayne Landscaping, Inc.

Page 1 (January thru June)

For the Year 2000

	Jan	Feb	Mar	Apr	May	Jun
BEGINNING CASH BALANCE	131,178	137,633	140,273	139,746	45,856	115,074
CASH RECEIPTS						
A. Sales/revenues	123,850	89,100	184,400	169,200	200,600	192,900
1. Landscaping — residential	0	0	41,000	21,000	23,000	24,000
2. Landscaping — small business	0	0	56,500	50,500	40,000	39,500
3. Landscaping — large corporations	0	0	73,500	57,200	55,100	51,000
4. Customized landscaping	0	0	13,400	40,500	82,500	78,400
5. Snow removal — residential	11,050	5,700	0	0	0	0
6. Snow removal — small business	66,900	53,000	0	0	0	0
7. Snow removal — large corporations	45,900	30,400	0	0	0	0
8. 5% Snow removal contracts	0	0	0	0	0	0
B. Interest income	108	110	109	110	109	110
C. Sale of long-term assets	0	0	0	0	0	0
TOTAL CASH AVAILABLE	255,136	226,843	324,782	309,056	246,565	308,084
CASH PAYMENTS						
A. Cost of goods to be sold						
1. Fertilizer	0	0	10,700	12,800	9,800	3,100
2. Pesticide	0	0	6,250	2,400	5,500	3,500
3. Plants/shrub	0	0	16,100	13,000	3,500	3,200
4. Salt/sand	5,375	0	0	0	0	0
5. Seed	0	0	21,000	41,500	24,500	5,000
Total cost of goods	5,375	0	54,050	69,700	43,300	14,800
B. Variable expenses						
1. Design specialists (2 w/taxes and benefits)	5,834	5,834	5,834	5,834	5,834	5,834
2. Machinery, tools, equipment	350	6,000	0	500	500	1,000
3. Marketing	3,500	6,500	6,500	3,500	3,500	5,000
4. Part-time worker salaries (w/taxes)	23,500	30,000	37,600	40,000	39,000	38,033
5. Sales bonuses	0	2,000	2,500	500		
6. Sales commissions	0	0	1,100	5,750	2,250	1,500
7. Supervisor salaries (w/taxes and benefits)	7,500	7,500	15,000	15,000	15,000	15,000
8. Travel expense	550	850	1,200	1,300	1,200	860
9. Miscellaneous selling expense	500	500	500	500	500	500
Total variable expenses	41,734	59,184	70,234	72,884	67,784	67,727
C. Fixed expenses						
1. Administration fees — legal/acct.	509	508	508	2,250	508	508
2. Insurance (liability, casualty, fire/theft, w comp)	704	714	735	739	737	736
3. Licenses and permits	100	200	750	2,350	1,300	1,025
4. Office equipment	1,750	8,650	1,100	900	825	525
5. Office salaries (w/taxes and benefits)	5,250	5,250	5,250	5,250	5,250	5,250
6. Owner's guaranteed payment	6,833	6,833	6,833	6,833	6,833	6,833
7. Rent expense	2,850	2,850	2,850	0	0	0
8. Utilities	480	463	360	376	247	378
9. Miscellaneous administrative expense	200	200	200	200	200	200
Total fixed expenses	18,676	25,668	18,586	18,898	15,900	15,455
D. Interest expense (vehicles, equipment)	406	397	389	380	371	362
E. Interest expense (land and buildings)	0	0	0	0	2,062	2,057
F. Federal income tax	0	0	33,249	0	0	33,249
G. State tax	0	0	7,199	0	0	7,199
H. Capital asset purch, cash (land and buildings)*	0	0	0	375,000	0	0
I. Capital asset purch, cash (vehicles, equipment)**	50,000	0	0	0	0	48,000
J. Loan repayment (1996) (land and buildings)	0	0	0	0	727	732
K. Loan repayment (1995) (vehicles, equipment)	1,312	1,321	1,329	1,338	1,347	1,356
TOTAL CASH PAID OUT	117,503	86,570	185,036	538,200	131,491	190,937
CASH BALANCE/DEFICIENCY	137,633	140,273	139,746	(229,144)	115,074	117,147
LOAN TO BE RECEIVED (land and buildings)	0	0	0	275,000	0	0
EQUITY DEPOSITS	0	0	0	0	0	0
ENDING CASH BALANCE	137,633	140,273	139,746	45,856	115,074	117,147

Note: * Building/Land purchased in April for $375,000 ($100,000 cash + bank loan for $275,000)

     ** Two 4x4 trucks purchased in January and August @ $50,000 cash each; Four U-hauls purchased for cash (July and August) @ $10,000 each

2000 Pro Forma Cash Flow Statement
Dayne Landscaping, Inc.

Page 2 (July thru December + 6 & 12-month Totals)

6-MONTH TOTALS	Jul	Aug	Sep	Oct	Nov	Dec	12-MONTH TOTALS
131,178	117,147	122,610	104,184	100,611	119,509	110,104	131,178
960,050	149,400	138,000	122,000	83,900	67,090	87,760	1,608,200
109,000	24,000	24,000	24,000	24,000	0	0	205,000
186,500	33,400	32,000	30,000	28,000	0	0	309,900
236,800	28,000	35,000	30,500	12,900	0	0	343,200
214,800	64,000	47,000	37,500	9,000			372,300
16,750	0	0	0	0	5,000	6,750	28,500
119,900	0	0	0	0	30,000	42,410	192,310
76,300	0	0	0	0	25,090	38,600	139,990
0	0	0	0	10,000	7,000	0	17,000
656	109	109	109	110	110	110	1,313
0	0	0	0	0	0	0	0
1,091,884	266,656	260,719	226,293	184,621	186,709	197,974	1,740,691
36,400	7,600	4,000	0	0	0	0	48,000
17,650	4,500	1,850	0	0	0	0	24,000
35,800	1,700	2,700	2,300	1,500	0	0	44,000
5,375	0	0	0	0	4,700	5,000	15,075
92,000	2,000	2,000	0	0	0	0	96,000
187,225	15,800	10,550	2,300	1,500	4,700	5,000	227,075
35,004	5,834	5,834	5,834	5,834	5,834	5,834	70,008
8,350	10,000	650	0	0	350	475	19,825
28,500	3,500	3,500	3,500	6,500	6,500	3,500	55,500
208,133	42,000	39,400	38,000	14,000	19,000	21,500	382,033
5,000					500	500	6,000
10,600	500	500	0	2,500	5,000	2,500	21,600
75,000	15,000	15,000	15,000	15,000	15,000	15,000	165,000
5,960	940	1,130	970	400	400	600	10,400
3,000	500	500	500	500	500	500	6,000
379,547	78,274	66,514	63,804	44,734	53,084	50,409	736,366
4,791	508	508	509	508	508	509	7,841
4,365	742	741	739	705	712	716	8,720
5,725	1,175	500	405	295	200	100	8,400
13,750	250	450	350	200	200	200	15,400
31,500	5,250	5,250	5,250	5,250	5,250	5,250	63,000
40,998	6,833	6,833	6,834	6,834	6,834	6,834	82,000
8,550	0	0	0	0	0	0	8,550
2,304	457	432	286	329	360	387	4,555
1,200	250	250	250	250	250	250	2,700
113,183	15,465	14,964	14,623	14,371	14,314	14,246	201,166
2,305	353	344	335	325	316	306	4,284
4,119	2,051	2,046	2,040	2,035	2,029	2,023	16,343
66,498	0	0	33,249	0	0	33,249	132,996
14,398	0	0	7,199	0	0	7,200	28,797
375,000	0	0	0	0	0	0	375,000
98,000	30,000	60,000	0	0	0	0	188,000
1,459	738	743	749	754	760	766	5,969
8,003	1,365	1,374	1,383	1,393	1,402	1,412	16,332
1,249,737	144,046	156,535	125,682	65,112	76,605	114,611	1,932,328
(157,853)	122,610	104,184	100,611	119,509	110,104	83,363	(191,637)
275,000	0	0	0	0	0	0	275,000
0	0	0	0	0	0	0	0
117,147	122,610	104,184	100,611	119,509	110,104	83,363	83,363

31

Three-Year Income Projection
Dayne Landscaping, Inc.

Updated: December 31, 1999	YEAR 1 2000	YEAR 2 2001	YEAR 3 2002	TOTAL 3 YEARS
INCOME				
1. Sales/revenues	**1,608,200**	**2,010,250**	**2,311,788**	**5,930,238**
a. Landscaping — residential	205,000	256,250	294,688	755,938
b. Landscaping — small business	309,900	387,375	445,481	1,142,756
c. Landscaping — large corporations	343,200	429,000	493,350	1,265,550
d. Customized landscaping	372,300	465,375	535,181	1,372,856
e. Snow removal — residential	28,500	35,625	40,969	105,094
f. Snow removal — small business	192,310	240,388	276,446	709,143
g. Snow removal — large corporations	139,990	174,988	201,236	516,213
h. 5% Snow removal contracts	17,000	21,250	24,438	62,688
2. Cost of goods sold (c – d)	**222,075**	**273,844**	**323,420**	**819,339**
Cost of goods (as a percentage of sales)	13.81%	13.62%	13.99%	13.82%
a. Beginning inventory	5,000	10,000	20,000	5,000
b. Purchases	**227,075**	**283,844**	**326,420**	**837,339**
(1) Fertilizer	48,000	60,000	69,000	177,000
(2) Pesticide	24,000	30,000	34,500	88,500
(3) Plants/shrubs	44,000	55,000	63,250	162,250
(4) Salt/sand	15,075	18,844	21,670	55,589
(5) Seed	96,000	120,000	138,000	354,000
c. C.O.G. avail. sale (a + b)	232,075	293,844	346,420	842,339
d. Less ending inventory (12/31)	10,000	20,000	23,000	23,000
3. Gross profit on sales (1 – 2)	**1,386,125**	**1,736,406**	**1,988,367**	**5,110,898**
Gross profit (as a percentage of sales)	86.19%	86.38%	86.01%	86.18%
EXPENSES				
1. Variable (selling) (a thru j)	**772,933**	**916,341**	**1,027,822**	**2,717,097**
Selling expenses (as a percentage of eales)	48.06%	45.58%	44.46%	45.82%
a. Design specialist salaries/payroll taxes	70,008	77,000	84,700	231,708
b. Machinery, tools, equipment	19,825	15,000	17,000	51,825
c. Marketing	55,500	55,000	55,000	165,500
d. Part-time worker salaries/payroll taxes	382,033	477,541	549,172	1,408,747
e. Sales bonuses	6,000	13,500	18,500	38,000
f. Sales commission	21,600	24,000	27,000	72,600
g. Supervisor salaries/payroll taxes	165,000	181,500	199,650	546,150
h. Travel expense	10,400	12,000	14,000	36,400
i. Miscellaneous selling expense	6,000	8,000	10,000	24,000
j. Depreciation (product/service assets)	36,567	52,800	52,800	142,167
2. Fixed (administrative) (a thru j)	**209,916**	**246,967**	**290,467**	**747,350**
Admin. expenses (as a percentage of sales)	13.05%	12.29%	12.56%	12.60%
a. Administration fees — legal/acct.	7,841	7,800	7,800	23,441
b. Insurance — liability, casualty, fire/theft, w. comp.	8,720	10,500	12,000	31,220
c. Licenses and permits	8,400	10,300	12,200	30,900
d. Office equipment	15,400	30,800	45,200	91,400
e. Office salaries/payroll taxes	63,000	77,000	91,000	231,000
f. Owner's guaranteed payment	82,000	90,000	100,000	272,000
g. Rent expense	8,550	0	0	8,550
h. Utilities	4,555	5,500	6,500	16,555
i. Miscellaneous administrative expense	2,700	3,400	4,100	10,200
j. Depreciation (facility, admin. assets)	8,750	11,667	11,667	32,084
TOTAL OPERATING EXPENSES (1 + 2)	**982,849**	**1,163,308**	**1,318,289**	**3,464,447**
NET INCOME OPERATIONS (GPr – Exp)	**403,276**	**573,098**	**670,078**	**1,646,452**
Net income operations (as a percentage of sales)	25.08%	28.51%	28.99%	27.76%
OTHER INCOME (interest income)	1,313	1,378	1,447	4,138
OTHER EXPENSE (interest expense)	20,627	28,105	25,844	74,576
NET PROFIT (LOSS) BEFORE TAXES	**383,962**	**546,371**	**645,681**	**1,576,014**
Taxes 1. Federal, s-employment	132,996	196,335	235,066	564,397
2. State	28,797	40,978	48,426	118,201
3. Local	0	0	0	0
NET PROFIT (LOSS) AFTER TAXES	**222,169**	**309,058**	**362,189**	**893,416**
Net profit (loss) (as a percentage of sales)	13.81%	15.37%	15.67%	15.07%

Projected Balance Sheet

Business Name:

Dayne Landscaping, Inc.

Projected for: December 31, 2000

ASSETS

		% of Assets
Current assets		
Cash	$ 83,363	12.41%
Petty cash	$ 0	0.00%
Accounts receivable	$ 0	0.00%
Inventory	$ 10,000	1.49%
Short-term investments	$ 0	0.00%
Long-term investments	$ 0	0.00%
Fixed assets		
Land (valued at cost)	$ 200,000	29.77%
Buildings	$ 163,050	24.27%
1. Cost	175,000	
2. Less acc. depr.	11,950	
Improvements	$ 0	0.00%
1. Cost	0	
2. Less acc. depr.	0	
Equipment	$ 92,833	13.82%
1. Cost	104,000	
2. Less acc. depr.	11,167	
Furniture	$ 0	0.00%
1. Cost	0	
2. Less acc. depr.	0	
Autos/Vehicles	$ 122,600	18.25%
1. Cost	160,000	
2. Less acc. depr.	37,400	
Other assets		
1.	$ 0	0.00%
2.	$ 0	0.00%
3.	$ 0	0.00%

TOTAL ASSETS $ 671,846   100.00%

LIABILITIES

		% of Liabilities
Current liabilities		
Accounts payable	$ 0	0.00%
Notes payable	$ 27,337	8.72%
Interest payable	$ 0	0.00%
Pre-paid deposits	$ 0	0.00%
Taxes payable		
Accrued federal income tax	$ 0	0.00%
Accrued state income tax	$ 0	0.00%
Accrued payroll tax	$ 0	0.00%
Accrued sales tax	$ 0	0.00%
Payroll accrual	$ 0	0.00%
Long-term liabilities		
Notes payable to investors	$ 0	0.00%
Notes payable others	$ 286,281	91.28%

TOTAL LIABILITIES $ 313,618   100.00%

NET WORTH (EQUITY)

		% of Net Worth
Proprietorship	$ 0	0.00%
or		
Partnership		
1. (Name 1), ___% equity	$ 0	0.00%
2. (Name 2), ___% equity	$ 0	0.00%
or		
Corporation		
Capital stock	$ 20,000	5.58%
Surplus paid In	$ 5,000	1.40%
Retained earnings	$ 333,228	93.02%

TOTAL NET WORTH $ 358,228   100.00%

Assets – Liabilities = Net Worth
and
Liabilities + Equity = Total Assets

1. See Financial Statement Analysis for ratios and notations

FINANCIAL STATEMENT ANALYSIS SUMMARY

The following is a summary of Dayne Landscaping, Inc.1999 and 2000 financial statement analysis information, as developed on the next 5 pages of spreadsheets (pages 35-39) :

*Author notation:
Writer must research industry standards.

	1999 HISTORICAL	2000 PROJECTED	INDUSTRY STANDARD
1. Net working capital	$119,846	$66,026	$80,000 + or -
2. Current ratio	8.34	3.42	2.0 +
3. Quick ratio	8.03	3.05	1.0 + or -
4. Gross profit margin	87.01%	86.19%	85.0%
5. Operating profit margin	23.21%	25.08%	25.0%
6. Net profit margin	14.28%	13.81%	14%
7. Debt to assets	30.93%	46.68%	33.0% -
8. Debt to equity	44.77%	87.55%	100% -
9. ROI (return on investment)	56.38%	33.07%	24% +
10. Vertical income statement analysis *			
Sales/revenues	100.00%	100.0%	
Cost of goods	12.99%	13.81%	15.0% + or -
Gross profit	87.01%	86.19%	85.0%
Operating expense	63.80%	61.11%	62.0% + or -
Net income operations	23.21%	25.08%	23.0% + or -
Interest income	0.16%	0.08%	N/A Variable
Interest expense	0.71%	1.28%	4.0% Variable
Net profit (pre-tax)	22.66%	23.88%	19.0% + or -
* All items stated as % of total revenues			
11. Vertical balance sheet analysis *			
Current assets	69.14%	13.90%	18.0% +
Inventory	2.54%	1.49%	2.0%
Total assets	100.0%	100.00%	
Current liabilities	8.29%	4.07%	15.0% -
Total liabilities	30.93%	46.68%	50.0% -
Net worth	69.07%	53.32%	50.0% +
Total liabilities + Net worth	100.0%	100.00%	

* All asset items stated as % of total assets;
Liability and net worth items stated as % of Total liabilities + Net worth

Notes:

Dayne Landscaping, Inc. has taken advantage of a rapidly-increasing marketplace, and has also neatly incorporated snow removal services to increase revenues significantly during winter months. The company earned an unusually high 1999 net profit for a start-up service business ($111,059). Debt Ratios (Debt:Assets, 30.93% and Debt:Equity, 44.77%) are better than industry average. A 2000 beginning cash balance of $131,178, with no current liabilities other than $16,332 of notes payable on a previous loan, give the company sufficient marketing funds to expand services into the corporate landscaping and design areas. The purchase of their present facility, currently under a lease agreement (using $100,000 cash + $275,000 loan funds) will not raise the Debt to Equity Ratio (projected at 87.55%) beyond a safe limit. Projections indicate high sales growth with the acquisition of new personnel, vehicles, and equipment to service the increased customer base. The company is experiencing rapid, but controlled growth. Financial projections indicate that the company will be more than able to fulfill its obligations to repay the $275,000 loan with interest and still maintain good cash flow and increased profitability.

Financial Statement Analysis
Ratio Table
Dayne Landscaping, Inc.

Type of Analysis	Formula	Historical: 1999		Projected: 2000	
1. Liquidity Analysis	**Balance Sheet**	Current Assets	136,178	Current Assets	93,363
	Current Assets	Current Liabilities	16,332	Current Liabilities	27,337
a. Net working capital	— Current Liabilities	**Net Working Capital**	**$119,846**	**Net Working Capital**	**$66,026**
	Balance Sheet	Current Assets	136,178	Current Assets	93,363
b. Current ratio	Current Assets	Current Liabilities	16,332	Current Liabilities	27,337
	Current Liabilities	**Current Ratio**	**8.34**	**Current Ratio**	**3.42**
	Balance Sheet	Current Assets	136,178	Current Assets	93,363
c. Quick ratio	Current Assets minus Inventory	Inventory	5,000	Inventory	10,000
	Current Liabilities	Current Liabilities	16,332	Current Liabilities	27,337
		Quick Ratio	**8.03**	**Quick Ratio**	**3.05**
2. Profitability Analysis	**Income Statement**	Gross Profits	676,834	Gross Profits	1,386,125
a. Gross profit margin	Gross Profits	Sales	777,864	Sales	1,608,200
	Sales	**Gross Profit Margin**	**87.01%**	**Gross Profit Margin**	**86.19%**
b. Operating profit margin	Income From Operations	Income From Ops.	180,564	Income From Ops.	403,276
	Sales	Sales	777,864	Sales	1,608,200
		Operating Profit Margin	**23.21%**	**Operating Profit Margin**	**25.08%**
c. Net profit margin	Net Profits	Net Profits	111,059	Net Profits	222,169
	Sales	Sales	777,864	Sales	1,608,200
		Net Profit Margin	**14.28%**	**Net Profit Margin**	**13.81%**
3. Debt Ratios	**Balance Sheet**	Total Liabilities	60,919	Total Liabilities	313,618
	Total Liabilities	Total Assets	196,978	Total Assets	671,846
a. Debt to assets	Total Assets	**Debt to Assets Ratio**	**30.93%**	**Debt to Assets Ratio**	**46.68%**
	Total Liabilities	Total Liabilities	60,919	Total Liabilities	313,618
b. Debt to equity	Total Owners' Equity	Total Owners' Equity	136,059	Total Owners' Equity	358,228
		Debt to Equity Ratio	**44.77%**	**Debt to Equity Ratio**	**87.55%**
4. Measures of Investment	**Balance Sheet**	Net Profits	111,059	Net Profits	222,169
a. ROI	Net Profits	Total Assets	196,978	Total Assets	671,846
(Return on Investment)	Total Assets	**ROI (Return on Invest.)**	**56.38%**	**ROI (Return on Invest.)**	**33.07%**
5. Vertical Financial Statement Analysis	**Balance Sheet** 1. Each asset % of Total Assets 2. Liability & Equity % of Total L&E **Income Statement** 3. All items % of Total Revenues	**NOTE:** *See Attached* **Balance Sheet and** **Income Statement**		**NOTE:** *See Attached* **Balance Sheet and** **Income Statement**	
6. Horizontal Financial Statement Analysis	**Balance Sheet** 1. Assets, Liab & Equity measured against 2nd year. Increases and decreases stated as amount & % **Income Statement** 2. Revenues & Expenses measured against 2nd year. Increases and decreases stated as amount & %	**NOTE:** **Horizontal Analysis** **Not Applicable** **Only one year in business**		**NOTE:** **Horizontal Analysis** **Not Applicable** **Only one year in business**	

35

1999 Historical
Vertical Income Statement Analysis
Dayne Landscaping, Inc.

Historical For the Year: 1999		Begin: January 1, 1999 End: December 31, 1999	
	AMOUNT		**% Total Revenues**
INCOME			
1. **Sales/revenues**		$ 777,864	100.00%
a. Landscaping — residential	216,000		27.77%
b. Landscaping — small business	160,700		20.66%
c. Customized landscaping	199,374		25.63%
d. Snow removal — residential	18,250		2.35%
e. Snow removal — small business	167,100		21.48%
f. 5% Snow removal contracts	8,500		1.09%
g. Miscellaneous accessories	7,940		1.02%
2. **Cost of goods sold (c – d)**		101,030	12.99%
a. Beginning inventory	**0**		**0.00%**
b. Purchases	**106,030**		**13.63%**
(1) Fertilizer	19,000		2.44%
(2) Pesticide	11,000		1.41%
(3) Plants/shrubs	23,000		2.96%
(4) Salt/sand	8,030		1.03%
(1) Seed	45,000		5.79%
c. C.O.G. avail. sale (a + b)	**106,030**		**13.63%**
d. Less ending inventory (12/31)	**5,000**		**0.64%**
3. **Gross profit on sales (1 – 2)**		$ 676,834	87.01%
EXPENSES			
1. **Variable (selling) (a thru j)**		318,000	40.88%
a. Design specialist salary/payroll taxes	20,000		2.57%
b. Machinery, hand tools, equipment	11,000		1.41%
c. Marketing	5,400		0.69%
d. Part-time worker salaries	182,000		23.40%
e. Sales bonuses	2,000		0.26%
f. Sales commission	10,800		1.39%
g. Supervisor salaries/payroll taxes	60,000		7.71%
h. Travel expense	10,400		1.34%
i. Miscellaneous variable expense	1,200		0.15%
j. Depreciation (product/services assets)	15,200		1.95%
2. **Fixed (administrative) (a thru j)**		178,270	22.92%
a. Administration fees—legal/accounting	3,050		0.39%
b. Insurance (liability, casualty, fire/theft)	11,600		1.49%
c. Licenses and permits	4,200		0.54%
d. Office equipment	7,700		0.99%
e. Office salaries/payroll taxes	42,000		5.40%
f. Owner's guaranteed payment	65,000		8.36%
g. Rent expense	39,900		5.13%
h. Utilities	4,320		0.56%
i. Miscellaneous fixed expense	500		0.06%
j. Depreciation (administrative assets)	0		0.00%
Total operating expenses (1 + 2)		496,270	63.80%
Net income from operations (GP – Exp)		$ 180,564	23.21%
Other income (interest income)	1,250		0.16%
Other expense (interest expense)	5,535		0.71%
Net profit (loss) before taxes		$ 176,279	22.66%
Taxes:			
a. Federal	51,999		6.68%
b. State	13,221	65,220	1.70%
c. Local	0		0.00%
NET PROFIT (LOSS) AFTER TAXES		$ 111,059	14.28%

1999 Historical
Vertical Balance Sheet Analysis

(All Asset percentages = % of Total Assets; All Liability or Equity percentages = % of Total Liabilities + Total Equity)

Analysis of Historical Balance Sheet			Date of Balance Sheet: December 31, 1999		
Dayne Landscaping, Inc.					

ASSETS		% of Total Assets	LIABILITIES		% of Total L + NW
Current assets			**Current liabilities**		
Cash	$ 131,178	66.60%	Accounts payable	$ 0	0.00%
Petty cash	$ 0	0.00%	Notes payable	$ 16,332	8.29%
Sales tax holding account	$ 0	0.00%	Interest payable	$ 0	0.00%
Accounts receivable	$ 0	0.00%	Pre-paid deposits	$ 0	0.00%
Inventory	$ 5,000	2.54%			
Short-term investments	$ 0	0.00%	Taxes payable		
			Accrued federal income tax	$ 0	0.00%
Long-term investments	$ 0	0.00%	Accrued state income tax	$ 0	0.00%
			Accrued payroll tax	$ 0	0.00%
Fixed assets			Accrued sales tax	$ 0	0.00%
Land (valued at cost)	$ 0	0.00%			
			Payroll accrual	$ 0	0.00%
Buildings	$ 0	0.00%			
1. Cost	0		**Long-term liabilities**		
2. Less acc. depr.	0		Notes payable to investors	$ 0	0.00%
			Notes payable to others	$ 44,587	22.64%
Improvements	$ 0	0.00%			
1. Cost	0				
2. Less acc. depr.	0		**TOTAL LIABILITIES**	$ 60,919	30.93%
Equipment	$ 12,800	6.50%			
1. Cost	16,000				
2. Less acc. depr.	3,200		**NET WORTH (EQUITY)**		
Furniture	$ 0	0.00%	**Proprietorship**	$ 0	0.00%
1. Cost	0		or		
2. Less acc. depr.	0		**Partnership**		
			1. Partner A	$ 0	0.00%
Autos/vehicles	$ 48,000	24.37%	2. Partner B	$ 0	0.00%
1. Cost	60,000		or		
2. Less acc. depr.	12,000		**Corporation**		
			Capital stock	$ 20,000	10.15%
			Surplus paid in	$ 5,000	2.54%
Other assets			Retained earnings, appropriated	$ 100,000	50.77%
1.	$ 0	0.00%	Retained earnings, unappropriated	$ 11,059	5.61%
2.	$ 0	0.00%			
			TOTAL NET WORTH	$ 136,059	69.07%
TOTAL ASSETS	$ 196,978	100.00%	**LIABILITIES + NET WORTH**	$ 196,978	100.00%
			Assets – Liabilities = Net worth -or- Liabilities + Equity = Assets		

2000 Projected
Vertical Income Statement Analysis
Dayne Landscaping, Inc

| Projected For the Year: 2000 | Begin: January 1, 2000   End: December 31, 2001 |

	AMOUNT		% Total Revenues
INCOME			
1. Sales/revenues		$ 1,608,200	100.00%
a. Landscaping — residential	205,000		12.75%
b. Landscaping — small business	309,900		19.27%
c. Customized landscaping	343,200		21.34%
d. Snow removal — residential	372,300		23.15%
e. Snow removal — small business	28,500		1.77%
f. Snow removal — large corporations	192,310		11.96%
g. 5% Snow removal contracts	139,990		8.70%
h. Miscellaneous accessories	17,000		1.06%
2. Cost of goods sold (c-d)		222,075	13.81%
a. Beginning inventory	5,000		0.31%
b. Purchases	227,075		14.12%
(1) Fertilizer	48,000		2.98%
(2) Pesticide	24,000		1.49%
(3) Plants/shrubs	44,000		2.74%
(4) Salt/sand	15,075		0.94%
(1) Seed	96,000		5.97%
c. C.O.G. avail. sale (a + b)	232,075		14.43%
d. Less ending inventory (12/31)	10,000		0.62%
3. Gross profit on sales (1 – 2)		$ 1,386,125	86.19%
EXPENSES			
1. Variable (selling) (a thru j)		772,933	48.06%
a. Design specialists salary/payroll taxes	70,008		4.35%
b. Machinery, hand tools, equipment	19,825		1.23%
c. Marketing	55,500		3.45%
d. Part-time workers salaries	382,033		23.76%
e. Sales bonuses	6,000		0.37%
f. Sales commission	21,600		1.34%
g. Supervisor salaries/payroll taxes	165,000		10.26%
h. Travel expense	10,400		0.65%
i. Miscellaneous variable expense	6,000		0.37%
j. Depreciation (products/services assets)	36,567		2.27%
2. Fixed (administrative) (a thru j)		209,916	13.05%
a. Administration fees — legal/accounting	7,841		0.49%
b. Insurance (liability, casualty, fire, theft)	8,720		0.54%
c. Licenses and permits	8,400		0.52%
d. Office equipment	15,400		0.96%
e. Office salaries/payroll taxes	63,000		3.92%
f. Owner's guaranteed payment	82,000		5.10%
g. Rent expense	8,550		0.53%
h. Utilities	4,555		0.28%
i. Miscellaneous fixed expense	2,700		0.17%
j. Depreciation (administrative assets)	8,750		0.54%
Total operating expenses (1+2)		982,849	61.11%
Net income from operations (GP-Exp)		$ 403,276	25.08%
Other income (interest income)	1,313		0.08%
Other expense (interest expense)	20,627		1.28%
Net profit (loss) before taxes		$ 383,962	23.88%
Taxes:			
a. Federal	132,996		8.27%
b. State	28,797	161,793	1.79%
c. Local	0		0.00%
NET PROFIT (LOSS) AFTER TAXES		$ 222,169	13.81%

2000 Projected
Vertical Balance Sheet Analysis

(All asset percentages = % of total assets; All liability or equity percentages = % of total liabilities + total equity)

Projected for: December 31, 2000	Date of Projection: December 15, 1999

Dayne Landscaping, Inc.

ASSETS			% of Total Assets	LIABILITIES			% of Total L + NW
Current assets				**Current liabilities**			
Cash	$	83,363	12.41%	Accounts payable	$	0	0.00%
Petty cash	$	0	0.00%	Notes payable	$	27,337	4.07%
Sales tax holding account	$	0	0.00%	Interest payable	$	0	0.00%
Accounts receivable	$	0	0.00%	Pre-paid deposits	$	0	0.00%
Inventory	$	10,000	1.49%				
Short-term investments	$	0	0.00%	Taxes payable			
				Accrued federal income tax	$	0	0.00%
Long-term investments	$	0	0.00%	Accrued state income tax	$	0	0.00%
				Accrued payroll tax	$	0	0.00%
Fixed assets				Accrued sales tax	$	0	0.00%
Land (valued at cost)	$	200,000	29.77%				
				Payroll accrual	$	0	0.00%
Buildings	$	163,050	24.27%				
1. Cost	175,000			**Long-term liabilities**			
2. Less acc. depr.	11,950			Notes payable to investors	$	0	0.00%
				Notes payable to others	$	286,281	42.61%
Improvements	$	0	0.00%				
1. Cost	0						
2. Less acc. depr.	0			**TOTAL LIABILITIES**	$	313,618	46.68%
Equipment	$	92,833	13.82%				
1. Cost	104,000			**NET WORTH (EQUITY)**			
2. Less acc. depr.	11,167						
Furniture	$	0	0.00%	**Proprietorship**	$	0	0.00%
1. Cost	0			or			
2. Less Acc. Depr.	0			**Partnership**			
				1. Partner A	$	0	0.00%
Autos/vehicles	$	122,600	18.25%	2. Partner B	$	0	0.00%
1. Cost	160,000			or			
2. Less acc. depr.	37,400			**Corporation**			
				Capital stock	$	20,000	2.98%
				Surplus paid in	$	5,000	0.74%
Other assets				Retained earnings	$	333,228	49.60%
1.	$	0	0.00%				
2.	$	0	0.00%	**TOTAL NET WORTH**	$	358,228	53.32%
TOTAL ASSETS	$	671,846	100.00%	**LIABILITIES + N. WORTH** $		671,846	100.00%

Assets – Liabilities = Net Worth -or- Liabilities + Equity = Assets

Dayne Landscaping, Inc.

IV. Supporting Documents

Competition Comparison

Owner's Resume

Letter of Reference

Business Plan Assumption Sheet

Note: For purposes of brevity, we have chosen to include only a portion of the supporting documents that would be found in Dayne Landscaping, Inc.'s business plan.

<u>Competition</u>

<u>Vendor</u>	<u>Garden Shop</u>	<u>Landscaping Plus</u>	<u>Dayne Landscaping</u>
Landscaping			
Design	Yes	Yes	Yes
Oriental design	No	No	Yes
Maintenance	Yes	Yes	Yes
Pest control	No	No	Yes

Snow Services			
Plowing	Yes	Yes	Yes
Removal	No	No	No
Response time	Whenever	Whenever	Designated
Guarantee	No	No	Yes

Servicing	NH only	NH, MA	NH, MA, CT
Price per hour	$25–30	$30–35	$20–30

41

Robin T. Dayne

181 Thoreaus Landing

Nashua, NH 03060

603-888-2020 (W) 603-889-2293 (H)

Summary

Five year's experience in the Landscaping Industry. Skilled in sales, support, and operations of new accounts for an established landscaping company. Managed an office of 10 employees related to customer service. Proficient in managing and workings of the landscaping service industry. Knowledgeable in landscaping, design, and planning.

Experience

Landscaping, Nashua, NH   **1993-1998**

Office Manager, January 1997–December 1998

Managed 10 employees that sold and serviced customer accounts. Responsible for planning scheduling, and managing inventory (equipment and tools) for the ten employees. Implemented the first "customer satisfaction survey" over the phone, to the entire base of customers.

- Developed a tool "check-in" process saving the company $10,000 a year in lost inventory.
- Organized the telemarketing necessary for the customer survey resulting in additional sales revenue of $25,000.
- Implemented and managed service issue "hot line" for dissatisfied customers.
- Responsible for all major accounts and employees that worked at the sites.

Account Supervisor, December 1995–December 1996

Managed 20 assigned accounts for landscaping and snow maintenance. Responsible for reporting to the President all account updates and potential revenue opportunities.

- Maintained the 20 accounts by scheduling all part-time workers.
- Trained part-time employees in proper lawn care maintenance.
- Managed the inventory, equipment, and supplies of each worker.
- Managed all customer service issues and received excellence award for all accounts at the end of the year.
- Scheduled all snow removal and coordinated snow emergencies.

Robin T. Dayne...Page 2

Account Landscaping Specialist, June 1992–November 1995

- Worked the landscaping contract of a large corporate account.
- Recommended landscaping design changes and secured additional contract with company.
- Provided snow removal during storm and emergencies.
- Learned the operation of all landscaping equipment, tools, and vehicles.

Equipment Rental, Inc.   1986–1992

Service Desk Manager, January 1986–May1992

- Responsible for handling any service issues related to the renting of the companies equipment or machinery.
- Managed all bill disputes to resolution.
- Interfaced with office manager on large account problems.
- Recommended improvements in the problem solving process that resulted in speedy results for the customers.

Personal Strengths

- Organized
- Excellent communication skills
- Strong management training and experience
- Dedicated to customer service excellence
- Strong knowledge of landscaping industry

Education

Completed Bachelors Degree in Horticulture at the University of New Hampshire. Independent studies at the Institute for Higher Learning majoring in Environmental Protection.

Affiliations and Interests

Board member of the Nashua Chamber of Commerce. Committee member of the City's "Beautification Program." Volunteer at Community Services of Nashua.

 rtd Marketing International, Inc. 81 Walden Pond Ave., Nashua, NH 03060

November 22, 1999

Dear Prospective Investor,

I am delighted to have the opportunity to write this letter of recommendation for Robin T. Dayne.

We have had a contract with Dayne Landscaping, Inc. since February. We came to them initially for snow removal because the company we were using could not guarantee our facility would be plowed by 7:00 AM, which we needed in order for our employees to park for work. Dayne Landscaping was able to provide us that guarantee and did an excellent job of fulfilling their commitment, during some very tough storms.

We have since contacted with them for landscaping maintenance and have found the same quality of service. They recommended changes that would save us money and our property hasn't looked this good in years.

Recently we secured their services to install an Oriental garden, which is unique and attractive. Our international clientele has even commented on our unique landscaping and in our business, first impressions can mean everything.

I would recommend them highly, based on their level of service, quality of work and commitment as well they should be considered for the funding they seek.

If you have further questions, feel free to contact me. I can be reached on my private number 603-882-2221, during business hours.

Cordially,

Heather Pope
President

Assumptions for Dayne Landscaping, Inc. Business Plan

Seeking Bank Loan

- **Purpose:** To purchase land and facilities currently leased by Dayne Landscaping, Inc.

- **Projected Terms:** $275,000 for 15 years @9%; need funding by April 1, 2000, repayments can begin on May 1, 2000 (see amortization schedule C).

Financial Assumptions

- $25,000 initial capital contribution by owner in corporation (not a loan).

- 5% required up-front fees for all snow contracts.

- 5% Sales Commission to be paid to sales representatives.

- Bonuses of $500 each to be paid for landing new corporate accounts.

- Salaries for (4) Supervisors @ $15,000, totaling $60,000 (+ benefits and payroll taxes).

- Salary for the President to be guaranteed @ $65,000 for 1999; projected raise to $82,000 for 2000.

- Salary for the Office Manager @ $22,000 (+ benefits and payroll taxes).

- Salary for the Administration Assistants (one in 1999, two in 2000) @ $15,000 (+ payroll taxes and benefits).

- Salary for part-time people @ $7 per hour. Hired as needed to meet volume.

- Licensing permit fees with City and State during the year.

- Rent deposit at $5,700 for first and last month.

- Heat and Electricity at $60 per sq. ft, totaling $360 per month, and $4,320 per year.

- Fire and Liability Insurance at $50 per sq. ft, totaling $300 per month, and $3,600 per year.

- All insurance at $8,000 per year. The total cost of insurance at $11,600.

- Two trucks purchased with 1999 loan: $60,000 @ 8%; interest five-year period = $12,955.05 (see amortizing schedule A).

- Four large mowers purchased with 1999 loan: $16,000 @8%; interest three-year period = $2,049.79 (see amortizing schedule B).

- State income taxes charges at 7.5% of net profits.

- Federal income taxes based on Federal Corporation Tax Schedule (15%-25%-34%-39% of net profits).

- Estimated taxes paid on schedule quarterly, based on actual and projected net profits for 1999 and 2000.

- Ending inventory: 1999 = $5,000; 2000 projected at $10,000.

Blank Forms and Worksheets

··

The forms on the following pages have been provided for you to copy and use in the writing of your business plan.

The forms that contain "Variable Expenses" and "Fixed Expenses" have spaces for you to fill in your own categories. They should be customized to your particular business. This will require you to decide on category headings when you begin the financial section of your business plan and follow through with the same headings throughout all financial statements.

The categories are developed by looking at your different accounts in your ledger or by using the categories from your revenue and expense journal. Those expenses that are frequent and sizable will have a heading of their own (i.e., advertising, rent, salaries, etc.). Those expenses that are very small and infrequent will be included under the heading "miscellaneous" in either the variable or fixed expenses section of each of your financial statements.

Cash to Be Paid Out Worksheet

Business Name: _____   **Time Period:** _____ **to** _____

1. START-UP COSTS   _____
   Business license   _____
   Accounting fees   _____
   Legal fees   _____
   Other start-up costs: _____
     a.   _____
     b.   _____
     c.   _____
     d.   _____

2. INVENTORY PURCHASES
   Cash out for goods intended for resale   _____

3. VARIABLE EXPENSES (SELLING)
   a.   _____
   b.   _____
   c.   _____
   d.   _____
   e.   _____
   f.   _____
   g. Miscellaneous variable expense   _____
   TOTAL SELLING EXPENSES   _____

4. FIXED EXPENSES (ADMINISTRATIVE)
   a.   _____
   b.   _____
   c.   _____
   d.   _____
   e.   _____
   f.   _____
   g. Miscellaneous fixed expense   _____
   TOTAL ADMINISTRATIVE EXPENSE   _____

5. ASSETS (LONG-TERM PURCHASES)
   Cash to be paid out in current period   _____

6. LIABILITIES
   Cash outlay for retiring debts, loans
   and/or accounts payable   _____

7. OWNER EQUITY
   Cash to be withdrawn by owner   _____

TOTAL CASH TO BE PAID OUT $ _____

Sources of Cash Worksheet

Business Name: _____

Time Period Covered: _____ ___, _____ to _____ ___, _____

---

1. CASH ON HAND _____

2. SALES (REVENUES)

Product sales income _____

Services income _____

Deposits on sales or services _____

Collections on accounts receivable _____

3. MISCELLANEOUS INCOME

Interest income

Payments to be received on loans _____

4. SALE OF LONG-TERM ASSETS _____

5. LIABILITIES _____

Loan funds (to be received during current period; from banks, through the SBA, or from other lending institutions)

6. EQUITY

Owner investments (sole prop/partners) _____

Contributed capital (corporation) _____

Sale of stock (corporation) _____

Venture capital _____

TOTAL CASH AVAILABLE

A. Without sales = $ _____

B. With sales = $ _____

Pro Forma Cash Flow Statement

Business Name:

Year: _____

	Jan	Feb	Mar	Apr	May	Jun	6-MONTH TOTALS	Jul	Aug	Sep	Oct	Nov	Dec	12-MONTH TOTALS
BEGINNING CASH BALANCE														
CASH RECEIPTS														
A. Sales/revenues														
B. Receivables														
C. Interest income														
D. Sale of long-term assets														
TOTAL CASH AVAILABLE														
CASH PAYMENTS														
A. Cost of goods to be sold														
1. Purchases														
2. Material														
3. Labor														
Total cost of goods														
B. Variable expenses														
1.														
2.														
3.														
4.														
5.														
6.														
7. Misc. variable expense														
Total variable expenses														
C. Fixed expenses														
1.														
2.														
3.														
4.														
5.														
6.														
7. Misc. fixed expense														
Total fixed expenses														
D. Interest expense														
E. Federal income tax														
F. Other uses														
G. Long-term asset payments														
H. Loan payments														
I. Owner draws														
TOTAL CASH PAID OUT														
CASH BALANCE/DEFICIENCY														
LOANS TO BE RECEIVED														
EQUITY DEPOSITS														
ENDING CASH BALANCE														

Quarterly Budget Analysis

Business Name: _____   **For the Quarter Ending:** _____ __, _____

BUDGET ITEM	THIS QUARTER			YEAR-TO-DATE		
	Budget	Actual	Variation	Budget	Actual	Variation
SALES REVENUES						
Less cost of goods						
GROSS PROFITS						
VARIABLE EXPENSES						
1.						
2.						
3.						
4.						
5.						
6.						
7. Miscellaneous variable expense						
FIXED EXPENSES						
1.						
2.						
3.						
4.						
5.						
6.						
7. Miscellaneous fixed expense						
NET INCOME FROM OPERATIONS						
INTEREST INCOME						
INTEREST EXPENSE						
NET PROFIT (Pretax)						
TAXES						
NET PROFIT (After Tax)						

NON-INCOME STATEMENT ITEMS

1. Long-term asset repayments						
2. Loan repayments						
3. Owner draws						

BUDGET DEVIATIONS	This Quarter	Year-to-Date
1. Income statement items:		
2. Non-income statement items:		
3. Total deviation		

Three-Year Income Projection

Business Name: **Updated:** _____ ___, _____

	YEAR 1 ____	YEAR 2 20___	YEAR 3 20___	TOTAL 3 YEARS
INCOME				
1. Sales revenues				
2. Cost of goods sold (c – d)				
a. Beginning inventory				
b. Purchases				
c. C.O.G. avail. sale (a + b)				
d. Less ending iventory (12/31)				
3. Gross profit on sales (1-2)				
EXPENSES				
1. Variable (selling) (a thru h)				
a.				
b.				
c.				
d.				
e.				
f.				
g. Miscellaneous selling expense				
h. Depreciation (prod/serv assets)				
2. Fixed (administrative) (a thru h)				
a.				
b.				
c.				
d.				
e.				
f.				
g. Miscellaneous fixed expense				
h. Depreciation (office equipment)				
TOTAL OPERATING EXPENSES (1 + 2)				
NET INCOME OPERATIONS (GPr – Exp)				
OTHER INCOME (interest income)				
OTHER EXPENSE (interest expense)				
NET PROFIT (LOSS) BEFORE TAXES				
TAXES 1. Federal, self-employment				
2. State				
3. Local				
NET PROFIT (LOSS) AFTER TAXES				

Break-Even Analysis Graph

Business Name: _____   **Analysis Date:** _____ __, _____

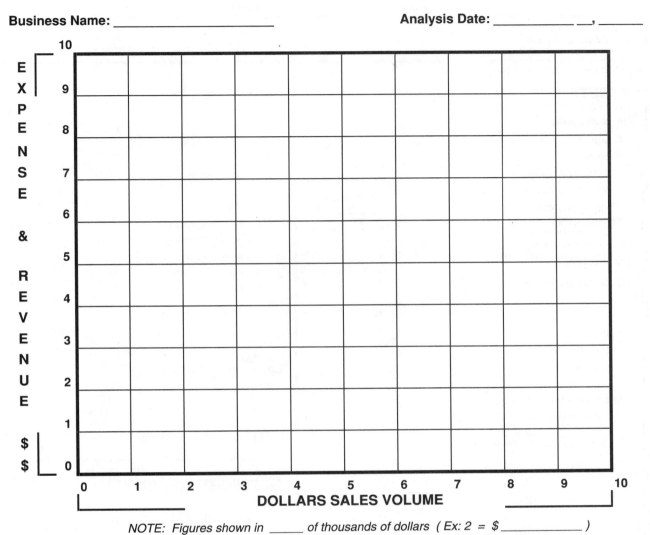

NOTE: *Figures shown in* _____ *of thousands of dollars (Ex: 2 = $ _____)*

Break-Even Point Calculation

B-E Point (Sales) = Fixed Costs + [(Variable Costs/Estimated Revenues) x Sales]

1. B-E Point (Sales) = $_____ + [($_____ / $_____) x Sales]

2. B-E Point (Sales) = $_____ + (_____ x Sales)

3. Sales = $_____ + _____Sales

4. Sales – _____Sales = $_____

5. _____Sales = $_____

6. Sales (S) = $_____ / _____

Break-Even Point
S = $

Balance Sheet

Business Name: _____ **Date:** _____ ___, _____

ASSETS

Current assets

Cash	$ _____
Petty cash	$ _____
Accounts receivable	$ _____
Inventory	$ _____
Short-term investments	$ _____
Prepaid expenses	$ _____

Long-term investments $ _____

Fixed assets

Land (valued at cost) $ _____

Buildings $ _____
  1. Cost _____
  2. Less acc. depr. _____

Improvements $ _____
  1. Cost _____
  2. Less acc. depr. _____

Equipment $ _____
  1. Cost _____
  2. Less Acc. Depr. _____

Furniture $ _____
  1. Cost _____
  2. Less acc. depr. _____

Autos/vehicles $ _____
  1. Cost _____
  2. Less acc. depr. _____

Other assets
  1. $ _____
  2. $ _____

TOTAL ASSETS $ _____

LIABILITIES

Current liabilities

Accounts payable	$ _____
Notes payable	$ _____
Interest payable	$ _____

Taxes payable
  Federal income tax $ _____
  Self-employment tax $ _____
  State income tax $ _____
  Sales tax accrual $ _____
  Property tax $ _____

Payroll accrual $ _____

Long-term liabilities
  Notes payable $ _____

TOTAL LIABILITIES $ _____

NET WORTH (EQUITY)

Proprietorship $ _____
  or
Partnership
(name)_____, ___% equity $ _____
(name)_____, ___% equity $ _____
  or
Corporation
  Capital stock $ _____
  Surplus paid in $ _____
  Retained earnings $ _____

TOTAL NET WORTH $ _____

Assets – Liabilities = Net Worth
and
Liabilities + Equity = Total Assets

Profit & Loss (Income) Statement

Business Name: _____

For the Year: _____

	Jan	Feb	Mar	Apr	May	Jun	6-MONTH TOTALS	Jul	Aug	Sep	Oct	Nov	Dec	12-MONTH TOTALS
INCOME														
1. Net sales (Gr – R&A)														
2. Cost of goods to be sold														
a. Beginning inventory														
b. Purchases														
c. C.O.G. available for sale														
d. Less ending inventory														
3. Gross profit														
EXPENSES														
1. Variable (selling) expenses														
a.														
b.														
c.														
d.														
e.														
f.														
g. Misc. variable expense														
h. Depreciation														
Total variable expenses														
1. Fixed (admin) expenses														
a.														
b.														
c.														
d.														
e.														
f.														
g. Misc. fixed expense														
h. Depreciation														
Total fixed expenses														
Total operating expense														
Net Income From Operations														
Other Income (Interest)														
Other Expense (Interest)														
Net Profit (Loss) Before Taxes														
Taxes: a. Federal														
b. State														
c. Local														
NET PROFIT (LOSS) AFTER TAXES														

Profit & Loss (Income) Statement

Business Name: _____

Beginning: _____ ___, _____   **Ending:** _____ ___, _____

INCOME		
1. Sales revenues		$
2. Cost of goods sold (c – d)		
a. Beginning inventory (1/01)		
b. Purchases		
c. C.O.G. avail. sale (a + b)		
d. Less ending inventory (12/31)		
3. Gross profit on sales (1 – 2)		$
EXPENSES		
1. Variable (selling) (a thru h)		
a.		
b.		
c.		
d.		
e.		
f.		
g. Misc. variable (selling) expense		
h. Depreciation (prod/serv. assets)		
2. Fixed (administrative) (a thru h)		
a.		
b.		
c.		
d.		
e.		
f.		
g. Misc. fixed (administrative) expense		
h. Depreciation (office equipment)		
Total operating expenses (1 + 2)		
Net income from operations (GP – Exp)		$
Other income (interest income)		
Other expense (interest expense)		
Net profit (loss) before taxes		$
Taxes		
a. Federal		
b. State		
c. Local		
NET PROFIT (LOSS) AFTER TAXES		$

Financial Statement Analysis
Ratio Table

Business Name: _____ **For the Year:** _____

Type of Analysis	Formula	Projected: Year 1	Historical: Year 1
1. Liquidity analysis a. Net working capital	**Balance Sheet** Current Assets — Current Liabilities	Current Assets _____ Current Liabilities _____ **Net Working Capital** $ _____	Current Assets _____ Current Liabilities _____ **Net Working Capital** $ _____
b. Current ratio	**Balance Sheet** Current Assets Current Liabilities	Current Assets _____ Current Liabilities _____ **Current Ratio** ____ . ____	Current Assets _____ Current Liabilities _____ **Current Ratio** ____ . ____
c. Quick ratio	**Balance Sheet** Current Assets minus Inventory Current Liabilities	Current Assets _____ Inventory _____ Current Liabilities _____ **Quick Ratio** ____ . ____	Current Assets _____ Inventory _____ Current Liabilities _____ **Quick Ratio** ____ . ____
2. Profitability analysis a. Gross profit margin	**Income Statement** Gross Profits Sales	Gross Profits _____ Sales _____ **Gross Profit Margin** ____ %	Gross Profits _____ Sales _____ **Gross Profit Margin** ____ %
b. Operating profit margin	Income From Operations Sales	Income From Ops. _____ Sales _____ **Operating Profit Margin** ____ %	Income From Ops. _____ Sales _____ **Operating Profit Margin** ____ %
c. Net profit margin	Net Profits Sales	Net Profits _____ Sales _____ **Net Profit Margin** ____ %	Net Profits _____ Sales _____ **Net Profit Margin** ____ %
3. Debt ratios a. Debt to assets	**Balance Sheet** Total Liabilities Total Assets	Total Liabilities _____ Total Assets _____ **Debt to Assets Ratio** ____ %	Total Liabilities _____ Total Assets _____ **Debt to Assets Ratio** ____ %
b. Debt to equity	Total Liabilities Total Owners' Equity	Total Liabilities _____ Total Owners' Equity _____ **Debt to Equity Ratio** ____ %	Total Liabilities _____ Total Owners' Equity _____ **Debt to Equity Ratio** ____ %
4. Measures of investment a. ROI *(Return on Investment)*	**Balance Sheet** Net Profits Total Assets	Net Profits _____ Total Assets _____ **ROI (Return on Invest.)** ____ %	Net Profits _____ Total Assets _____ **ROI (Return on Invest.)** ____ %
5. Vertical financial statement analysis	**Balance Sheet** 1. Each asset % of Total Assets 2. Liability & Equity % of Total L&E **Income Statement** 3. All items % of Total Revenues	**NOTE:** *See Attached* **Balance Sheet &** **Income Statement**	**NOTE:** *See Attached* **Balance Sheet &** **Income Statement**
6. Horizontal financial statement analysis	**Balance Sheet** 1. Assets, Liab & Equity measured against 2nd year. Increases and decreases stated as amount & % **Income Statement** 2. Revenues & Expenses measured against 2nd year. Increases and decreases stated as amount & %	**NOTE:** *See Attached* **Balance Sheet** **&** **Income Statement**	**NOTE:** *See Attached* **Balance Sheet** **&** **Income Statement**

Insurance Update Form

Business Name: **Updated as of** _____ ___, _____

	Company	Contact Person	Coverage	Cost Per Year
1.				$
2.				$
3.				$
4.				$
5.				$
6.				$
7.				$
1. TOTAL ANNUAL INSURANCE COST				$
2. AVERAGE MONTHLY INSURANCE COST				$

NOTES:

1.
2. .
3.

Target Market Worksheet

1. WHO ARE MY CUSTOMERS?_____

    a. Economic level (Income range): _____

    b. Sex: _____

    c. Age range: _____

    d. Psychological makeup (Lifestyle): _____

    e. Buying habits: _____

2. LOCATION: _____

    a. Where do my customers live? _____

    b. Where do they work? _____

    c. Where do they shop? _____

3. PROJECTED SIZE OF MARKET: _____

4. WHAT ARE THE CUSTOMERS' NEEDS? _____

    a. _____

    b. _____

    c. _____

    d. _____

    e. _____

5. HOW CAN I MEET THOSE NEEDS? _____

    a. _____

    b. _____

    c. _____

    d. _____

    e. _____

6. WHAT IS UNIQUE ABOUT MY BUSINESS? _____

_____

Note: Complete the questions asked on the worksheet in outline format. Then formulate the information gathered into text.

Location Analysis Worksheet

1. Address: _____

_____

2. Name, address, phone number of realtor/contact person: _____

_____

3. Square footage/cost: _____

_____

4. History of location: _____

_____

5. Location in relation to your target market: _____

_____

6. Traffic patterns for customers: _____

_____

7. Traffic patterns for suppliers: _____

_____

8. Availability of parking (include diagram): _____

_____

_____

9. Crime rate for the area: _____

_____

10. Quality of public services (e.g., police, fire protection): _____

_____

Location Analysis Worksheet
continued

11. Notes on walking tour of the area: _____

_____

_____

12. Neighboring shops and local business climate: _____

_____

_____

13. Zoning regulations: _____

_____

14. Adequacy of utilities (information from utility company representatives): _____

_____

15. Availability of raw materials/supplies: _____

_____

16. Availability of labor force: _____

_____

17. Labor rate of pay for the area: _____

_____

18. Housing availability for employees:_____

_____

19. Tax rates (state, county, income, payroll, special assessments): _____

_____

20. Evaluation of site in relation to competition: _____

_____

_____

Competition Evaluation Worksheet

1. COMPETITOR: _____
   _____

2. LOCATION: _____
   _____

3. PRODUCTS OR SERVICES OFFERED: _____
   _____

4. METHODS OF DISTRIBUTION: _____
   _____

5. IMAGE: _____
   a. Packaging: _____
   b. Promotional materials: _____
   c. Methods of advertising: _____
   d. Quality of product or service: _____

6. PRICING STRUCTURE: _____
   _____

7. BUSINESS HISTORY & CURRENT PERFORMANCE: _____
   _____

8. MARKET SHARE (number, types, and location of customers): _____
   _____

9. STRENGTHS (the strengths of the competition can become your strengths): _____
   _____

10. WEAKNESSES (looking at the weaknesses of the competition can help you find ways of being unique and of benefiting the customer):
    _____
    _____

Note: A Competition Evaluation Worksheet should be made for each competitor. Keep these records and update them. It pays to continue to rate your competition throughout the lifetime of your business.

Glossary of Business and Financial Terms

The following glossary will define business and financial terms with which you may not be familiar. Use of these terms will help you to speak and write in a language that will be understood by potential lenders and investors as well as business associates with whom you may be dealing.

account A record of a business transaction.

accountant One who is skilled at keeping business records. Usually, a highly trained professional rather than one who keeps books. An accountant can set up the books needed for a business to operate and help the owner understand them.

accounts receivable A record of what is owed to you. All of the credit accounts taken together are your "accounts receivable."

amortization To liquidate on an installment basis: the process of gradually paying off a liability over a period of time.

analysis Breaking an idea or problem down into its parts: a thorough examination of the parts of anything.

articles of incorporation A legal document filed with the state which sets forth the purposes and regulations for a corporation. Each state has different regulations.

asset Anything of worth that is owned. Accounts receivable are an asset.

bad debts Money owed to you that you cannot collect.

balance The amount of money remaining in an account.

balance sheet An itemized statement which lists the total assets and the total liabilities of a given business to portray its net worth at a given moment in time.

bookkeeping The process of recording business transactions into the accounting records.

break-even analysis A method used to determine the point at which the business will neither make a profit nor incur a loss. That point is expressed in either the total dollars of revenue exactly offset by total expenses or in total units of production, the cost of which exactly equals the income derived by their sale.

budget A plan expressed in financial terms.

business venture Taking financial risks in a commercial enterprise.

capital Money available to invest or the total of accumulated assets available for production.

capital equipment Equipment that you use to manufacture a product, provide a service, or use to sell, store, and deliver merchandise. Such equipment will not be sold in the normal course of business, but will be used and worn out or consumed in the course of business.

cash Money in hand or readily available.

cash discount A deduction that is given for prompt payment of a bill.

cash flow The actual movement of cash into and out of a business: cash inflow and cash.

cash receipts The money received by a business from customers.

collateral Something of value given or held as a pledge that a debt or obligation will be fulfilled.

contract An agreement regarding mutual responsibilities between two or more parties.

controllable expenses Those expenses which can be controlled or restrained by the business person.

corporation A voluntary organization of persons, either actual individuals or legal entities, legally bound together to form a business enterprise; an artificial legal entity created by government grant and treated by law as an individual.

co-signers Joint signers of a loan agreement, pledging to meet the obligations in case of default.

customs broker Licensed individual, who for a fee, handles the necessary papers and steps in obtaining clearance of goods through the customs.

customs duty Tax levied on goods imported into the United States. In some nations it may also refer to the tax on goods exported from that country.

debit Monies paid out.

debt That which is owed.

debt capital The part of the investment capital which must be borrowed.

depreciation A decrease in value through age, wear, or deterioration. Depreciation is a normal expense of doing business which must be taken into account. There are laws and regulations governing the manner and time periods that may be used for depreciation.

entrepreneur An innovator of business enterprise who recognizes opportunities to introduce a new product, a new process, or an improved organization, and who raises the necessary money, assembles the factors for production, and organizes an operation to exploit the opportunity.

equity The monetary value of a property or business that exceeds the claims and/or liens against it by others.

financial statements Documents that show your financial situation.

fixed expenses Those costs that don't vary from one period to the next. Generally, these expenses are not affected by the volume of business. Fixed expenses are the basic costs that every business will have each month.

freight forwarder Company responsible for handling transport of imported and exported goods; deals with documentation, permits, and transport.

gross Overall total before deductions.

income statement A financial document that shows how much money (revenue) came in and how much money (expense) was paid out. See also profit & loss statement.

interest The cost of borrowing money.

inventory A list of assets being held for sale.

lease A long-term rental agreement.

letter of credit Instrument issued by a bank to an individual or business by which the bank substitutes its own credit for that of the individual or business.

liability insurance Risk protection for actions for which a business is liable.

limited partnership A legal partnership where some owners are allowed to assume responsibility only up to the amount invested.

liquidate To settle a debt or to convert to cash.

loan Money lent at interest.

management The art of conducting and supervising a business.

marketing All the activities involved in the buying and selling of a product or service.

merchandise Goods bought and sold in a business. "Merchandise" or stock is a part of inventory.

net What is left after deducting all expenses from the gross.

net worth The owner's equity in a given business represented by the excess of the total assets over the total amounts owing to outside creditors (total liabilities) at a given moment in time. The net worth of an individual is determined by deducting the amount of all personal liabilities from the total of all personal assets.

nonrecurring One time, not repeating. "Nonrecurring" expenses are those involved in starting a business, which only have to be paid once and will not occur again.

operating costs Expenditures arising out of current business activities. The costs incurred to do business: salaries, electricity, rental, deliveries, etc.

partnership A legal business relationship of two or more people who share responsibilities, resources, profits, and liabilities.

payable Ready to be paid. One of the standard accounts kept by a bookkeeper is "accounts payable." This is a list of those bills that are current and due to be paid.

profit Financial gain; returns over expenditures.

profit & loss statement A list of the total amount of sales (revenues) and total costs (expenses). The difference between revenues and expenses is your profit or loss. Same as income statement.

profit margin The difference between your selling price and all of your costs.

pro forma A projection or estimate of what may result in the future from actions in the present. A pro forma financial statement is one that shows how the actual operations of the business will turn out if certain assumptions are achieved.

ratio The relationship of one thing to another. A "ratio" is a shortcut way of comparing things that can be expressed as numbers or degrees.

receivable Ready for payment. When you sell on credit, you keep an "accounts receivable" as a record of what is owed to you and who owes it. In accounting, a "receivable" is an asset.

retail Selling directly to the consumer.

service business A retail business that deals in activities for the benefit of others.

share One of the equal parts into which the ownership of a corporation is divided. A "share" represents a part ownership in a corporation.

stock An ownership share in a corporation; another name for a share. Another definition would be accumulated merchandise.

takeover The acquisition of one company by another.

target market The specific individuals, distinguished by socio-economic, demographic, and interest characteristics, who are the most likely potential customers for the goods and services of a business.

tariff Duties imposed on exports and imports.

terms of sale The conditions concerning payment for a purchase.

trade credit Permission to buy from suppliers on open account.

volume An amount or quantity of business; the "volume" of a business is the total it sells over a period of time.

wholesale Selling for resale.

working capital, net The excess of current assets over current liabilities.

Index